Praise for

*Too High to Fail*

"Fine has written a well-researched book that uses the clever tactic of making the moral case for ending marijuana prohibition by burying it inside the economic case."
— Bill Maher in *The New York Times Book Review*

"Fine examines how the American people have borne the massive economic and social expenditures of the failed Drug War, which is 'as unconscionably wrong for America as segregation and DDT.' A captivating, solidly documented work rendered with wit and humor."
— *Kirkus Reviews* (Starred Review)

"A well-researched journey into the world of legal cannabis farming and a funny, maddening account of [American] farmers' travails under federal persecution on an island of legality."
— *Outside*

"In his entertaining new book . . . [Fine] successfully illuminates an unusual world where cannabis growers sing 'Happy Birthday' to [friendly law enforcement] while crossing their fingers against the threat of federal raids. This informative book will give even hardened drug warriors pause."
— *Publishers Weekly*

"An important book."
— Michael Pollan

"*Too High to Fail* covers everything from a brief history of hemp to an insider's perspective on a growing season in Mendocino County, where cannabis drives 80 percent of the economy (to the tune of $6 billion annually)."
— *Boing Boing*

Thomas Balogh

When not writing and reporting from wherever needs
be—half a dozen continents so far—**Doug Fine** medi-
tates with goats on his Funky Butte Ranch in New
Mexico. Rufous hummingbirds are his alarm clock.
Some day he'd like to be an astronaut. He lives.

# TOO HIGH TO FAIL

Cannabis and the New
Green Economic Revolution

## DOUG FINE

GOTHAM BOOKS

GOTHAM BOOKS
Published by the Penguin Group
Penguin Group (USA) Inc., 375 Hudson Street,
New York, New York 10014, USA

USA | Canada | UK | Ireland | Australia
New Zealand | India | South Africa | China

Penguin Books Ltd, Registered Offices: 80 Strand, London WC2R 0RL, England

For more information about the Penguin Group visit penguin.com.

Published by Gotham Books, a member of Penguin Group (USA) Inc.

Previously published as a Gotham Books hardcover

First trade paperback printing, August 2013

10  9  8  7  6  5  4  3  2  1

Gotham Books and the skyscraper logo are trademarks of Penguin Group (USA) Inc.

Kurt Vonnegut quote from *Cat's Cradle* on page 245 reprinted
with permission from Dell Books.

The Library of Congress has catalogued the hardcover edition as follows:

Fine, Doug.
  Too high to fail : cannabis and the new green economic revolution / Doug Fine.
    p.  cm.
  ISBN 978-1-592-40709-5   978-1-592-40761-3 (pbk.)
  1.  Marijuana—Economic aspects.   2.  Marijuana industry.   I.  Title.
  HD9019.M38F56 2012
  338. 4'7362295—dc23                                    2012014437

Printed in the United States of America
Set in Janson Text
Designed by Spring Hoteling

To the people of Mendocino County, California.

Thanks to your openness and trust, this book is written from the inside. Some of you, in inviting me into your lives and farms, expressed a desire to avoid the "drawing the federal bead" phenomenon that still exists as of this book's initial publication. Therefore, some names, dates, locations, and menu choices have been changed herein to protect privacy. Many more have not.

*Here's to a safer world in the Drug Peace Era —*

*Doug* A.

God said, "See, I give you every seed-bearing plant that is upon all the Earth . . . they shall be yours for food."

—Genesis, 1:29


It is vastly desireable to be getting under way with our domestic cultivation and manufacture of hemp, flax, cotton and wool.

—Thomas Jefferson, July 4, 1790


Grow up. It's just a plant.

—Henry Rollins

# CONTENTS

# AUTHOR'S NOTE

## Hey, Bro, It's the Return of the Greek

> We smoked and respected tight gage. That was our cute little name for marijuana.... We always looked at pot as a sort of medicine ... with much better thoughts than one that's full of liquor.
>
> —Louis Armstrong, in *Louis: The Louis Armstrong Story*, by Max Jones and John Chilton, reviewed in the Summer 2010 issue of *O'Shaughnessy's: The Journal of Cannabis in Clinical Practice*

**A**fter some delightful etymological time travel through the catalog of possible appellations, from the "Tea" of the 1930s jazz scene to the "Chronic" of '90s hip-hop, I decided to go botanical with the name I use for the actual plant discussed in this book. In the course of my year-long research, it became clear that the likely enduring term for the plant is *cannabis*, which is the genus name (neo-Latin, from the Greek) for both the psychoactive/medicinal "marijuana" plant and industrial/nutritional "hemp." No other term seemed to cover the scope of this plant as broadly as the second decade of the millennium unfolds.

The two branches of psychoactive (delta-9-tetrahydrocannabinol- or THC-containing) cannabis are "sativa" (tropically descended, thin-leaved, taller-growing) and "indica" (originally from the mountains of Asia, thick-leafed and bushy). A third, nonpsychoactive branch of the plant family is called "ruderalis." Today nearly all strains of medicinal/social cannabis are a blend of the first two, though genetics researchers are hard at work retracing lineages, often for the purposes of maximizing medicinal, nutritional, or industrial qualities found in particular strains. In the field, humans have been selectively breeding strains for at least five millennia, for clothing, housing, spiritual use, and food.

For all of these varieties and uses, "cannabis" appears to be working in a debate that has ramifications for everything from the U.S. national debt to soil health in sub-Saharan Africa. As of this writing, cannabis is being used as door material in Dodge Vipers and is one of the primary components in a British construction material company's "Hemcrete: Carbon Negative Hemp Walls." One place cannabis is not yet found: the aboveground U.S. economy. That's thanks to its listing as a Schedule I narcotic under the federal Controlled Substances Act (CSA).

The Schedule I listing is very important. By explicitly declaring that there are no legitimate uses for the cannabis plant, it prevents businesses like Hempcrete from developing Stateside. That means cannabis's status deprived U.S. treasury coffers of up to $6.2 billion in taxes in 2011, according to Harvard economics professor Jeffrey Miron. After legalization, Miron told CNBC, he sees the tax benefit at $46.7 billion annually, with $41.3 billion additionally pumped into the economy in saved enforcement and incarceration costs. So for dollar reasons alone, I figured that a dignified name was necessary.

I indeed had many choices. That is to say, we humans sure like to give nicknames to things we're close to. In 1991, I snapped awake during an otherwise less-than-jolting college lecture on phonemes when my professor mentioned that linguists often use a culture's word for cannabis to determine when key language changes have occurred throughout history.

"They found that the plant has been both vital to and nearly ubiquitous in human society for as far back as the historical record goes," Professor Lerer lectured. When I first heard that, at age twenty, I thought, "Really? Kind bud? Huh. It's not just for river trips and Dead shows anymore." For unrelated reasons, I soon asked Professor Lerer to be my advisor.

Four years later (1995), a budding journalist wandering across Asia in search of a particularly elusive barking deer which—my

NGO contacts told me—was going to force the stalling of a questionable World Bank hydrodam project in rural Laos, I stumbled across an herb hanging between the turmeric and the dried pepper in a tent bazaar. It smelled, to use a phrase of Lisa Simpson's, "like the art teacher's office." I pointed.

"*Gansa*," explained the woman tending the booth, miming a scooping-with-spoon motion. "Tasty. In soups."

"Ah, using the Sanskrit root, I see," I thought, hoping, seven thousand miles away, that my parents somehow sensed that the Stanford tuition had just been justified in the field. If only I knew that, had I purchased the hanging cannabis flower that day for my evening tentside soup, it would prove, seventeen years later, to be tax deductible.

Ah, well, I think the market stall's sarong-wearing proprietress had wanted an exorbitant nineteen cents per pound, anyway, prior to haggling. Tourist prices. And the dollar has depreciated against the Lao kip in the ensuing years anyway. Probably close to forty cents per pound in Laos these days. U.S. wholesale prices as of this writing range from two thousand to six thousand dollars per pound.

Plus, I didn't know how the accounting folks at *The Washington Post*, which ran my hydrodam exposé, would look at "*gansa*" on my expense report. What struck me even at the time was the absence of what you might call "culture war stigma" surrounding the plant in Asia—and I've since read, in dense economic analyses aimed at venture capitalists, that "familiarity with the value of industrial hemp fiber among Asian immigrants" is another reason that a revitalized U.S. market will take off. That is, if dollars triumph over rhetoric and cannabis gets reclassified under the Controlled Substances Act.

In a place like Laos where the Earth, not the supermarket, determines the diet, cannabis was just another herb, no matter what the 1961 Single Convention on Drugs—which banned production and supply of cannabis and other substances worldwide, or at least amongst the 181 current signatories—said.

Forget "when in Rome." Throughout human history, cannabis has been a "when on Earth" plant. *The Columbia History of the World* says that the earliest known fabric was hemp cloth from China, made ten thousand years ago. And we can see clearly that our word *canvas* (originally from the Arabic) derives from the same root as *cannabis*—thanks again, Professor Lerer. The oldest surviving paper, also from China and manufactured in the second century BCE, is likewise cannabis-derived. A few hundred years later, an early Chinese medical manual includes treatments made from cannabis.

By the dawn of the Industrial Age, cultures from Mongolia to Peru were using the plant for food, shelter, clothing, baskets, medicine and/or spirituality, on every continent except Antarctica. Thomas Jefferson's draft of the Declaration of Independence was famously scribbled on Schedule I felonious paper—that's tree-free paper, fellow environmentalists, unlike our current "Save the Rain Forest" junk-mail solicitations. And the coverings that put the "covered" in the "covered pioneer wagons" that facilitated America's nineteenth-century westward expansion were made of cannabis fiber. Indeed, as many have pointed out, the importance of cannabis to early European settlement in North America can be seen in the dozens of municipality names that remain today: For much of their lives, my grandparents lived in the town of Hempstead, New York.

Thus you'll be seeing the word *cannabis* as the go-to term in these pages. It covers all uses of the plant. For today's loafer-wearing registered cannabis lobbyists, it's a "seize the name" identity politics issue—they cringe when they hear a tie-dye–wearing peace-sign flasher urge a reporter—no doubt referred to as "brother" or "sister"—to "legalize weed" or profess the joys of "smoking herb." For legal reasons alone prior to federal decriminalization, *medicine* would be a preferable soundbite.

Indeed, drum circles and hacky sacking are discouraged at the more buttoned-down cannabis-industry investment conferences, where entrance fees can top a thousand dollars. For legislators and lawyers, the scientific connotation makes sense. It even has a nice, sophisticated ring to it at law enforcement seizure press conferences. Though those, as we shall see, might be as endangered as the monikers *dope* or *Lao barking deer*.

To give a comparison to another issue, the *marijuana* in the elder advocacy group National Organization for the Reform of Marijuana Laws (NORML)'s name feels as outdated to some of its members as the word *colored* in the NAACP's. You still hear the term *marijuana* out there in the field and in the sheriff's vehicle, but it could be on its way out. The new K Street national lobby group for the plant is called the National Cannabis Industry Association (NCIA).

# THE PLAYERS

## THE SHERIFF

A locally raised law enforcement professional of three decades' experience, the twice-elected, quite popular Mendocino County, California, sheriff Tom Allman had what he told me was a "startling revelation" following the passage of California's 1996 ballot initiative Proposition 215 (the Compassionate Use Act of 1996), which allowed for medicinal use of the plant in the Golden State. While to this day he maintains that he is simply "required to enforce the law" and is "neither pro- nor anticannabis," what he noticed was that, contrary to what he'd been raised and trained to believe, "the sun still rose, and there was still an America" in the days and years after the 1996 election. "Suddenly the T-rex in the economy was being acknowledged."

Allman, in his words, is "simply obeying county nuisance regulations" by implementing the nation's first cannabis permitting ordinance, called 9.31 officially (that's the county code chapter) and the "Zip-Tie" Program colloquially, for the expensive registration anklets that must be attached to the stalk of every permitted plant. In 2011, the program cost about $8,500 per farmer for ninety-nine plants with a final cannabis dispensary value of close to one million dollars.

In its second full year following a 2010 revamping, revenue from the voluntary 9.31 Program (that is to say, cannabis taxes) saved Sheriff Allman from laying off seven deputies. At least two neighboring (and similarly economically struggling) California counties were considering a similar program as of mid-2011.

Of other law enforcement or prosecutorial minds not open to his "the sun still rose" realization (what he calls his professional law enforcement "evolution"), Allman says, "Maybe it's time for them to retire. My dad ran a liquor store. He raised me to believe the damn hippies were ruining the county. I see now that they're helping save it. My dream is to be able to stop talking about cannabis—get it off the headlines—so I can fight the real problems in this county: meth and domestic violence. I care about this even more than raising my own kids right."

## THE FARMER

Tomas Balogh is a thirty-three-year-old cannabis farmer who grew the plant named "Lucille," which I followed from "birth" to patient in this book. A first-year sustainable cannabis farmer in the Mendocino hills, Balogh previously had paid for his UC Berkeley education by cultivating the far more energy-demanding indoor-grown variety of the plant. The Cal University bursar had a special room for Balogh to enter so she could run his tuition money through an automatic cash counter.

"Forty-five hundred dollars three semesters in a row," Balogh explains proudly, pointing to his meat-and-potatoes Super Silver Haze strain (which we'll see and especially smell more of in these pages). Balogh canvassed for Obama in Florida in 2008 and was undergoing a self-described "organic awakening" when we met in 2011. Now, he says, he "just wants to pay" his taxes and provide medicine for patients while demonstrating the economic and social legitimacy of the chosen crop of which he is, judging by his reputation in California cultivation circles, a talented farmer.

## THE PLANT

A female, Mendocino-developed cannabis plant of the strain Cashmere Kush, Lucille III is affectionately named after a less-than-friendly human neighbor of Balogh's (who happens to be the new, out-of-county wife of a possible former cannabis farmer, now, like many cannabis retirees, a vintner). The botanical Lucille's medicinal properties were believed by her Gregor Mendel-esque breeder, a second-generation Mendocino County cannabis geneticist named

Rock (whom we'll also meet in these pages), to include a high CBD count: this nonpsychoactive "cannabinoid" chemical is all the rage in medicinal circles these days. We'll see how Lucille tested.

She is "the third" Lucille because the first two died as cuttings. Hence, big thanks to area farmer Leif, who suggested Tomas grow backups of any variety I wanted to follow. "When's your book deadline?" was Leif's first question for me. Lucille had, in fact, eighty-seven sisters and cousins in her garden at Tomas's "Eagle Nest" property, named for its high-altitude remoteness.

That the 9.31 Zip-Tie permitting program allows for ninety-nine plants is not accidental: One hundred is the number at which federal sentencing minimums for conspiracy kick in. The plan among 9.31's drafters on the Mendocino County Board of Supervisors (one of whom was actually trying to curb plant numbers in his town-based district, and another of whom believed passionately the number is much too low), was to "respect" the federal limit and hence avoid interference in their nascent decriminalization program. We'll see if it worked.

## THE SERGEANT

Sergeant Randy Johnson (not the All-Star pitcher), or Sergeant Randy as he is known in Mendocino County, is a Dennis Franz look- and act-alike who administers the 9.31 Zip-Tie Program for Mendocino County. A zero-tolerance drug warrior as of 2009, he now believes that permitted cannabis farmers are "valuable members of our community." Armed with a clipboard, he bounces around the remote Northern California county he serves, making sure permitted farms are properly signed, fenced, and clean.

"The first word in this program is *medical*," Randy likes to say whenever he finds, say, a juice bottle in a flower-processing room. "Wear gloves and white coats," he advises. "There are people who don't want our program to work." In other words, he is a law-enforcement officer who does. He is already fielding consulting offers from out of state.

## THE GANJAPRENEUR

The 9.31 poster child and a favorite putative partner of venture capitalists who salivate at the prospect of the end of cannabis prohibition, Matt Cohen is on the national board of the new D.C.-based National Cannabis Industry Association (NCIA) lobbying organization and is executive director of a Mendocino-centric cannabis trade organization called MendoGrown. This he hopes will brand local cannabis "the way Napa became synonymous with fine wine." Cohen also runs a cannabis medicine delivery non-profit, onto which he initially tried to tack a Community Supported Agriculture produce-delivery program. "Folks wanted the medicine, mainly," he said, shelving the broccoli "for now." He is the most public face of the 9.31 Program, even appearing openly on the PBS program *Frontline*. Will the feds let such flaunting continue?

## THE AMERICAN PEOPLE

One hundred million of whom have used cannabis (twenty-seven million in the past year), and 70 percent of whom support medical use, according to an October 2011 Gallup poll. The number is just over 50 percent supporting full (all-use) legalization in that poll, the first time more than half of Americans so polled. Cannabis's current listing under Schedule I of the federal Controlled Substances Act means that it officially possesses "no currently accepted medical use in treatment in the United States." Cocaine and methamphetamine are listed under the less restrictive Schedule II. Cannabis's not-very-effective synthetic substitute, dronabinol (brand name Marinol) is in Schedule III.

The American Medical Association (AMA)'s official position since 2009, actually reflecting a return to the physician group's 1937 stance opposing cannabis prohibition in the first place, has been that "smoked cannabis reduces neuropathic pain, improves appetite and caloric intake especially in patients with reduced muscle mass, and may relieve spasticity and pain in patients with multiple sclerosis . . . the Schedule I status of Marijuana [should] be reviewed with the goal of facilitating clinical research and development of cannabinoid-based medicines, and alternate delivery methods."

California's largest medical group, the California Medical Association, went further. On October 14, 2011, its trustees, representing thirty-five thousand physicians, called for cannabis's full legalization.

Many of the venture capitalists who study the potential American cannabis market see the medicinal/social uses of the plant as simply one sector. As one attorney representing ganjapreneurs told me, "There are billions of dollars in this plant that don't involve smoking, from domestic energy to textiles to construction material to food."

# INTRODUCTORY
# POSITION PAPER

## If You Were Inclined to Stereotype,
## Incline the Other Way

The global war on drugs has failed, with devastating consequences for individuals and societies around the world. Fifty
years after the initiation of the UN Single Convention on Narcotic Drugs, and 40 years after President Nixon launched the
U.S. government's war on drugs, fundamental reforms in
national and global drug control policies are urgently needed.

Vast expenditures on criminalization and repressive measures directed at producers, traffickers, and consumers of illegal
drugs have clearly failed to effectively curtail supply or consumption. Apparent victories in eliminating one source or
trafficking organization are negated almost instantly by the
emergence of other sources and traffickers. . . . Our principles
and recommendations can be summarized as follows:

End the criminalization, marginalization, and stigmati-
zation of people who use drugs but who do no harm to others.
Challenge rather than reinforce common misconceptions about
drug markets, drug use, and drug dependence.

Encourage experimentation by governments with models
of legal regulation of drugs to undermine the power of organized crime and safeguard the health and security of their citizens. This recommendation applies especially to cannabis, but
we also encourage other experiments in decriminalization and
legal regulation that can accomplish these objectives and provide models for others.

—Global Commission on Drug Policy,* June 2011. Signatories
include George P. Shultz, Ronald Reagan's secretary of state,
César Gaviria, former president of Colombia, Ernesto Zedillo,

---

* The eleven suggestions of the Commission's much-publicized 2011 report,
released upon the fortieth anniversary of the modern War on Drugs, can be
read at http://www.globalcommissionondrugs.org/Report

> former president of Mexico, Fernando Henrique Cardoso, former president of Brazil, George Papandreou, prime minister of Greece, and Paul Volcker, former chairman of the Federal Reserve
>
> No longer should the federal government's laws supersede the wishes of local citizens who have decided that their fellow neighbors ought to have the right to legitimately use medical marijuana. As we have seen for years, seriously ill patients will attempt to obtain their medication however they can and it is unconscionable for the [Department of Justice] to use its limited resources to endanger the lives of patients who are simply seeking to ease their suffering. We respectfully request that your administration reschedule marijuana as a Schedule II or III drug administratively, or publicly support the adoption of legislation that would change federal statute to achieve this same goal.
>
> —October 31, 2011, letter to President Obama from U.S. representatives Sam Farr, Pete Stark, Steve Cohen, Lynn Woolsey, Barbara Lee, Dana Rohrabacher, Mike Thompson, Jared Polis, and Bob Filner

> Am I willing to pursue a decriminalization strategy as an approach? No.
>
> —President Barack Obama, July 2011

For those who may be wondering what bias or agenda I might have tucked in my hard drive as I write this book, wonder no longer. It's a fair question, because we all believe something, don't we? And cannabis is "one of those issues" that some folks still imagine provide a window into where someone stands on a whole cluster of other "moral" issues important in making a basic "friend or foe" determination.

Like a filibuster-stopping percentage of my countryfolk—67 percent, according to a 2011 Angus Reid Public Opinion poll—I believe that by any reasonable journalistic standard, the War on Drugs is a failure. It is bad for America. Bad for its economy. Bad for its society. Not great for Mexico's, Central or South America's, the Caribbean's, Canada's, or Afghanistan's, either, to name just a few places.

To state otherwise would be like covering the 1960s Civil Rights Movement and making arguments in favor of Jim Crow in the name of balance. Even if it were waged efficiently, the Drug War can't work. Not when cannabis is one of the targets (I don't discuss dangerous drugs like heroin and methamphetamines in this book). Human ties to the plant have been too strong on six continents for too many millennia to try to enduringly convince enough people that its negatives (and there are negatives) outweigh the positives.

I say that professionally. I don't have a cousin Lenny in prison for possession of a joint or any other personal bone to pick. It's just that I, like Ronald Reagan's secretary of state George Shultz, former president Jimmy Carter, NAACP president Benjamin Todd Jealous, and free market Nobel Laureate economist Milton Friedman, believe that prohibition of something people very much want doesn't work. Never has. Never will. This goes for anything for which there's strong demand, let alone one of humanity's longest-utilized and most valuable plants.

We have both the rise of organized crime and these silly little postscripts in our otherwise elegant Constitution (amendments eighteen and twenty-one) to remind us what happens when hysterical zealots try to tell a nation what its citizens can and cannot ingest. And don't let anyone tell you that alcohol prohibition is in some way different from cannabis prohibition, in that alcohol has "always been socially accepted." I've got three thousand years of linguistic proof and a shopkeeper in Laos to show the typical human response to the cannabis plant. It's the current Western model that's atypical.

The Drug War is as unconscionably wrong for America as segregation and DDT. It's more costly than President Reagan's "Star Wars" Strategic Defense Initiative (SDI), which didn't spend sixty billion taxpayer dollars annually (between state and federal Drug War expenditure) during a down economy. Congress allocated only forty-four billion for SDI over ten years.

But keeping the discussion away from the moral and on the

practical for the moment, our incomprehensible policy, our nation's longest war, has done more than cost you and me (as American taxpayers) a trillion dollars just since Richard Nixon declared a War on Drugs on June 17, 1971. It has turned our nation into the most highly incarcerated society in history. By far—2.3 million Americans, or 1 percent of us, are behind bars, according to the International Centre for Prison Studies. That's three quarters of a million more than China imprisons. A quarter of our inmates are in for drug offenses. Even Antonin Scalia and Pat Robertson call that "a great mistake" and "not a good thing," respectively.

Want to know how deeply the Drug War has wormed its way into your pocket? In a time of fiscal crisis, with more than a trillion needing to be cut from the federal budget, Drug War spending, including interdiction and law enforcement, actually *increased* 3.3 percent to record levels in 2010, according to the Associated Press: $15.5 billion. That's just federal.

All in exchange for seizure of 1 percent of contraband. That's a generous estimate, actually. No one knows how much cannabis Americans enjoy. In one week in September 2011, though, Border Patrol agents in Arizona carted off thirty-two hundred pounds worth more than $1.6 million, according to CBS News. Every time I watch the continuous wobbly caterpillar of identical white semitrucks rolling through the Border Patrol checkpoint nearest my New Mexico ranch, I wish I had X-ray vision. And every American contributes three hundred wasted dollars per year to the dubious eradication effort, according to retired Missouri Supreme Court chief justice Ray Price. Even the Dallas Cowboys sometimes win when they throw *that* much money at a problem.

Though it's stifling what could be a key industry sector in America's economic recovery, the continued Drug War spending is not accidental. If you wonder why, despite 70 percent of Americans' supporting medical cannabis and overwhelming mainstream research backing it up, President Obama, in July 2011, called decriminalization off the table, just recite the words "Follow the money." In fact, you should probably tape those words to the masthead of your newspaper or newsreader every morning: It's useful when trying to understand most issues, including the NFC East.

A decriminalized, regulated cannabis industry, that is to say, an end to cannabis prohibition, is at least perceived to be a threat by:

- The hugely politically influential pharmaceutical industry. Whether its executives like it or not, health care costs are becoming so ubiquitously out of reach for average Americans that entire cottage industries of below-the-insurance-radar treatments, some ancient and even—gasp—*effective*, are springing up.

- The private prison industry.

- Some law enforcement lobbies.

- The especially disingenuous banking industry. This is the industry that makes billions laundering illegal cartel profits while repeatedly denying bank accounts to several of the cannabis-farming, taxpaying Americans you'll meet in these pages. In fairness, bank managers often truthfully claim to have been threatened by the Justice Department with unfriendliness if they accepted these folks' often nonprofit funds. Why the threats aren't directed at the cartel accounts is anyone's guess.

Still, as emphatically as I believe that America will be stronger economically and healthier as a society when the post–Drug War Era begins to unfold, I want to state my respect for individual members of law enforcement, and not just the local Northern California law enforcement pioneers that I profile in this book. California cannabis farmer Jim Hill said it best of the Drug Enforcement Administration (DEA) agents who sashayed into his house one day in 2009 to "politely pilfer through my underwear drawer": "They were just guys doing their job, and trying to do it well. Just like me: working to feed their family."

The DEA was established two years after the 1971 War on Drugs was declared. Today its budget is nearly two and a half billion dollars and it employs more than nine thousand people. That, folks, is an industry. And it's just one federal agency. Thirty billion dollars of the Drug War's annual budget comes from state coffers. Thus some people argue that the whole forty-year effort has actually been a success: It's created thousands of reliable jobs. In law enforcement and prison management.

From this starting point—the trillion-dollar failed Drug War must end, for the good of the country, for the good of the world— I wanted to see if something better might come next. In other words, I came to examine the legitimate cannabis industry, not necessarily to praise it. For a location I chose what you might call the home base of top-shelf domestic cannabis production. There North America's first local-governmental attempt to regulate sustainable cannabis farming was unfolding.

I'll use this season-long local study as a launchpad for a higher-altitude look at a multibillion-dollar plant that could have a staggeringly large and positive impact on the American economy in sectors far beyond the agricultural; beyond the cannabis field itself. Think domestic energy. Think South Carolina textile industry. Think Nebraska family farmer. One media report puts cannabis revenues at $35.8 billion annually. No wonder the seminal 1970s Oakland funk band Tower of Power sang:

> I got some friends,
> Who like to stay high,
> Think of the tax potential,
> If it was legal to buy.

Today, of course, the singer would maintain, perhaps with less metrical suavity, that he has some friends "who like to stay medicated as recommended by their doctor." Or "who process hemp

seed into an immensely profitable health shake." Because of cannabis's potentially valuable role in a broad range of American com-
modities markets, we may eventually come to see its greatest value
in energy production (or food production, or textiles), with smokable cannabis proving to be a niche market, like cigars in the
tobacco market.

Added together, we're talking about billions of dollars that
could and should be added to the American economy. Like any
promising industry, though, cannabis is not all upside. You will
find in these pages interviews with psychiatrists talking about
what they feel is the largely ignored addiction issue with today's
powerful cannabis. You'll find second-generation cannabis farmers frustrated by what they feel is the past decade's "out of control"
growth in cannabis farming by newcomers. These folks also fear
that cannabis legalization will mean production will be seized
from small farmers by Merck or Coors.

What you won't find by way of "objectivity" in this book is a
defense of the patently absurd and economically devastating War
on Drugs, which actually started against cannabis on the federal
level in 1937 by way of the Marihuana Tax Act. A lot went into the
start of federal cannabis prohibition. Some Western state politicos
feared Latino political influence and decided to demonize what
they characterized as a Mexican herb. There were other such crusaders inside the Beltway, including Harry J. Anslinger: Originally
an alcohol prohibition crusader, he helped popularize the "Save
our kids from the demon weed" mantra in the 1930s as the first
commissioner of the Federal Bureau of Narcotics. His demographic
breakdown of users of the plant was "Most are Negroes, Hispan-
ics, Filipinos, and entertainers. Their Satanic music, jazz and swing,
result from marijuana usage."

But the anticannabis smear campaign every procannabis blog
likes to lament is the one media baron William Randolph Hearst
allegedly launched in support of his own timber investments and
Pierre Dupont's chemical and petroleum-based synthetics. The
amazing yield and harvest properties of cheap cannabis *were* a

threat to these and to the cotton industry as well (today, cotton uses a quarter of the world's pesticides, while cannabis needs few). Whether it was fear of hemp's market superiority or just yellow journalism, thus began the infamous and often racist "Reefer Madness" era, which produced the unintentional cinematic comedy of the same name starring an—in real life—cannabis-friendly actress, Thelma White,* pretending to be ruined by the plant.

Cannabis prohibition didn't get off to a good start. Within five years, it was called off abruptly (if temporarily), when our at-war nation needed the best rope in the world. The U.S. War Department's procannabis 1942 propaganda film *Hemp for Victory*, a click away on YouTube, is a must-see both for its historical overview of the plant and its Orwellian "now we're at war with Eastasia" flip-flop in federal policy.

The reason the film was made is not difficult to discern: Japan had cut off the American supply of Filipino cannabis. Over footage of the Acropolis, a narrator correctly informs us that "long ago, when these ancient Grecian temples were new, hemp was already old in the service of mankind."

Legalized (or decriminalized, or exempted, or regulated—some people make a lot of the differences among these) cannabis has the potential to return thousands of American small family farmers to the land, while helping the soil heal from a century of monoculture abuse that threatens to end the prolific harvests that were instrumental in our nation's ascension as a world power.

What Iowa wouldn't give for that! North Dakota too. That state's agriculture commissioner, Roger Johnson, said on CNN in 2007, "What an opportunity we're throwing away, not being a part of this [industrial cannabis] industry. . . . We really ought to be in this business. It's economics."

For proof about how correct he is, Mr. Johnson can point to the facts on the ground starting one inch north of his North

---

* According to an unbylined article in the Summer 2010 issue of *O'Shaughnessy's: the Journal of Cannabis in Clinical Practice*.

Dakota. Across the prairie provinces, Canada's rejuvenated industrial (nonpsychoactive) cannabis industry, representing a tiny percentage of rapidly increasing world production and only twelve years old, harvested 13,837 acres worth fifteen million dollars in 2010, according to the government. And that's just raw material value at the source, and not value-added products like food and textiles. This is a crop with ten times the per-acre yield of corn, and nine times the value. Imagine if that yield went not only into the food supply but also into the energy supply. You'd see a lot fewer Middle Eastern monarchs buying sports teams.

Toronto's *Globe and Mail* reported in 2011 that the industrial cannabis market in Canada is growing 10 percent annually, with exports (meaning to the United States, mainly) increasing by 500 percent over the past four years. The trade balance ledger isn't lost on the industry, whose goal, the article said, is "to generate more than $100 million for the Canadian economy by 2015."

When researching this book, I scoped around for an area in the United States where the Drug War was accordingly declared over—although in the States, given the federal quagmire, the declaration would have to be unilateral. I found that cannabis cultivation had been effectively decriminalized in Mendocino County, California, the northern coastal paradise where much of this book is set, explicitly because three generations of civil disobedients now overwhelmingly dominate local government and juries.

The first and most important thing you need to know about Mendocino County is that a local jury convicting on a cannabis case is a rare event. Roughly as likely as a Napa County jury convicting someone for growing a grape. A parade of seemingly slam-dunk prosecutions get covered in the regional press with sentences like (and I quote the April 8, 2011, *Willits News* coverage of a typical trial), "*The jury apparently also believed Graves's assertion that all [169 pounds] of the marijuana on his property . . . was medicinal in nature.*"

One way to understand this is to, yes, follow the money again. Only, this time on the grassroots (literally), not the corporate, level. The more formerly middle-class people are pushed out of the mainstream economy (paying a mortgage, owning stocks), the more open they are to join locally based economic rebuilding efforts. Out of necessity. This is not 401(k) country. If you're a cannabis farmer, the bank won't even *take* your money, let alone give you a loan.

Whether you believe the cannabis flower (colloquially: "bud") to be the miracle medicine that returned your Aunt Sally from a semidormant arthritic to a bike-riding companion, or you believe it is the Devil Weed that leads to promiscuity, there is, in the words of a septuagenarian cannabis farmer named Sarah who has been growing since the Carter administration, "only one direction this war can go. We won. We grow. It's over." Like alcohol prohibition before it, common sense, human desire, and economic inevitability will eventually prevail and the Drug War will end.

Good policy eventually wins out. Presumably, maybe even hopefully, the tens of thousands of publicly funded Americans employed to "fight" (that is to say, "lose") it, from DEA agents to prison guards, will find new bureaucratic teats on which to latch. It's already happening, on the budgetary end: The California Department of Justice saw its budget cut by thirty-six million dollars in 2011. Thus endeth state participation in the longtime CAMP (Campaign Against Marijuana Planting) raids, which since the 1980s have been as much an annual rite for Northern Californians as migrating geese.

Good thing the *Capitol Weekly* reported in September 2011 that that state's *"crime rate dropped across the board in every major measured category, with violent crimes—including murders and rapes—at their lowest comparable levels in more than forty years."*

A drop in cannabis enforcement hasn't resulted in the end of the world, but rather a move toward fixing it. But what will a nationwide Pax Cannabis entail? Making packs of cannabis joints available to adults at every convenience store like so many Coors twelve-packs, with all the accompanying licensing and age requirements? Is it that simple? Regulate it like alcohol and tobacco? I think that might be the plan of one of California's putative 2012 cannabis-related ballot initiatives. It's called the "Regulate Marijuana Like Wine Act of 2012."

In the Golden State's far-north and ruggedly progressive Mendocino County, in whose remote mountains I've just lived and researched for a year, legislators aren't waiting for federal or even statewide policy to change. Folks here know what their number-one cash crop is, and they've decided to bring it aboveground and derive municipal revenue from it. Today.

# PREFACE

## Yes, But Does the Topic Pass the Rwanda Test?

The hemp plant . . . has been so generally cultivated the world over as a cordage fiber that the value of all other fibers as to strength and durability is estimated by it. . . . The plant is an admirable weed killer, and is sometimes employed . . . because it puts the soil in good condition. . . . The value of hemp for fiber . . . and oil would seem to make its cultivation a very profitable one.

—*Yearbook of the United States Department of Agriculture*, 1895

I really don't think we would exist without it.

—Thirty-seven-year-old Mendocino County, California, wine and garden shop owner Nicole Martensen, speaking of the local cannabis industry in a July 19, 2009, Associated Press article

There's an episode of the *Seinfeld* television program wherein Everyman George Costanza, considering his job prospects after yet another layoff, reflects, "I like sports. Maybe I could be the general manager of a baseball team."

It's funny because it's ridiculous, right? Well, the self-help merchants at the headquarters of *The Secret* would no doubt like us to remember that George does, eventually, come to work for the Yankees.

So in the spirit of aiming high when considering the follow-up to my previous book, *Farewell, My Subaru*—a project that compelled me to abandon petroleum for vegetable oil and the dairy aisle for endearingly mischievous goats—I similarly thought, from a "journalist who wants to go where the zeitgeist is" perspective, "I'd sure like to be paid to learn about cannabis. How it works botanically. Its history and roles in various human societies. Because it's sure got folks worked up in this one. And it *is* far and away my nation's number-one cash crop, with almost none of its revenue taxed in a time of debt crisis."

Seriously, anyone who crunches the numbers can see that simple decriminalization of cannabis can almost immediately act as, if not a cornerstone, then at least a significant piece of a national economic recovery. In the nineteenth and early twentieth centuries, alcohol taxes at times provided more than 70 percent of federal revenue. So far, because "drugs" represent such a hot-button issue, enough key people on the political side haven't crunched (or admitted to crunching) the numbers, which include $100 million in California tax revenue in 2006, according to CNBC, and $105 million in 2011, according to the California Board of Equalization, whose employees collect and count it.

Those on the economic side, though? Oh, yeah. "Greenest" people around. And I don't mean Sierra Club green. A Mendocino-based cannabis trade group received free legal advice from an attorney who just wanted to gain experience in a soon-to-be lucrative industrial space. "The financial world is betting on an end to [cannabis] prohibition," he told me.

The political world might be forced to catch up, and soon. With many state budgets looking like California's—in mid-2011, *The California Report* called state revenues down $539 million from earlier projections, and the state's 2011 unemployment rate was around 12 percent—all bets are off. This reality is spurring some ideologically rigid California Republicans like Fullerton state assemblyman Chris Norby to advocate for cannabis decriminalization in the name of economic development and personal freedom.

Even on the federal level for a while there, some pundits were saying that Barney Frank and Ron Paul's Ending Federal Marijuana Prohibition Act (HR 2306), which mimics legislation that covered the repeal of alcohol prohibition and which was laughed off the Beltway when initially proposed in early 2011, might actually make it out of committee. I know—desperate times seem to breed moments of electoral nonhypocrisy. There are only so many refueling options left for the American economic plane right now.

So that's why the cannabis plant was initially journalistically, botanically, and especially nutritionally, interesting to me. I include this last adverb because when I did a prebook assessment, I found that the plant was already in an astonishing number of components in my life, and several of them were edible or related to home economics: Every morning I squeezed the perfectly Omega-balanced cannabis (hemp) seed oil (produced in Canada) into my family's health shake. We pounded the stuff.

Then I put on my cannabis sun hat and went for a run. My Sweetheart and I diapered our kids in organic hemp (the only material that held up to repeated washing and brutal New Mexican line drying) and hung our curtains with cannabis twine (Walmart–purchased, made in Romania). We then bathed our children in Doctor Bronner's Fair Trade hemp soap (lavender variety usually, though sometimes rose). I mean, one tries not to sound like one of those "cannabis can do anything including bring about world peace and an end to Ring Around the Collar" people, but by the time I finished the assessment, I felt I deserved some kind of Canadian tax rebate.

All of these uses were unintentional and nonpolitical, and resulted simply because cannabis won out in the marketplace. And all of them represented economic value I could be contributing to the American economy. If, you know, cannabis were legal to grow here. Because if forty years of failed Drug War have taught us anything, it's that cannabis is going to be grown, one way or another. It's really our choice among three options: establish a legal framework that provides tax revenue, watch other countries reap the benefits instead, or allow the homicidal organized-crime network that doesn't contribute to the tax base to continue to operate.

Nothing new about the idea of hemp as an industrial material, by the way—Henry Ford used it in an experimental 1941 model. But I was astounded when I added up my family's cannabis industry investments. Take that unintentional two-thousand-dollar consumer contribution and multiply it by three hundred million Americans. You get a big number, without a single joint being lit. And also a lot less foreign oil once hemp's biomass potential is exploited. "It's magnitudes more productive than corn- or soy-based ethanol as a biofuel," a USDA biologist told me at a 2010 sustainability festival. "But it's not even on our blackboard because it's a federal crime."

Here's a curious fact that highlights the absurdity of the war on industrial cannabis. The United States isn't allowed to do business with any nation that violates the 1961 Single Convention on Drugs. But that treaty specifically exempts the increasing numbers of nations that are, wisely, starting to repair their relationship with the renewable industrial uses of the plant. If only we could apply such a policy domestically and free that USDA biologist to do honest research! We'd have billions more dollars in our economy and a more balanced trade ledger. We might even wean off foreign oil.

Even after nearly a half century of relentless eradication efforts, this innocent-looking plant finds itself indeed firmly in the crosshairs of the cultural zeitgeist. By 2010, fifteen U.S. states plus the District of Columbia, and counting, often spurred by citizen initiative and budgetary imperative, had already created medicinal cannabis programs. It'll be seventeen in 2012. Fourteen had decriminalized minor possession of the plant's psychoactive flowers for any purpose. So when I was offered a book contract following multiple publisher interest, I was being told that I was on to a burning hot topic.

If I accepted a book advance, I could pay my mortgage, indirectly, care of the plant that my folks had raised me to believe would cause my head to explode, or, if I was lucky enough to survive and one day emerge from both rehab and the associated cultural banishment, would narrow my career options to "bus driver" and something in the "sanitation engineer" space. If I found myself in the same room as a joint, I was instructed to leave.

Within my family's suburban circle of friends, we had nervous breakdowns, anorexia, dentists going to jail for fraud. Even divorce.

But short of actual homicide, just about the worst thing you could say about someone (say, over a glass of sangria at the pool party) was "I hear Louise's kid is smoking pot." This was a cornerstone of my civics education, the ultimate boogeyman, Orwell's Emmanuel Goldstein lurking as the "At All Costs Do Not Open This Door" in the labyrinth of my upbringing. Mine and a hundred million others' kids in the 1980s. "Just Say No" was First Lady Nancy Reagan's issue.

So I wasn't sure how my now-retired folks would react when I told them I was considering spending a year not running from joints in the room, but rather living among the growers and providers of the material in the joints. Oh, well, in these tough times, you do what you have to do to feed the family. Or to quote the jubilant George Costanza as he announced his new job to his friends, "The New York Yankees!"

From this tempting financial starting point—only getting paid to learn about cannabis *while being* the general manager of the Yankees would be better—the idea still had to pass what I call the Rwanda Test. In 1994 I reported from that tiny, gorgeous country for *The Washington Post*. The Switzerland of Africa, it had been called, before people turned on their neighbors. What I came away with was that the most underreported contributor to the recent ethnic horror there was the fact that it is the most densely populated country in a densely populated continent. I watched folks find fertile sides of rocks. Not a molecule went uncultivated. Soil health is a major issue in everyday lives.

Now, no one plant is going to singlehandedly end resource scarcity in sub-Saharan Africa or anywhere else. But as a fellow who likes to think his work is at least trying to nudge the cosmos in a positive direction, I had to ask myself: Was it worth spending a year of my working life, which after my family is the major component of my waking day, to "researching weed"? How does *that* help the seventh child of a Rwandan family in need of protein?

And you know what? After preliminary research, the topic passed rather easily and with flying colors. Cannabis is really that important economically, nutritionally, medicinally, and ecologically: 1,170 trees would be saved if this book were printed on hemp paper, provided it sells the hundred thousand first-run copies I've promised my accountant it will. The seed and pulp provide at once omega-complete food, fuel, textiles, and a competitively durable industrial fiber. And it can be grown in more marginal land than many other crops thanks to the millennia of botanists, priests, and health care providers who've bred strains to survive in every ecosystem. Alaska's "Matanuska Valley Thunderfuck" is one of the most famous strains in the world. Sixty degrees of latitude to the south, every reggae song ever written reminds us that cannabis likewise grows quite well along the equator.

This can help free climate-change-ravaged villages in, say, Mbazi, Rwanda, from resource wars, not to mention putting America back to work in a vertical, domestic, multibillion-dollar industry. Additionally, it helps in topsoil restoration thanks to foot-long taproots that grow in a month. And the industrial varieties of cannabis, in particular, have extremely low fertilizer and pesticide needs, which is both a cost and health factor, particularly in less developed agricultural communities.

OK, I was convinced that Rwanda and a thousand other such subsistence-based societies could tangibly be helped by the resurgence of cannabis. That just left my folks to explain all this to. These were the now seventy-year-old liberal Democrats who, as forty-year-olds, had introduced me to the "your head will explode and forget Stanford" theory of cannabis's effects. These days, they had bridge tournaments and alumni association dinners to attend. I figured that schedule afforded them some thinking time. So even if it nearly caused *their* heads to explode, I wanted them to be aware of the facts I was unearthing. Partly thanks to that Stanford (and Grateful Dead concert) education.

Turns out, I needn't have worried. Clutching a *New Yorker* magazine with an evidently relevant article as she approached my New Mexico ranch gate on a visit just before I started research on this project, one of the first (and unprompted) things my retired teacher mother said, even before greeting the grandkids, was "Boy, this Drug War sure has been a waste of money. All those kids in jail! All that wasted tax revenue!"

So if you want to know why, in the end, I spent a year talking to cannabis farmers and patients and collective managers, I'll point to two reasons, really. 1) I came to realize that wider research into the cannabis plant as a legal economic engine could help both America and the developing world—the several billion people whose communities have been devastated by the compounding effects of climate change, overpopulation, cultural disruption, and both political and soil mismanagement, and, 2) even my mother realized federal drug policy must change. She'd evolved from magic head explosions to "Legalize It." It told me, "Boy, the truth has reached critical mass. You may speak it publicly."

Assuming her unfamiliarity with Tower of Power, Mom appeared to be paraphrasing Nobel Laureate economist Milton Friedman, writing in *The Wall Street Journal* in 1991 of the human desire to feel good: "It is demand that must operate through repressed and illegal channels. Illegality creates obscene profits that finance the murderous tactics of the drug lords; illegality leads to the corruption of law enforcement officials."

*Obscene profits* should get politicians' attention. The way Mendocino County, California, sheriff Tom Allman put it after revealing overflights of his county early in his tenure was "Ah, so *that's* how that conservative Republican pays for three kids' college tuition."

I'm comfortably certain that even my newly enlightened folks would never have considered cannabis cultivation as a long-term college investment plan. It's a when-in-Rome issue. The laws people unthinkingly break back East are more abstractly financial: stock tips and the like. Not my folks, of course. But that's the kind of thing, rather than cannabis, that earns the local cultural wink. In Northern California, it didn't take the collapse of Lehman Brothers to inspire distrust of the banking industry. Nothing like stashing your kids' tuition in a shoe box to lead to a wide variety of alternative cultural norms. Such as a sheriff protecting his taxpaying cannabis farmers from thieves.

In case I had any lingering doubts about relocating my family to another time zone for a yearlong, largely goat-free examination of a legal American cannabis economy, an astonishing news story sealed the deal. Six months into my research for this project, federal authorities announced that they had arrested eleven people, including the mayor, in Columbus, New Mexico, one of the closest towns of any size to my remote Funky Butte Ranch. The defendants were allegedly Mexican cartel members. We're talking about the mayor of a U.S. town.

This is a hamlet that has been sleepy since the moment of its founding, except for those disruptive couple of days in March 1916 when Pancho Villa's army invaded and burned it. It is also a town through which my family heads, fuels up, and sometimes hangs out en route to hikes after nearby Italian food.

And the Drug War's failure had now spilled over there?* Putting my family at risk in our backyard?!? This, adding insult to ineffective policy, was two years after my nearest neighbor, a retiree, was arrested in a massive, terrifying, air-supported bust for something like thirteen cannabis plants (Mendocino County, California, authorities seized six hundred thousand in 2010, a figure the official press release estimates as 10 percent of the crop but which most growers tell me is closer to 1 percent).

That was a hassle, since I expect to be awakened by hummingbirds buzzing the feeder, not by choppers rattling my canyon. Plus my neighbor didn't spend a minute in jail, not that he should have. And I (as a taxpayer) funded the daylong nuisance that had nearly

---

* A 2011 report by *USA Today* concluded that the overall U.S. border region is safer than it was a decade ago. I believe this (it better be, since I'm paying for twenty-one thousand Border Patrol agents), but "my" border isn't. It's the people of Palomas, of course, the once somnolent, good-vibed border town across from Columbus, who are suffering most intensely from the violence (of the "too barbaric to describe" variety) and the absence of tourists and government services. I'm pretty sure, at least, that the Columbus-based Our Lady of Palomas hunger charity to which I donate is not cartel controlled.

fifty guys with wires in their ears, but otherwise trying to look inconspicuous, hanging out in the riverbed I have to cross to get to my mailbox. All that effort, and I find it's still no longer safe to take my family on our favorite outing, which includes one of the only decent Italian food joints in the Land of Enchantment.

Now it was personal, let me tell you. When you're used to hearing your goats braying for breakfast and instead, one Thursday, you find yourself in the climactic scene to *Goodfellas*, you start asking how much longer this forty-year-long Drug War farce is going to continue. Then you find out that your taxes are being used to go after the wrong people. That'll make any journalist worth his salt investigate the alternatives.

# ONE

## The Day a Cannabis Farmer Cried Out, "Thank God, the Police!"

The prestige of government has undoubtedly been lowered considerably by the prohibition law . . . for nothing is more destructive of respect for the government and the law . . . than passing laws which cannot be enforced. It is an open secret that the dangerous increase of crime in this country is closely connected with this.

—Albert Einstein, 1921

Late on the afternoon on a windy (and the blusteriness is important) summer Sunday in 2010, Mendocino County, California, deputies under the command of twice-elected sheriff Tom Allman were dispatched to a Redwood Valley farm, about twenty minutes from the county hub and two-sushi-bar city of Ukiah.

According to the dispatcher, a burglar alarm had gone off—one of those jobs where the alarm company calls the authorities. It turned out the alarm's red laser sensors were protecting a fairly fragrant one-acre, ninety-nine-plant cannabis crop. The two deputies responding to the call parked beside a three-story flagpole that was displaying what can fairly be called superlatively patriotic (in fact, sheet-size) versions of both the Stars and Stripes and the California state flag. There they were met by the farm's chamber of commerce member owner, thirty-three-year-old Matt Cohen, and all three proceeded to his no-longer-beeping field, which also happened to be just past his medical cannabis cooperative's processing room.

Other than that, though, the farm looked like it could have been owned by a Reaganite, or perhaps a fairly meticulous graduate of the local 4-H Club. Sure, there was the overwhelming, unmistakable, and locally ubiquitous *eau de cannabis*. But you can't breathe in Mendocino County without that. There was a Farm Bureau Member sign affixed to the farm's front gate. There were even a couple of friendly goats. The grounds were immaculate, and the lettuce was leafing out in the front vegetable garden.

One of the deputies at the alarm sensor powwow noticed the nearby "9.31" registration permit issued by his own department hanging rather nicely framed on the processing room wall. Chapter 9.31 is the county land-use ordinance that created the functionally named Zip-Tie Program that bands every registered cannabis plant in the county in a bright yellow anklet. For a total annual cost to the farmer of about $8,500.

These zip ties, in turn, allow Cohen's not-for-profit, Internet-based cannabis delivery cooperative, called Northstone Organics, to grow the ninety-nine plants (worth close to a million dollars in the down buyer's market of 2010), as far as the County of Mendocino was concerned. The peace officers could also see the chamber of commerce member-in-good-standing certificate posted next to the cannabis cultivation permit.

So the deputy in charge did what he does when checking up on any law-abiding citizen: He asked Cohen if everything was all right, learned that the buzzer had been a wind-tripped false alarm (no one was trying to burgle the crop this day, though it happens),*

---

* A farmer I followed in 2011 named George Fredericks heard the gunshots from a lethal garden grab gone bad on a nearby ranch in 2010. To even mention such rare incidents in an era where meth and alcohol violence is a daily occurrence is to overemphasize it significantly. Still, it happens about once per year in Mendocino County, explicitly because the plant is illegal. And while any violence is deplorable, unacceptable, and cause for reflection, it is worth asking what other multibillion-dollar business claimed one life or fewer in the past year. While you've read this footnote, someone has been killed or injured in an alcohol-related motor vehicle accident and by the time you finish this chapter someone will have died from a prescription drug.

When it comes to the safety of living with my family in Mendocino County for a year, I think it's worth noting that I left my keys in my truck throughout my county tenure and never locked my cabin. It's one of those places where wallets get returned by Good Samaritans calling the radio station. In fact, Mendocino County has low enough crime to ensure that when there is the annual wished him a good evening, and departed, presumably feeling a sense of a job well done.

Oh, and then the same thing happened again three weeks later. With the same result.

Today, the aboveground and locally legal cannabis cultivators of Mendocino County think of those alarm bells roughly the way the denizens of Philadelphia treated the peals of the Liberty Bell in 1775. Because not only had local law enforcement fundamentally (and seemingly impossibly) reversed its stance on the Drug War (even the current sheriff had busted 9.31 permittees in the past, before the ordinance), but also the 9.31 badge could be used as a valuable marketing tool for, say, Bay Area cannabis dispensaries eager to find a legal, sustainably grown source for their cannabis medicine supplies. In other words, 9.31 could serve as a high-end brand. Like Cristal, or "Cuban seed." But fairly traded. 9.31. Remember that number. We're going to be hearing a lot about it in these pages.

At least in Mendocino County, Matt Cohen was as aboveground as the hardware store owner or the vintner, and thus was protected from "rippers" (as cannabis thieves are known) by the law enforcement professionals he funded—"as I *should* be," he maintained in one of our first conversations, sounding like a conservative great uncle.

"We're growing the best quality, sustainably grown medicine in the world," Cohen told me. "Why is that something to hide at a chamber of commerce meeting? People like me are the businesspeople helping America remain competitive in the world economy." The overall professional and cultural soundtrack of the county, in other words, is no longer "I Fought the Law" but "All Together Now."

---

cannabis-related violent incident, media can trot out the ex-logger curmudgeon for the reliable "this used to be a nice place to raise kids" quote. Guess what? It still is an extraordinarily great place to raise kids. When I took my late-afternoon writing break each day, my oldest darted ahead of me to the nearby creekside park to play with whatever new or old friends were there.

If you can accept the lucrative internal logic in that rarified space, then you realize that *of course* the Sheriff's Department comes to check that everything's copacetic with Cohen.

They were explicitly on the same side, you see, Cohen and the deputies and the chamber of commerce—even if this last organization didn't know it yet: promoting a high-end, regulated, Mendocino County–branded cannabis industry.

Now, that might not be what Sheriff Tom will publicly tell you. He's a law enforcer, not an economic booster. And, as he reminded me more than once, he has other sheriffs calling to ask about the 9.31 Program. His spin has to emphasize law and order. So his soundbites generally stick to the "I'm just following the law, whether I like it or not" line. Or the "I'm trying to keep my deputies out in the field, tackling this county's real problems" argument. Or, at most, the populist "I'm giving legitimate medical marijuana growers the opportunity to comply with the law—but I'm not going to stand for punks coming up here to pollute our county and make an easy million" Rambo take.

To someone who grew up in the Just Say No Era, by contrast, in fact in an East Coast suburb where you're still, today, probably going downtown for a joint and might lose your kids, the Mendocino County situation that would allow such a cannabis/law-enforcement partnership immediately struck me as astonishing and important. The landmark Zip-Tie permitting experiment thus forms the narrative backdrop as I examine the potential for a legal nationwide cannabis economy to replace the massive, current largely illegal one. I conducted this examinaton by following a single plant over nine months from birth (that is, not from seed but from mother-plant clone cutting) to patient.

And that final medical destination was something I tried to keep firmly in mind over the course of the 2011 growing season. This was not always easy, since it sure takes a long time and a borderline excessive amount of work to get it there. But I knew it was crucial to remember that the entire raison d'être for the Mendocino cannabis industry as it existed in 2011 was to help people who use the plant as part of their medical treatment. That's what state law demanded.

It's important to understand, though, and the venture capitalists who are watching the industry very closely do understand, that the model on which I focus is mappable to other uses for cannabis: Other parts of the country might similarly benefit by growing cannabis as part of a domestic textile or food production resurgence, or for a domestic fuel source. Industrial varieties can also be useful in the building-supply, cosmetics, and paint industry. But in the famous Emerald Triangle region of Northern California I studied, the cannabis varieties grown are, well, potent.

Even beyond medical limitations, farmers in Mendocino County, that charging front edge of the cannabis Green Rush, that first American county to fully end the Drug War, can (for now) only aspire to be legal if adhering to what the California courts (if not the governing cannabis legislation) seem to be shaping as a "not-for-profit collectively cultivated medicine by-and-for-patients" model. Some other medical cannabis states, like Colorado, currently run a state-regulated for-profit model.

So, "medical" it is in Mendocino County in 2011. Even if you believe, wrongly, that the whole idea of medical cannabis is a load of bunk, that is frankly irrelevant, from a "bailing out bankrupt governmental coffers at all levels from the federal to the local" perspective. In fact, the fellow whose department benefits from the proceeds of the Zip-Tie Program, the very fellow evangelizing Ordinance 9.31 in neighboring counties and states, more or less agrees with you.

The first time I met with Sheriff Allman, in his office full of valor citations and flanked in the hallway by framed photos of every other county sheriff since Mendocino's 1850 incorporation, he told me that, in his view, "maybe five percent" of medical cannabis claims were legit.

That's his view, not the law's: The wording of California's successful 1996 Proposition 215 ballot initiative allows for medical use of cannabis to treat "any . . . illness for which marijuana provides relief." Some other state programs are much more restrictive—in cases like New Jersey and New Mexico perhaps too much so, as a glance at the body of medical research indicates.

During our second interview, Sheriff Tom (it's an informal county) said something telling while giving me what I had learned is the standard honest law enforcer's line about how much he'd rather get a call that involves someone using cannabis than an alcohol-related one, let alone one involving cocaine, meth, or prescription drug abuse. I think the way he phrased it was "I've never seen a stoned man beat his wife—he generally just plays video games."

With those words, a thought occurred to me. I asked him if that might be considered effective medicinal use and therefore bump up his 5 percent legitimate use estimate.

"What?" he asked. "Playing video games?"

"Cannabis—what would you call it?—mitigating potentially violent tendencies in, say, an undiagnosed chronically depressed person."

"OK, maybe twenty percent," the sheriff amended curtly but with typical good humor. Tom Allman likes his job. Our third interview had to be delayed twenty minutes while he cradled office and cell phones and resolved a violent dispute at a local indigenous casino. Then he clapped his hands once, apologized, sat down, and said, "Where were we?"

In 1984, the U.S. Supreme Court ruled that allowing VCRs to record programming did not in itself violate the federal Copyright Act of 1976 unless the copied material was used for a "commercial or profit-making purpose." In other words, even if huge numbers of people didn't use the devices legally (you know, without the express written consent of Major League Baseball or HBO), those who did still had a right to own them. The ruling is widely considered to have launched the multibillion-dollar home entertainment revolution that today brings us, for better or for worse, *Ishtar* via instant download from nearly any spot on Earth.

Similarly, with cannabis, I discovered that assertions that many essentially "healthy" people (baseball-game tapers, in the

VCR example) were obtaining doctor referrals for cannabis is irrelevant. For one thing, if production of the plant we're discussing becomes legal for broader uses, from housing insulation to poison-ivy tincture to Middle East dispute resolution, you can just add on a few zeros to the billions in value you'll see it already generates within the confines of its medicinal designation. So that's just an additional upside. For another, even within that medical realm, all I needed was one Carl Reid to know that medical cannabis brings people genuine relief that they can't find elsewhere. If those who use it "just" for stress relief tag along with that, it's a small price to pay. Totally worth it. Here's why:

Carl being a New Mexico friend, I knew his long medical story before I embarked on my research for this book. The most recent chapter concerned his difficult, yearlong saga getting access to reliable cannabis in the Land of Enchantment even after his Veterans Administration doctor acknowledged it was a wise course.

A sixty-three-year-old Vietnam veteran with a titanium ladder in his back, Carl is not faking his pain. I was introduced to him by a mutual friend in 2009, when we went for a hike. About a mile in, I heard a heartrending groan and saw on Carl's face a harrowing scrunched-like-a-dried-apple expression. He was just trying to stand up following a water break under the shade of some yuccas. I guess I kind of leapt skyward in surprise.

"Sorry 'bout that," he apologized. "Gotta keep movin' or things start cramping up in the ol' spine."

Ours was a short, flat hike that day, and Carl's gait was best described as "hobbled." Though he didn't complain a bit about the pace or the heat or the rattlesnakes, he did later tell me he was "on his ass" for a week afterward. This is a guy who spent much of his working life after the military as a railroad engineer, and who didn't consider a day started until he was outside.

Carl hurts. A lot. Always. For three excruciating decades now. He remembers the 110-pound pack "in the jungle" that did it—the first "click" that progressed by stages and finally caused his back to "give out" during an ice-cream-churning incident several years after he left Vietnam. This started a series of surgeries, each designed, Carl says, "to remedy the damage caused by the previous one."

Later that same day after our hike, I praised one of Carl's truly incredible turned wooden bowls that I saw in a display case at our mutual friend's house. He managed to make the grain almost a narrative part of the piece.

"You take commissions?" I asked.

"Afraid those days're behind me, my friend," Carl said. "I can't stand up long enough anymore to work at my lathe."

Having "maxed out" on the quite legal Vicodin, to which he considered himself dependent even though "it wasn't helping anymore," Carl spent much of 2010 trying to do something he never imagined he would: become a part of New Mexico's fledgling medicinal cannabis program. He'd heard about its anti-inflammatory benefits for injuries such as his, and he'd been informally experimenting on a black market supply of the plant. He'd heard the clinical benefits, in fact, from his doctor.

One problem was, he said, that "my VA doc knew cannabis could help, but she couldn't sanction it. She's federal." (In December 2010, the biotech company Cannabis Science, Inc., announced that it had formed a Military Advisory Board, which, according to the company press release, "will help identify and develop actionable policies to help ease the burden on veterans serving with debilitating injuries and illnesses. The board will provide an institutionalized conduit for the evolving concerns of military veterans to be brought to the attention of senior policymakers and the public.")

Fast-forward through a year of bureaucratic-labyrinth wandering and two hundred dollars in out-of-pocket doctors' fees from multiple "nonfederal" caregivers—when it started, New Mexico's was not one of the easier programs to join. I called Carl in mid-2011 to assess his progress. He'd been accepted in the New Mexico program, and was using a home-delivered oral tincture of cannabis-infused olive oil, which he administered sublabially (under his tongue) in a thirty-milligram dose twice a day.

Actually, I had to wait a week to speak with him, because when I first called he was away on a weeklong backcountry horseback trip.

"I was on a horse for the first time in a dozen years—and it's monsoon wildflower season," he told me in a tone that sounded like a much younger man than the fellow I remembered hearing groan more than a year earlier. "It was phenomenal. It was a dream I didn't dare to have." And it was federally felonious. Not that Carl gave the Federal Scheduling Quagmire much of a thought. He was feeling too good.

"I feel the most mobile I can remember feeling in thirty years," he gushed. "It's such a huge pain reducer. And even if it wan't (Carl drops the *s* in words like *wasn't*), if it just got me off the Vicodin, then I'd be ahead of the game. But it's done more'n that. It's given me my life back."

"Should I ask? Should I ask?" I wondered. Horseback riding was impressive enough—I knew that after his combat posting Carl had served in a ceremonial calvary unit, and missed it. Maybe that was enough. Ah, heck, I asked anyway.

"So, are you taking bowl commissions?"

"I'm looking to rent studio space downtown with some good natural light," he said, referring to the Yankee Street artsy section of his hometown of Silver City. "Better ambiance with all those other studios around. When you came back, maybe you can help me move my lathe. There might be something in it for you."

# TWO
## Adventures with Vioxx

> Between 1985 and 2008, sales of antidepressants and antipsy-
> chotics multiplied almost fiftyfold, to $24.2 billion. Prescrip-
> tions for bipolar disorder and anxiety have also swelled. One in
> eight Americans, including children and even toddlers, is now
> taking a psychotropic medication. . . . Over time, [author Rob-
> ert] Whitaker argues, [prescription psychiatric] drugs make
> many patients sicker than they would have been if they had
> never been medicated.
>
> —John Horgan, director of the Center for Science Writings
> at the Stevens Institute of Technology, from a review entitled
> "Are Psychiatric Medications Making Us Sicker?" in
> *The Chronicle of Higher Education*

**M**ore and more verifiable stories like Carl's flooded over me
during the next year once I knew where to look: medical
cannabis collectives. Whatever the politics behind its medical designation, that's where I heard dozens of apolitical (or sometimes
conservative) patients fervently assert that cannabis actually does
possess broad and effective medicinal properties without danger
of overdose and without major side effects. To ask if that's abused
is like asking if wine's medicinal properties are ever abused. Of
course, but do you ban resveratrol?

In (to put it mildly) right-leaning Orange County, California,
I saw senior ladies—the largest demographic component of a cannabis collective therein called Wilbur OC—being schooled in
modern delivery methods (such as the vaporizor and the lozenge)
so as to stimulate their appetite and deliver the only treatment that
makes their arthritis bearable.

Craig Raimondi, Wilbur OC's tie-wearing manager, told me,
"We see a lot of folks returning in desperation to the cannabis of

their college days. They have positive memories of the plant, and feel comfortable giving it a shot when prescription medicines don't provide relief for their symptoms. In the communities of people living with various ailments, word gets around that it's effective."

Wilbur OC and its sister collective in San Diego have 5,050 patient members, several dozen of whom annually take a field trip to the sustainably minded Mendocino County farm that is the source of 100 percent of the collectives' medicine. This is known in the industry as a "closed loop" model, which has marketing value during federal cannabis prohibition because it shows that an outfit can be relied on not to divert cannabis to, say, gravity-defying Cincinnati Bengals wide receiver Jerome Simpson (whose 2.5-pound California shipment was nabbed upon delivery to his home in 2011) or a college dorm in Missouri (where, by the way, prices for California bud in 2011 were about three times higher—six thousand dollars per pound—than they were inside the Golden State).

The two collectives were so popular that their executive director and Mendocino farm manager, forty-seven-year-old Jim Hill (he of the polite DEA underwear-drawer raid), closed membership in 2010. The collective simply couldn't produce any more medicine than Hill and his full-time botanist already did and Hill didn't want to risk getting it from outside sources. Only members could receive medicine.

"Orange County needs its medicine too," Raimondi told me when I pointed out that this was where Richard Nixon retired. "That's our motto." And Wilbur offers it less expensively than any other collective or dispensary I'd seen in California too—an important consideration for veterans or seniors on a fixed income whose insurance, if they have it, can't (yet) cover a federal "drug." The Wilbur OC online menu in 2011 listed a price of two hundred dollars for an ounce of medical cannabis—considerably lower than California street levels, which could push three hundred. It's safe to say an ounce might be a reasonable monthly supply for pain control. A monthly supply of the generic version of Vicodin, by comparison, can cost six hundred dollars for the uninsured. Now, the fact that many vets and seniors do have coverage is beside the point if the covered remedies are either ineffective, addictive, or causing debilitating side effects.

"We've put all of the other collectives and dispensaries in this area out of business," Raimondi said.

That was meaningful to me, because Hill, a former greyhound breeder and current small plane owner who said he'd paid more than a hundred thousand dollars in legal fees successfully fighting his various raids, was so effervescent and unwaveringly passionate in his "I'm in it for the patients" line that my native East Coaster's Cynic Meter had kicked in. What I'm trying to say is that it took me several months of visits to Hill's Northern California farm and the Southern California collectives they supply before I realized that he wasn't full of shit.

Coming from a family of medical doctors and thus imbued with a sensor that goes off like Matt Cohen's cannabis alarm at the slightest hint of quackery or what you might call "crystal whoo whoo" medicine, I naturally had to see the collective situation for myself, so I cruised to one of Hill's collectives in April 2011. Everything in the neighborhood was so homogeneous that it took me several circles before I identified the long, low, mirrored, typically OC office building where Wilbur is housed, with its good landscaping and lawyer and defense-contractor neighbors.

Raimondi said that the collective's location was explicitly chosen to provide convenient access to residents of the nearby and senior-heavy "Leisure World" development—now incorporated as Laguna Woods. Average resident age in the seventies. The quiet lobby I entered was adorned with a wall-size, patient-painted mural. Two patient/members were in the back among rows of labeled jars of herbal medicine, carefully trimming flowers into their final form as part of their "reimbursement" for their medicine. For legal reasons, many California cannabis collectives avoid the term *payment*. They love that verb *reimburse*. Patients reimburse the collective for its operating costs, which is what you do if you belong to a food cooperative. At Wilbur, patients could also help other, less mobile members make it to doctor appointments as part of their reimbursement. The point was to meet the state's requirements for "collective cultivation."

All told I met a half-dozen patients receiving Hill's Mendocino medicine, and all spoke of positive results for ailments ranging from arthritis to cancer to pain from war injuries to PTSD. In fact, what I saw in Orange County was an eye-opener for me: There are people there who like both Bill O'Reilly *and* cannabis.

At the San Diego collective Hill founded, the patient who most intrigued me was thirty-year-old Iraq War vet and retired army sergeant Jamie Brown, who is also the collective manager. There's no less graphic way to describe his shrapnel injury than to say what he says: "You could fit two fingers into the dent in my back." That was because of the rocket that exploded five feet from his tent in 2003.

Two months of in-patient, sometimes touch-and-go intensive care followed for an injury that his doctor told him he "wouldn't have survived if this was Vietnam." The entry wound was an inch and a half from Brown's spine, took out his left kidney, his spleen, and the distal portion of his pancreas. During the acute phase of his recovery, he had multiple chest tubes.

And yet six months later his real problem was prescription painkillers. "I got great care that saved my life, no question, but when you tell the VA you have pain, they toss you a pill. None of the painkillers is positive for your body, and I was on every one of them at some point. If I hadn't tried cannabis as a kid, I'd probably never have thought of it as a medicine. But I moved to California [from Indiana] in large part because of the medical cannabis law, and today I take no pharmaceuticals at all. Cannabis isn't just helpful to me for pain and the remnants of any PTSD. It's a motivator to eat well and exercise, which is crucial to staying healthy with my injury. I'm a lucky man to have access to this plant. I thank God for it, actually. I think about the other injured vets I knew in Indiana every day and I wish they had access to the medicine that I do."

When I asked him how he handled his cannabis medication within the federal constraints faced by his VA doctor, Brown said, "You're the first person I've ever told outside of my family, this collective, and close friends that I medicate with cannabis."

Another San Diego patient/member at Hill's collective, fifty-four-year-old former Navy SEAL Mike Knox, was prescribed methadone for an aorta tear, a medication that made him lethargic and obese before he kicked it with cannabis. "I lost a hundred thirty-five pounds when I got off that stuff," he said. "I just bought me a new motorcycle. I'm back. In my age group especially, we Medicaiders at fifty-plus years old, we need this medicine—and education about it."

Continuing to hear such troubling claims about our economy's most profitable federally legal industry, Big Pharma, caused me to recall with palpable distaste, even fear, my own single experience with prescription pharmaceutical painkillers. It was unspeakable— without exaggeration one of the most horrible episodes in my life, and that includes covering, just out of high school, the 1988 Republican Convention when Dan Quayle was announced as the vice-presidential offering.

I had been prescribed Vioxx, Merck's (now-banned) painkiller for joint pain that turned out to be a luckily early-diagnosed case of Lyme disease in 2001. I took one pill in my Alaskan cabin and I suppose you could argue that it worked because indeed my joint pain became secondary. But that was because I became severely disoriented and violently sick to my stomach for the good part of a day. At times my heart began racing and I felt panic.

I remember making one of those promises to the Creator never to take another of these pills if I pulled through, preferring even a brief coma, forget about joint agony, to Vioxx's side effects. The memory of that adventure rather kept my mind open this past year whenever I heard a cannabis patient who was dealing with a long-term or chronic illness tell me, "Nothing else works." Been there, brother, and I know your "else" was probably even worse than mine.

Vioxx is far from the only questionably approved pharmaceutical that is having disastrous effects on large numbers of people. To give a current example, Seven Counties Services, a mental health center in Tennessee, is refusing to give its thirty thousand patients the antianxiety medications known as benzodiazepines (brand name Xanax) because abuse and overdose is so widespread, according to *The New York Times.*

So that's why, whenever I hear someone point out, accurately, that in states like California, Colorado, and Montana it's a piece of cake to get a doctor's recommendation for cannabis, I know we're about to venture into the territory of Mark Twain's famous adage that there are lies, damned lies, and statistics. One patient's "social," "spiritual," or "akin-to-morning-coffee" relationship with the plant might be another's "stress reduction," "PTSD mitigation," "occasional insomnia treatment," "Irritable Bowel Syndrome inflammatory relief," or even "component of a homeostatic wellness regimen." It's an herb that humans have been working with for millennia. It genuinely has a lot of beneficial uses.

Not that the medical-recommendation situation isn't humorous. I saw multiple physician referral vendors enjoying long lines and in fact engaged in something of a price war at the June 27, 2011, *High Times* Cannabis Cup in San Francisco. In addition to being another event I can't believe I can tax-deduct, it was also one at which a Mendocino-based dispensary called the Leonard Moore Cooperative won in the concentrates (hash) category for its Ingrid indica strain. Go American entrepreneurialism.

Yes, obtaining a doctor's recommendation for cannabis in many medical cannabis states in 2011 is as easy as asking your doctor for Viagra or Ambien. Except cannabis doesn't seep into the water supply when discarded or expired. And no corporations are paying doctors to prescribe cannabis. Yet. Also, as I was learning from speaking to patients, it's much safer than many less-stigmatized "legal" drugs.

So why isn't there 100 percent support for medical cannabis in the United States, instead of 70 percent? The most comparatively

coherent argument I've heard against broad, California-style medicinal exceptions to existing cannabis laws came from a Carnegie
Mellon professor, Jonathan Caulkins, writing in the August 8, 2011,
*Christian Science Monitor*. Caulkins, who has also written a drug
policy book, observes that one study showed that California cannabis patients "most commonly reported seeking . . . cannabis . . . to
relieve pain, improve sleep, or relax," rather than treat what
Caulkins tells us are the afflictions that "motivate voters to support medical marijuana programs (HIV/AIDS, cancer, or glaucoma)."

Now, Caulkins seems to think Californian voters are incapable
of understanding the words *any . . . illness for which marijuana provides relief* on their ballot. I don't know where arthritis, MS,
Crohn's disease, or hospice care went, or whether, in his view, cancer treatment includes both promising research into tumor cyto-
toxicity and cannabis's famous and irrefutable postchemotherapy
appetite stimulation (aka it allows otherwise nauseated patients to
eat). But, OK, let's accept those stated academic stats of Professor
Caulkins, writing from a non-medicinal-cannabis state, Pennsyl-
vania. Even though they don't even slightly correlate with the facts
I witnessed on the ground over the course of a year of full-time
field research in California.

Given the fact that the legal situation surrounding medical
cannabis has evolved as it has, and it isn't going away, it seems to
me more valid to frame the discussion another way. What I want
to know is, for most users, does the plant do more good or harm?
This "is it Medicine or is it Poison?" question seems to me, when
you erase the rhetoric on all sides, the essential question. And it's
one I was delighted to research in depth, and not just because of
the massive economic value at stake in the answer.

In fact, I've always considered the word *Pharmakon* to be one
of my key life-guiding mantras. In Greek, the root can mean both
*medicine* and *poison*. I believe it is important, in any endeavor, to
attempt to tip the scale toward the medicinal side of things in life.
Which was it, when it came to cannabis? I know I've heard people

screaming both "This medicine saved my life!" and "Drugs killed my niece!"

Could it be both? Did the answer simply depend on the dose or frequency of use? Like aspirin, was too much medicinal cannabis poison? Since "psychoactivity" is concerned and potential addiction is in play, I asked that last question both chemically and socially.

It's a complicated discussion. On the one hand, cannabis activists love to post comparatively huge death statistics for alcohol and other dangerous drugs next to cannabis's "deaths caused" number of "0." But that's just physical overdoses. A Mendocino County–based clinical psychiatrist named Mark Kline told me that in his "poor coastal community with high unemployment and associated social problems," he sees the same potential behavioral and genetic associations that can lead to abuse of any compounds, medical or otherwise, at play in cannabis, especially in today's potent strains, and that in particular he finds it problematic that cannabis is generally self-prescribed.

"I'd rather see it treated as an herbal remedy than a pharmaceutical," he told me. "It's not really something you can put in an orange pillbox and label with 'Take three times daily as needed for stress.'" The drug Kline believes it most closely resembles in its psychological effects is not cocaine, heroin, or alcohol, but Valium, "because of the way it integrates into a patient's life sometimes without him even fully realizing its effects." This, Kline feels, is not a good thing.

Confounding my hopes nearly immediately for a simple answer to the Medicine or Poison issue was an interview in his Willits, California, office with Dr. William Courtney, an M.D. and cannabis researcher. There I learned how much there is to learn. Courtney was a man who, I was warned by my referrer (the county sheriff), spoke in such dense clinical language that I should consider myself brainy if I comprehended "ten percent of what he says." I therefore can report with some pride I believe I pegged as much as 12 percent, but only after checking out some of the research on his foundation's website (cannabisinternational.org). And he was being concise during our hour-long interview in late April 2011, because his wife was about to go into labor.

I'll have to hope that the reader will independently delve into the research (Courtney's and others': the University of California at San Diego's Center for Medicinal Cannabis Research at http:// www.cmcr.ucsd.edu/ is also a respected resource, with a recent sample study on the home page titled "A Two-Part Study of Sativex Oromucosal Spray for Relieving Uncontrolled Persistent Pain in Patients With Advanced Cancer"). There anyone can gain at least a coherent layman's understanding of concepts like "cannabinoid receptors" (CB1 and CB2 and their ilk) and "isolation of endogenous cannabinoids."

A really good compound with which to familiarize yourself is CBD (cannabidiol), a nonpsychoactive cannabinoid (component of the cannabis plant), which in study after study is showing wide-ranging promising medicinal effects, most significantly in tumor reduction. In my truck the other day, I heard an underwriter on a local public radio station hawk lab testing of cannabis harvests for "THC, CBD, potency, and molds."

I'll sum up the journalistic challenge of trying to establish if cannabis does more good than harm this way: Even the famous THC, just one of eighty or so known cannabinoids for which we humans have associated receptors (up from around sixty known a few years ago), is one heck of a complex molecule. The way it reacts with the human brain varies by the moment (it changes based on anatomical biochemistry over time) and by the individual.

This is why farmers will always be part of this industry and why Big Pharma's isolating and synthesizing one component of the cannabis plant, as in prescription Marinol, used for appetite stimulation, doesn't work very well. When a San Francisco dispensary manager I interviewed is asked by a patient, such as his father (a newcomer to the plant), which strain will be most effective for (in this case) his periodic spates of insomnia, he finds it difficult to answer.

"First off, this is an issue for a patient to discuss with his or her doctor, but what I've found basically corroborates the research," he told me. "If an indica strain shows dramatic sleep-aid value in eighty percent of patients, it can have the opposite effects in five percent, and no effect on fifteen percent. Patients have to understand their systems, and sometimes try multiple dosages and strains to find what works for them. Everyone's biochemistry interplays with cannabinoids uniquely."

The good news is, if you're among the 5 percent for whom that indica strain is contraindicated for insomnia, it's not going to kill or even harm you, and its effects will wear off in two hours. You'll know if you're among the 80 percent because you'll be asleep. In a very small percentage of people, the dispensary manager told me, in his experience less than 1 percent, cannabis can cause anxiety. Studies I subsequently checked seem to confirm this, and usually in people predisposed to anxiety or mental illness. Many FDA-approved pharmaceuticals have much more common side effects.

And if that weren't enough to complicate the discussion, cannabinoid receptors are further unusual in that they are systemic: They're not limited to just the brain or just the pancreas—they're everywhere in our bodies, even the skin. If you have inflammation in a muscle in your foot, cannabinoid receptors somehow know to spring up nearby. If you introduce the right cannabinoids into your system in the right way, pain is reduced.

"When their work is done, they can even blow themselves out," Dr. Courtney told me, meaning the receptors will shut up shop until needed again. You hear the fascination in the voice of Courtney when he lists recent studies about the human endocannabinoid system. And the studies are often recent, because cannabis research has stagnated for so long in the United States due to the plant's Schedule I classification.

To obtain cannabis samples or funding for research, some researchers have resorted to applying for grants with negative-sounding hypotheses suggesting addictive qualities or postulating that cannabis interferes with AIDS cocktails (with the actual studies, unsurprisingly, finding that it actually augments the efficacy of AIDS treatments).

In one famous case, Donald Tashkin at UCLA began investigating the harmful effects of inhaled marijuana on the lungs of 243 cannabis smokers. After eight years, he found in 1997 that "the long-term study of heavy, habitual marijuana smokers argues against the concept that continuing heavy use of marijuana is a significant risk factor for the development of chronic lung disease."* In fact, other studies have concluded that cannabis use may actually be associated with a decreased risk of lung cancer.

And so Dr. Courtney, who was dressed in a Mr. Rogers cardigan when we met and looked a little bit like Carl Sagan, believes that despite the hampered trickle of research, there is no disguising the naked reality: There is very little evolutionary, botanical, neurological, anatomical, or anthropological (or even archaeological) doubt that we as a species have to some degree evolved with this plant. Or, to use a concept of Michael Pollan's, it's bred us. But let's be fair: It's been mutual. So when it comes to the question of "Is cannabis more helpful than harmful to the greater human population?," I could at least answer, "Well, it sure has been an enduring relationship."

Courtney's sense of human/cannabis coevolution is rather cutting edge. He believes that one possible avenue for such interspecies genetic exchange over time is via plasmids—loops of independent DNA about the size of a virus. "It would be difficult to find a number large enough for how improbable it is that [the human symbiosis with cannabis] is happenstance," he told me. The two species have helped each other over time, in other words. Mendocino County, California, in fact, is essentially one big human effort to nurture cannabis DNA.

---

* As reported in Volume 155 of the *American Journal of Respiratory and Critical Care Medicine.*

# THREE

## If Your Cancer Treatment Options Can Cost You Your Job, You Might Be Living Under a Policy in Need of Change

The tumors regressed over the same period of time that cannabis was consumed via inhalation, raising the possibility that cannabis played a role in tumor regression. . . . Further research may be appropriate to elucidate the increasingly recognized effect of cannabis/cannabinoids on gliomas (brain cancers).

—From a 2011 study by Mansoor Foroughi, Glenda Hendson, Michael A. Sargent, and Paul Steinbok, entitled "Spontaneous regression of septum pellucidum/forniceal pilocytic astrocytomas—possible role of Cannabis inhalation," in the journal *Child's Nervous System*

Smoked marijuana has not withstood the rigors of science—it is not medicine, and it is not safe.

—First paragraph, U.S. Drug Enforcement Administration (DEA) "Position on Marijuana" paper, 2010

Marijuana, in its natural form, is one of the safest therapeutically active substances known. . . . It would be unreasonable, arbitrary, and capricious for the DEA to continue to stand between those sufferers and the benefits of this substance.

—U.S. Drug Enforcement Administration chief administrative law judge Francis L. Young, in 1988, ruling that the Controlled Substances Act required the transfer of cannabis from Schedule I to Schedule II. Twenty-three years later, that has not happened.

The main reason that we still have a Drug War, and the major reason that Mexican cartels are profitable, is because of the DEA's assertion (per the first paragraph in its 2010 position paper) that smoked cannabis has no medical value at all, not even the smidgeon that would facilitate easier research Stateside. Drug

Czar Gil Kerlikowske says the same thing a lot too. But I found out from Dr. Courtney that right across town from the DEA and Kerlikowske's Office of National Drug Control Policy (ONDCP), the equally federal Department of Health and Human Services had in 2003 been awarded Patent Number 6,630,507, titled "Cannabinoids as antioxidants and neuroprotectants." Another patent, this a nongovernmental one from 1999, titled "Cardiovascular uses of cannabinoid compounds," was awarded to George Kunos et al (Patent Number: 5,939,429), and has the following abstract:

> Hemorrhagic shock and in other conditions associated with excessive vasoconstriction, such as hypertension, peripheral vascular disease, cirrhosis of the liver, or certain forms of angina pectoris can be treated by using agonists of CB1 receptors as well as other cannabinoid receptors.

These patents and dozens of others like them sounded more than slightly medicinal to Jim Hill, who manages the Southern California collectives with all the nonliberal grannies. So much so that when his Mendocino County farm was raided by those polite DEA agents in 2009, Hill printed out some of these medical cannabis patents and asked the agent in charge why he was there at all, since his administration's stated position that cannabis has no medical value contradicts its sister agency's patent.

"He told me," Hill in turn told me, "'the right hand doesn't know what the left hand is doing.' I think he learned something that day."

That's all well and good, unless you have a sick friend who might benefit from a medicine but wants to (or has to) play by the rules. Which is another way of saying that, forget about the billion-dollar economic roadblock, our government's internally contradictory policies are almost certainly costing lives.

"If the little old lady in our collective who got her appetite back after chemo understands that cannabis is a vital medicine, I would think our policymakers could get the memo," Hill said. Conventional Mendo wisdom, incidentally, has it that Hill's own federal raid was spurred by his prominent quotes and farm photos in a nationally syndicated 2009 Associated Press article headlined "California Sprouts Marijuana Green Rush."

Although I earlier said that I don't have a cousin in jail for possession of a joint, I confess that after speaking with Dr. Courtney, this medical thread of the cannabis issue suddenly began to acquire a personal connection for me. I mean, the industrial side of cannabis felt important because I would love to see the nation's economy get any kind of viable jump-start. But after I delved just a bit into the cancer research, I had a decision to make vis-à-vis an ill family friend we'll call Fred. A government-funded scientist, no less, who was dealing with several new tumors from his long-suppressed non-Hodgkin's lymphoma.

When I referred him to Dr. Courtney's site, after some "I don't want to send false hope or sound like a miracle-cure crackpot but a life is at stake here" internal debate of my own, Fred's reply (reproduced in part here) was thoughtful but in no small measure scary to me:

| | |
|---|---|
| From: | Fred'sNotMyRealName@gmail.com |
| Subject: | Re: You Came to Mind |
| Date: | April 29, 2011 6:18:30 PM MDT |
| To: | fine@well.com |

Hi Doug:

I do realize this is a serious topic and it would be a lot better if the federal government would get out of the way and let people get onto the real work. And the difference between the CBDs and THC is not something I had seen yet.

Strangely, this topic recently came up on the lymphoma forum I frequent. The National Cancer Institute Complementary and Alternative Medicine Center posted something fairly positive about the anti-cancer effects of cannabis but then made it vaguer a few days later.

As a federal employee I would be risking my job if I got caught (even if I moved to a state like CA and got a medical marijuana card, which would be easy). But I never mind when people give me ideas. Heck, it's not like you are suggesting oils from the organs of endangered Asian bears (and yes, someone really suggested that to me).

So thanks for thinking of me and I'm definitely looking forward to the book.

Cheers,
Fred

I'll never forget the tableau of the airport terminal in which I read that note, because my blood ran cold. I tried to imagine inveighing Fred, "You mean, even if it's effective for reducing your tumors, stimulating your appetite, and reducing pain from your conventional regimen, you're avoiding a treatment because it might not currently be the best decision for your *job*?" Yikes.

In our exchange, Fred also made some points about not wanting to mix and match treatments (which could violate agreements he'd made to be part of clinical trials). So his hands were tied, because of roadblocks to clinical cannabis research. Later, touring Jim Hill's picturesque Potter Valley farm in the heart of Mendocino County's river-hugging eastern end near harvest time, I was thinking for the thousandth time about the powerful prescription painkillers Fred sometimes has to take following his treatments. Alongside the collectives' full-time botanist, Sharif Moye, I gestured at a foot-long cannabis bud hanging from an "Apricot Kush" plant, and blurted out, "Like it or not, this doesn't seem to me to be the likely source of a trillion-dollar war."

"It says a lot," Moye, who had obviously given the issue some thought, said with a series of resigned nods, "that we've banned flowers."

One reason thirty-two-year-old Moye had given the issue some thought is that he describes his mother's mind as "returning from zombie to coherent, allowing us closure," when he and his father shut off the morphine drip that had caused her to "check out" and replaced it with a sativa cannabis strain that worked far better for the final weeks of her late-stage cervical cancer. "We knew she wasn't going to make it," Moye told me. "But she snapped back to life, she ate, and we got to talk about things I can't imagine not having discussed. Plus I got to see her smile again."

Pretty easy to see where that falls in the medicine/poison debate. This was all years before Moye's own farm was raided. As with his boss Hill's raid, all charges were dropped, though Moye, even with a fifty-thousand-dollar investment in the Drug War's legal subsidiary, never got his wife's computer back. You see this pattern, called Punishing with the Process, a lot in cannabis country. It often affects the business plans of entrepreneurs who expect to wake up one morning soon to find their crop as legal as wine.

Moye, by the way, with a chemistry degree, went from doing pharmacology and drug development research at the University of Arizona to doing nonprofit botanical research in Mendocino County. His friends and colleagues thought he was crazy— dropping a promising phamaceutical career to "go grow dope in California." But Moye says the decision was an easy one. "My academic work wasn't helping anyone. It was about tenure for the professor. My work here helps several thousand patients every day, some of whom are going to survive where my own mother couldn't."

A few days after Moye told me that story, I got a Google News heads-up containing a Bloomberg article about a Massachusetts company called Medicinal Genomics, whose founder, Kevin McKernan, had just sequenced the entire cannabis plant genome, for purposes of aiding research—such as CBD's tumor-shrinking properties—that he believes will eventually help patients like Fred all over the world.

McKernan told Bloomberg that he embarked on the sequencing project—in his house, by the way—essentially as a matter of duty (or, if you insist on being cynical, since his start-up *is* called Medicinal Genomics, as a win-win investment). "Any compound that's nontoxic and shows hope [in tumor shrinking], we should be all over," he said. "The only way I knew how to do that was to sequence the genome."

Even in a world full of important stories like teetering Middle East dictators and massive national debt, cannabis is top-tier crucial to brilliant people like McKernan who could be doing anything. They know it's connected to the economy, health care reform, civil liberties, climate change, domestic energy, the federal budget, ending violence in Mexico, and finding food for nine billion fellow humans. Little issues like that. And, as the wealth of cataloged studies on Dr. Courtney's website indicates, the plant is a potentially valuable tool in the medical treatment of anyone who has to get rid of cancerous growths.

Similarly, progressive billionaire investor George Soros had plenty of other issues to choose from when he became a major sponsor on Proposition 19, the full cannabis decriminalization and regulation effort in California that narrowly failed in 2010. Organizers of one of the 2012 legalization efforts in the Golden State (which they promise is worded much better and will pass if it makes it to the ballot, though this is more likely in 2014) tell me it requires about two dollars per signature just to get the issue on the ballot, not counting election canvassing. That's a total of about three million dollars to have a chance to succeed in California. When you talk to electoral activists in a democracy, you learn that change has a price tag, just as apples and car repairs do.

However it happens, I hope federal policy changes quickly enough for Fred, or that the other, more federally sanctioned, chemical- or radiation-based and debilitating experimental treatments he is undergoing work. His situation, though, made me gladder than ever that I had just relocated to the home base of post–Drug War experimentation. With some other spots in California and Colorado close behind, Mendocino County was the one place in North America where, in February of 2011, cannabis was being treated essentially like just another regulated industry.

Thanks to that county ordinance called 9.31. The Zip-Tie Program is to the American War on Drugs what the New Deal was to the Great Depression. The beginning of the end.

Yes, as the economic and medical evidence piled up I got even more relaxed about having hired some goat milkers and bumped my Sweetheart and two bouncy ranchers-in-training west a couple of states in late winter via a ridiculously oversize, vegetable-oil-powered truck connected to a wobbly U-Haul trailer. To, you know, begin my research in earnest. Hopefully meet some locals. Make connections. If they'd talk.

Inside of six weeks I was in police custody for the first time in my life. It was only twenty minutes in the back of a police car and I wasn't in friendly Mendocino County. But still. There's nothing like having your pockets emptied with your hands held behind your back and wondering if your kids are going to grow up fatherless due to a plant not even in your possession to generate the following, almost inevitable question:

"Let me get this straight. A flower so valuable to humans that the oldest surviving medical book included a cannabis physician's desk guide, a plant that provides relief to patients, astronomical economic benefit to growers, ecological benefits to fields, nutritive benefits to humans on every continent (except Antarctica, unless they have greenhouse 'grows' I don't know about), this . . . this is why I'm currently being led into the back of a Sonoma County sheriff's deputy's vehicle?"

Somebody, I realized while, at age forty, getting my first look at the wrong side of a patrol car door, ain't telling it like it is. It wasn't until later that evening that I chilled out enough to determine that if my new journalistic subject was similar at core to, well, every other single topic I've covered over two decades on five continents, then it'd probably be a good idea to follow the money.

For instance, I soon learned that one cannabis dilemma faced by the revolving door of senior government regulators and Big Pharma executives is that a plant that's relatively easy to grow in your backyard can prove an impediment to shareholder value if your business model calls for patenting much more expensive, usually much less effective synthesized or derivative pills.

And that's just the admittedly lucrative biotech side of the cannabis plant. The nutritive, industrial, social, and environmental restoration angles (not to mention post–Drug War taxpayer savings and budget-balancing benefits from incarceration drops) add tens of billions more to the value of this simple flower.

Even during my little incident with the deputies, I suspected I was onto something when the blood drained out of the face of the officer in charge of my brief incarceration that April day in 2011, Sonoma County narcotics detective Andy Cash (yes, Cash), after I informed him that although I was not in possession of any cannabis, as his colleague Deputy Londo had intimated by saying my truck (or perhaps its admittedly kung-pao-chicken-derived exhaust) "smelled like marijuana," I *was* in fact a journalist writing a book about the topic.

A late arrival to the scene, Cash had sauntered over to the locked police car (yes, I checked, while the officers were tangled in some of my infant's car-seat blankets) in an effort to play Good Cop ("This can be really quick if you just tell us whether you're transporting a little or a lot of pot"). He also contradicted Deputy Londo's stated reason for pulling me over, telling me that I had been late in signaling for a lane change.

While Cash and Londo fruitlessly ransacked my sons' life jackets and river booties not far from an almost impossibly ironic Anheuser-Busch billboard featuring a San Francisco Giants tableau and the enormous slogan "Grab Some Buds," I thought but wasn't quite brave enough to say, "So, you know, thanks for the chapter."

In other words, once again it looked to me like I had a book here. And so as soon as I had regained my freedom, I dove back in. I've met Cash since, and he really seems a decent fellow. When I heard him testify in another case I was following, he struck me as honest. Still, my Sonoma misunderstanding reminded me that some people are still, incredibly, fighting the Drug War, and that my choice of topic carried with it some danger. It still feels surreal when I think that for the past year, each day I'd wake for work, kiss my family, exercise, eat some local eggs, and hear my Sweetheart say, as she handed me my lunch, "Have fun on the cannabis farm."

# FOUR

## Reporting to You from Inside the
## Bubble within the Bubble within the Bubble

We are Californians associating to collectively cultivate. We do not purchase. We do not sell. We . . . pay tax on all transactions. We do not accept vendors. Membership is closed-loop, limited to qualified Californians age 21 and over, who are allowed by state law to use cannabis.

> —One hundred percent Mendocino-supplied Orange County, California, "Wilbur OC" Cannabis Collective website

The women involved in the case, who grew marijuana in their own backyard . . . had strong medical justification for using the drug—I thought it was most unwise to prohibit them from doing so, but I think that it was equally clear that the federal constitution did authorize the federal government to enforce the statutes on the books."

> —Retired U.S Supreme Court justice John Paul Stevens, referencing a 2005 High Court case, *Gonzales v. Raich*, October 19, 2011

Every regional subculture requires a period of residency before a newcomer can in good faith publicly declare himself a local. In Maine, I learned from a friend who moved there a few weeks too late, it's a generation. No exceptions. If you arrived in the Pine Tree State when you were one second old, it doesn't count. You're from "away."

Alaska, my home for many years and, incidentally, the first U.S. state (in 1975) to legalize cannabis for all uses during the Drug War, sets the meter at a more reasonable one winter. The more grizzled of the Last Frontier's denizens figure if you survive a few ditch skids and wet-firewood emergencies, you're not just a wide-eyed, eagle-snapping tourist anymore.

In California in general, the Local Badge is pinned on upon the real estate closing. The Golden State, despite the fact that the bear that adorns the state flag has been hunted to extinction, is North America's place of and for newness, to this day. The whole End of the Line mind-set.

It's how you can tell Californians from other humans: by their acceptance of and frequent adherence to a variety of left- and right-wing absurdness, often combined in odd hybrids within a single resident's politics. Burning Man, Silicon Valley, Rush Limbaugh: All started here. And to be sure, we should be grateful for the genuine intellectual and lifestyle fertility that is cushioned by these wide, some might say cosmically wide, parameters for what passes as acceptable behavior.

It's this open-mindedness that explains why Elon Musk, PayPal-founder-cum-rocket-scientist, believes that despite everything, the Golden State will always be the world center of innovation. Despite the taxes, despite the wacky ballot initiative system, despite even the putting forth of the Terminator as a gubernatorial candidate so folks would be distracted enough to let the Enron brownout matter go away.

And yet in the far northern, vast, geographically diverse and profoundly rural county of Mendocino, in whose redwoods I rented a moldy cabin to research this book (not an easy task at the cusp of planting season, what with all the "Will pay top dollar for 215-friendly property" postings you see on Craigslist here),[*] there's a unique twist to this "owning of space" philosophy.

Here, four hours from Google headquarters, you're not a local until a new generation of cannabis growers moves in with even more offensive driving habits and hairstyles, and against whose fashion and general grooming you can bond with the generation that used to resent you.[†]

---

[*] A reference to the 1996 ballot initiative that exempted medicinal cannabis from other drug laws in California.

[†] Some of whose members have by now cashed in and become organic vintners. In an arguably unintentional double entendre, Mendocino is in fact officially

This might sound like a trite summary of the local zeitgeist, but not only is it three generations into active sociological fact, it's only human—merely a version of how people judge other people in every cultural ecosystem. And it has one other crucial quality: It is, in the end, inclusive. Once you're in, you're in. Without further judgment, no matter your politics, musical tastes, or view of the current sheriff.

This is why you can have a county that holds a "Frontier Days" rodeo weekend (including throbbing country music of the Show Me the Birth Certificate variety) and at the same time spawns a local alternative advice columnist who calls herself "Super Slut." It also makes outside penetration—by anything from wayward hikers to federal law enforcement choppers—extremely difficult. Especially when one of the region's community-supported radio stations, KMUD, openly announces the latest helicopter sightings on the air during harvest season.

As a longtime habitué of red counties where viewing a female nipple traditionally occurs shortly prior to marriage (or at least shortly prior to first conception), I knew things were different here by the end of my first day of local interviews. That was when a member of the Mendocino County Board of Supervisors railed to me over an organic beer that local land-use ordinance 9.31, in permitting up to ninety-nine cannabis plants per (nontownsite) parcel, wasn't permissive *enough*. We're talking about between one hundred and six hundred pounds per harvest, at about twenty-five hundred dollars per pound in 2011. That's a lot of medicine. If it doesn't get seized or rained on at the wrong time.

Turns out, I had not yet *begun* to be blown away by the Men-

---

America's Greenest Wine Region™. The Mediterranean climate here works for both of these number-one and far distant number-two local crops. Or, as my Sweetheart put it after a month of fair-trade farmers' markets and a brutal massage-therapist advertising war: "It's like the Alps here: beautiful, progressive, and highly taxed." Indeed, in my New Mexico valleys, some of my neighbors would rather die from copper-mine-poisoned water than say a nice thing about the Earth. Mendocino County, by contrast, hosts the annual "Gaia Festival" on Wavy Gravy's Hog Farm.

docino Normal. Shortly after that pubside "Legalize it" chant from an elected cannabis farmer, Mendocino sergeant Randy Johnson, who manages the Zip-Tie Program full-time-plus for his boss, Sheriff Allman, invited me—with the owner's permission— to accompany a 9.31 inspection to a local farm.

He was heading to a cannabis appointment, in a relatively civilized (read: almost reachable by two-wheel-drive) part of the county to make sure that the field had been secured by the ordinance-mandated fencing. Hands were shaken. Smiling photos taken. Regulatory suggestions made.

The grower, already certified USDA Organic for his duck eggs and produce, was thirty-one-year-old George Fredericks. He shrugged at my astonishment at the scene in a "welcome to Northern California" kind of way and said, "I just want to be able to pay my taxes instead of being treated like a criminal. I farm a medicinal plant [loud quacking behind us]. Sorry. And ducks." George sent me home after a subsequent visit with a just-picked watermelon. In his family's personal garden, that vine was between the cannabis and the spinach.

This kind of botanical integration is more than a conscious lifestyle decision. The utter county-wide relaxation about it is horticultural civil disobedience. Mendocino's experiment, though it looked to be replicated in at least two other California counties in 2012, was and is radical even by Golden State standards. One county over, as I already knew all too well, people were getting arrested for the exact same crop choice.

"Mendo" life, in short, is about Mendo. It's Mendo-centric. When you're inside the 3,878-square-mile county, you're among family. When you're outside the county, you're not. There's even a specific county pace, called Mendo Time, best described as "fifteen minutes late is OK, except for hair-cutting appointments."

This is a place not yet fully given over to digital devices as the human endgame in communication. Discovering this was incredible to me, being just those four hours from Google headquarters, though sometimes one hour from getting clear Verizon cell coverage. This, in fact, is a place not yet fully given over to the telephone. Sometimes if you really need to talk, you go and find a person. Or try, and often as not wind up leaving scrap-paper handwritten messages at what someone has told you is his favorite haunt.

For a guy with a new smartphone, this method of investigative journalism, from the technical perspective, feels about as advanced as consulting the *I Ching*. But it does get you out there; forces you to speak with people. And, boy, what you learn immediately is "do they ever speak." As long as they're pretty sure you're not a narc, you can't get them to stop.

From the county's deservingly well-remunerated mechanics to the sheriff, everyone's an insider, and everyone knows The Issue. My haircutter tipped me off that a much-touted interagency aerial raid then quite loudly under way in the county was overcrowding the local jail. Her in-law works there, you see.

Three decades of such insularity has resulted in a lot of parents inflicting names like Vision, Phase Change, and Sunrise on their kids, to the detriment of any future college application or Senate campaign. But it also makes it about the easiest place in North America to hitchhike, which is particularly useful when your vegetable-oil-powered truck is buried axle-deep in a backwoods ditch.

It is, as Mendocino County Board of Supervisors member and recently converted champion of permitted cannabis farming John McCowen puts it, "a bubble within a bubble within a bubble." Meaning Mendo inside progressive NoCal inside generally accepting California.

Another, more sociological way of phrasing the Mendocino County mind-set is that, in landing here, I've had the pleasure of experiencing what one model of functional economic localism really looks like in practice. A lot of places talk about honing a local economy. Mendo lives it. The place, from Boonville to Covelo, is a community. It has a sense of "we." The neighborhood zoning feud matters much more than the presidential debates.

I thought such cohesiveness had gone out with shamanism.

One cannabis collective I visited, for example, had also doubled as an organic Community Supported Agriculture farm. Another gave cultivation and legal seminars, right in the upscale coastal village of Mendocino. I had eaten George Fredericks's duck eggs (they're sold at local markets) before I met him on Sergeant Randy's inspection and learned that he just as legally grows medical cannabis.

And thus in these mountains, where there exists the social space that allows cops and pot growers to even communicate, let alone be open allies on any issue, one shouldn't be too surprised that Ordinance 9.31 sprang forth.

The Drug War essentially had to end here first. You hear a lot of talk about how the Northern California sunlight and Mediterranean-like soil are ideal for cannabis (and grape, and raspberry and mushroom) cultivation, and they are. But the real reason Mendocino is to cannabis what Silicon Valley is to high tech is not agricultural: it's political. Sonoma to the south is too populated, too wealthy from other pursuits. Humboldt to the north is too disorganized.

If California is America's progressive lab, Mendocino is California's. New ideas brought in by new people are allowed to take root (literally) here more quickly than most other places in the United States. In other words, to paraphrase Mrs. Clinton and Supervisor McCowen, it takes a bubble within a bubble within a bubble to engender societal change as significant as legalizing cannabis. You simply have to not care what the rest of the world thinks. Plymouth, Massachusetts, in 1620 was a bubble within a bubble within a bubble.

Perhaps not quite to the degree that the Pilgrims lacked one, there's not much of a safety net for Mendo, on paper one of California's poorest counties. Very little help is coming from the fiscally bankrupt state of California. This is another reason Mendo-style rugged individualism blew me away. Usually, in my experience in rural Alaska especially, the places that talk the most Libertarian talk tend to, if you peel back a few layers, have the most high-level dependence on federal government largesse. In Mendo, they're genuinely weaning from that teat, but not at the behest of the NRA. More like Earth First!

Locals here "in the hills" have a long history of clamming up to strangers (at least until local references are provided). The genuine hippie back-to-the-landers who started the top-shelf domestic cannabis industry after scooping up dirt-cheap slices of Utopia in the 1970s get most of the credit. But the children of loggers and ranchers were also returning from Vietnam at the same time and were newly cannabis friendly. This slice of the demographic pie had lessons to teach the newcomers when it came to repelling the Man. Especially in the art of camouflage.

The town where I lived for most of 2011, Willits, is widely regarded as the epicenter of the American localization movement. It is the home, thanks to the Yuppification of some of those Utopians, of the original Real Goods store, which in the 1970s was America's first solar-panel retailer. It is also a town with a five-to-one massage-therapist-to-physician ratio and, perhaps unsurprisingly, given its specialty local crop, possibly an even higher herbalist-to-physician ratio.

By now the culture has thirty years' experience sniffing out dangerous outsiders like Narcs, East Coasters or, worst of all, Southern Californians. Today, the putative transplant would be wise to avoid too much reliance on e-mail and wearing tennis shoes. Nothing says "narc" like white Nikes.

The upside, regionally, is that a seven-year-old stopped mid-jump-rope by a stranger asking about Mom's garden knows to say nothing and run right home to report the incident. Mom will check into it, and if you don't ooze narc vibes, know her neighbor, and can meet her eye, you'll probably be invited for dinner.

The downside, for me, is that it's still hard to find a store that'll take a dang credit card. For obvious reasons, this has traditionally been a cash economy. Often a fragrant cash economy. When I got my new phone in the county's big city of Ukiah (population 14,857)

and apologized for a crumpled twenty, the saleswoman laughed
and said, "You're either joking or new around here."

"What do you mean?" I asked, as yet unaware that Mendo,
with its windy, hilly line-of-sight problems, still has more dropped
call spots than rural New Mexico—heck, than the Bat Cave.
Three-G, 4G, no matter how many Gs they throw at it.

"Dude, if it's not soaked in hash oil I put it at the top of the
pile," she told me. "I knew your money wasn't going to be an issue
at the bank when I couldn't smell you the minute you entered the
store.* I mean, personally I think it makes money smell better, but
I'm the one who has to drop the cash bag off at the end of the day.
And these [holding one of my twenties up to the light], are the
cleanest Jacksons I've seen all week."

"I guess the money in Georgia must smell like peaches, or pea-
nuts, or whatever," I observed.

"What, now? Peaches?"

"Just noticing that I'm in an agricultural community."

Unlike many heartland agricultural communities, the county
overall votes highly Democratic, though its beloved sheriff and
DA are both registered Republicans. As for the spotty cell-phone
coverage, I have come to feel that even that is crucial to Mendo
having a powerfully distinctive There there. In fact this, I now
realize, is why Google might as well be in Mongolia. There's an
atmospheric Great Wall keeping Mendocino County a "let's meet
face to face" place. A place where folks notice whether you make
eye contact and shake hands with respect. You should introduce

---

\* I was to learn that the famous "Green" smell of cannabis is the result of the
botanically important compounds known as terpenes. Disguising terpenes (from
which we get the word *turpentine*, though your hardware store's brand of paint
thinner today almost certainly does not contain cannabis resins) for purposes of
cannabis transport is no easy feat. Due to their molecular structure, they can
seep through concrete. Thus you see billboards in Ukiah advertising the giant,
specialty-plastic "turkey bags" that provide smell suppression for up to six hours.
Long enough for an aboveboard farmer to safely get medicine to collective or
dispensary, or for a black market farmer to get it to an in-state wholesaler.

yourself at a first meeting, and explain why the heck you're there. Otherwise, as Jim Hill told me, "everyone will wonder where you're growing, or who you're investigating."

For my purposes, having to do the legwork, having to pound the hillsides, got me invited to observe the lives and fields of a lot of cannabis farmers who were ready to tell their stories. Who were ready to come aboveground and declare that they are hardworking small American farmers who grow a valuable crop for a living.

Unfortunately, there are still thousands of farmers in the Emerald Triangle of Northern California's prime cannabis-growing counties who are, to put it mildly, less ready to discuss what they do. Less ready to start paying payroll taxes on their seasonal hires, the bud trimmers. Less ready to address challenging questions about pesticide runoff or indoor diesel generator use. These are unsustainable techniques that longtime cannabis farmers say were brought into existence by the covert farming methods made necessary during the Drug War and its helicopter raids.

It's hard to totally blame the gray or black market growers for their resistance to change, if change means cooperating with law enforcement: There is probably not a Mendocino County family that hasn't had some entrepreneurial member get his or her door bashed down by a troop of armed men who weren't fans of the crop. It's scary when that happens. Makes an impression. The invaders yell and wave guns, sometimes shoot pets, and then they go away. Cash and plants are rarely returned even though charges, if any are actually filed, hardly ever go anywhere.

"My wife was eight months pregnant when they crashed through our garage door without a warrant," Sharif Moye said of his raid, which occurred in 2008, before 9.31 was enacted in its current form. "Every room in the house and the gate to the garden was labeled [indicating compliance with medical cannabis laws]. They knew they weren't dealing with criminals."

Indoor growing versus outdoor growing—especially intentionally sustainable outdoor growing—is a very big issue in the multibillion-dollar industry as cannabis approaches inevitable decriminalization nationally. Cannabis awaits its spot in the farmers' market. In the Community Supported Agriculture box. Maybe even on Whole Foods' shelves. Laos's markets, for crying out loud, are two decades ahead. Not a bad marketing slogan: "Tasty in Soup."

And, evidently, healthy. A sixty-five-year-old second-season Mendocino cannabis farmer, Buffy Madison, told me she's growing the plant so that she can, on her doctor's advice, treat a three-decade-long internal inflammation syndrome—brought on by workplace chemical exposure. She's doing this with a daily shake containing edible, nonpsychoactive cannabis flowers and leaves.

"We lost our insurance when my [systems analyst] husband was nudged into early retirement," Madison told me when I saw her, in bifocals and a dragonfly necklace, taking studious notes at a cultivation seminar. Having assumed I'd be meeting farmers forty years her junior, I just had to approach her. "So this treatment is affordable. I hope it's effective. All the research I've seen has me optimistic. It saved a neighbor of mine."

Buffy has no particular activist connection to cannabis. She's not even been a smoker "since the sixties." She's just exhausted her mainstream medical options and has better access to current cannabis medical research than 99 percent of Americans. In her case, economic necessity is forcing her to explore local medical invention. And locally, raw cannabis shakes play the role that my Nana's chicken soup did for me as the go-to folk remedy. Interestingly, science is backing up the effectiveness of both.

# FIVE

## The End of "Green, Leafy" as Cultural Profanity
## and the Birth of the Redneck Hippie

> During my thirty-six years as a Denver cop I arrested more
> people for marijuana than I care to remember, but it didn't
> amount to one bit of good for our citizens. Keeping marijuana
> illegal doesn't do anything to reduce marijuana use, but it does
> benefit the gangs and cartels who control the currently illegal
> marijuana trade.
>
> —Tony Ryan, board member, Law Enforcement
> Against Prohibition (LEAP)

During my first several weeks as a Mendocino County resident,
I didn't completely get the lifestyle memo. People kept trying
to send it, but my mind couldn't grasp the extent of this truth: The
cannabis industry isn't just here to stay in the economy. It *is* the
economy. Buffy's story alone should have taught me that cannabis
is as accepted in Mendo life as hops are in Bavaria. She told me she
had called the sheriff after planting in 2010, "to make sure my crop
was OK."

The problem was I grew up in a place and era where *Newsday*
made it clear that a "green, leafy" Baggie found on a suspect impli-
cated him in every unsolved criminal case on Long Island including the McKinley girl's disappearance. This is why the absolute
absence of local stigma took a while to sink in. Sensing my resistance, even the chief law enforcer was trying to school me. The
biggest problems in the county, Sheriff Tom told me in our first,
second, and third interviews, are "meth and domestic violence.
Marijuana isn't in the top three."

The first time, while I was still in awe of such statements, he
wanted to make sure I didn't miss the point. The elected sheriff of

an American county dramatically pointed out his office window toward the puffed emerald mountains beyond and said to me, a journalist on the record, laptop open, "If you told me that there's a fellow in my parking lot right now with a pound of marijuana tucked under his arm, I wouldn't get off my ass to do something about it."

This statement does not reflect a Hydrogenation Era aversion to exercise. Rather it reflects the embedded regional shrug surrounding anything green and leafy. If not embrace of same. Green is a good, healthy color. Where you really see it is in the basic assumptions embedded in regional media coverage of the cannabis crop. Notice, in this June 8, 2011, article about a brouhaha from *The Willits News*, that the only possible charges the cannabis grower faces are for shooting a burglar who was running away:

> By Linda Williams/TWN Staff Writer
>
> In a new first for Mendocino County, an alleged thief got some birdshot in his backside after attempting to steal pot at arrow point from a Round Valley grower.
>
> Mendocino County sheriff's deputies were called to Covelo at 6:45 a.m. Friday morning by a 46-year-old man reporting an attempted pot robbery at his Henderson Lane home. The robbery victim told deputies Hank Johnson Whipple, 24, of Covelo, came to his home with a bow and arrow and attempted to steal some of his marijuana plants. The unidentified victim responded first with pepper spray, and then fired four blasts with a shotgun loaded with birdshot at the fleeing Whipple.
>
> Law enforcement is familiar with Whipple, a parolee who has been arrested for parole violations five times in the past 2.5 years. Whipple was located that evening, with the help of Round Valley Tribal Police, at a Tabor Lane residence. Whipple climbed

onto the roof to escape capture, but was later convinced to turn himself in.

He was taken to Frank R. Howard Memorial
Hospital for removal of dozens of birdshot pellets
from his back, and then arrested on suspicion of
violating parole and robbery.

No information about whether charges are
expected to be filed against the Covelo grower for
shooting the alleged robber was available as of
press time.

That's the whole article, people. In Mendocino County, the
green, leafy possessor is not the problem. The guy who tries to
steal it is.

And seemingly far outside the Bubble[3], the wider financial
world is rather enthusiastically hopping on the Green, Leafy band-
wagon. Wall Street is betting with real money on the triumph of
the change being fomented in little Mendocino County and a few
other places like it across the nation. Not just the legal triumph,
but the perceptual one. The complete erasing of any stigma associated with cannabis. The jockeying about who will prevail in
whatever regulatory model emerges has long since begun.

When you look at the financial statements for a company like
Orange County–based General Cannabis, Inc., which owns the
popular WeedMaps website, the only "safe harbor" disclaimer you
see surrounds the elasticity of financial projections, not the federal
legal status of the plant from which the company's revenue is indirectly derived. It seems a nonissue. In 2011, I watched two giggling,
stoner-joke-making Bloomberg reporters give very serious "buy"
recommendations to publicly traded cannabis industry corporations. Even Miracle-Gro is now openly marketing to cannabis
farmers.

Yet when a sheriff told me a pound of cannabis is kosher in his
jurisdiction, I imagined he was being hyperbolic, maybe even
kidding—trying to fool the new guy. Although his statement made

me laugh, it didn't make me a believer that the Drug War was essentially over in Mendocino County.

The "ah-ha" moment occurred in May during a supermarket run with an employee of the food bank where I volunteered a few hours per week in the town of Willits. Pointing out the van's window, I observed to Leslie, the food bank helper and a non–cannabis user (one of those smiley people who always *seem* like they're medicated, and who once allowed a renter to cultivate the plant on her property), that Willits sure had a thriving five-block downtown, considering, you know, "this down economy."

We were crawling along the main drag at the strictly enforced twenty-five miles per hour,* past colorfully hand-painted restaurant signs, an organic market (where we picked up nearly expired Greek goat milk yogurt for the county's hungry), three pizza joints, and a community garden based at the high school.

"You still don't get it, do you?" Leslie said, slapping her hand on the driver's seat. "That's not just a vintage clothing store. [Ooh! Look at that fuzzy vest!] It's a cannabis wife's hobby shop. The market, the garden supply store. The tax base. Nothing in this town would be here without herb."

Perhaps activated by the telltale *eau de terpene* emanating from a small farm behind somebody's shop, I at that moment recalled that upon my first visit to Willits's exceptional Zaza Bakery a month earlier (get the berry cheese croissant), the baker had asked me chattily, "Here for the season?"

I blinked, and said, "Yep—my first year in grapes."

This memory, compounded by Leslie's assertion, evoked in my mind the scene in Hawthorne's "Young Goodman Brown," in which the World's Only Honest Man discovers that while he gathers wood, his whole Puritan town is out at a pagan barbecue:

---

* They mean it: It's a lifestyle issue to yield to pedestrians and bicyclists right on Highway 101, which runs from Port Angeles, Washington, all the way to Los Angeles. Or, as the local bumper sticker expresses it, "Back Off, City Boy." And it's in fact "outsider" black market cannabis buyers who most often, judging by the headlines, seem to fail to heed Mendo Time in the 3:14 A.M. range. Willits is one of those towns that is a lot easier to navigate once you know the back roads.

*Among them, quivering to and fro between gloom and splendor, appeared faces that would be seen next day at the council board of the province, and others which, Sabbath after Sabbath, looked devoutly heavenward, and benignantly over the crowded pews, from the holiest pulpits in the land. Some affirm that the lady of the governor was there.*

Or at least the lady of the County Board of Supervisors, which in 2009 passed the cannabis regulation ordinance (actually a revision of an earlier one that wasn't working as well) that drew me here. While easily 85 percent of Mendocino County's economy is generated by cannabis—a figure that could push $8.1 billion annually,* which represents a value of $258.04 per county resident, per day—it's possible that only one in four of its eighty-six thousand residents is directly involved in cannabis farming. So it's not as ubiquitous as poor Goodman Brown found sin in early nineteenth-century New England. And, to be fair, a small minority—the county sheriff calls it 5 percent—is adamantly opposed to cannabis in all its forms, value to local coffers be darned.

There's a group called the Anderson Valley Action Coalition, for example, whose members from the Boonville area show up at public meetings to put forth the old-school "who will think of the children?" view that wine tasting rooms are preferable to putative cannabis tasting rooms in their community, the same community

---

* How I arrived at that number: The Mendocino County Sheriff's Department announced record cannabis seizures of six hundred thousand plants in 2010, and estimated that to be 10 percent of the overall crop. Growers unanimously say it's actually much closer to 1 percent, but let's be generous. Prices were low in 2010 because of high supply, so we'll calculate the value of the cannabis at an unheard of, below historic low of one thousand dollars per pound. We'll also pretend that each plant only gave a very low 1.5 pounds per plant. That's where the $8.1 billion figure comes from. And it represents only Mendocino County's stake, with many lucrative gardens encompassing a single acre. Add in neighboring Humboldt and Trinity counties (which comprise, along with Mendocino, the famous Emerald Triangle cannabis production region), much of Oregon and Washington, and British Columbia, and you start to see why a cannabis-unfriendly (read: seizure-hungry) narcotics squad believes it can throw a dart at, say, an innocent writer's truck and nab some medicine and maybe some property. The potential sales tax revenues alone provide sufficient economic explanation for this book.

that produced three Emerald Cup cannabis competition winners in 2010.

"Someday," local cannabis collective manager and farmer Laura Hamburg asserts, drawing the comparison with the architects of Napa's grape empire, who garner *New York Times* obituaries, "these farmers will be tenured sustainable agriculture professors."

They're sure not statistically problem parents. A 2011 study by researchers at Toronto's Hospital for Sick Children concluded that children of cannabis growers have no more health risks than those whose parents do anything else in the world. Presumably including those who sell America's deadliest drug—alcohol—or those who market off-label antipsychotic drugs like Seroquel to children.

Oh, and then there's the *Los Angeles Times* headline of September 21, 2011, which sums up the obvious when it comes to neighborhood safety in a world of legal cannabis: "RAND [Corporation] study finds *less* crime near pot dispensaries" (italics theirs—look it up, even though law enforcement complaints in Los Angeles later caused RAND to disavow it).

Some of the Action Coalition folks appear not yet to understand the difference between cannabis and meth. Once it's not alcohol or tobacco, they oppose it.

To intentionally settle in Mendo with this view would be exactly like settling in Silicon Valley and opposing computers. You have every right to your opinion, of course, but if you seek inner peace, you might want to consider moving elsewhere.

Or, as the local joke has it, a directory of Mendocino County cannabis growers has long been in print. It's called the phone book. And why not? It doesn't take much space to grow even the twenty-five plants that Mendocino County code says you can grow, for any reason, permitted or not.* If only there was such a glut of small-town wellness doctors or AIDS medicine.

---

* This is a result of a series of county ballot initiatives. Some would say, "That's all you need to know—twenty-five plants are fine in Mendocino County." But it isn't all you need to know, even discounting federal law. To give one example of something more you need to know, the moment you harvest and process those

Why would anyone complain about the crop that provides the local economic base? Mostly because of *Reefer Madness* brainwashing. But also because while most Mendo farmers "do it right," some are like bad neighbors anywhere: The worse the behavior, the less they care. For example, I first smelled and then—several months later—saw that my closest neighbors at the second cabin I had rented were cultivating a thriving cannabis garden in a former hot tub area not fifty feet from my driveway. My truck was (and, as I type, is) the closest working vehicle to the garden by a wide margin. I can see two dozen Kelly green plants today from my porch.

This was a little troubling, since I and my Sweetheart had specifically chosen this not-inexpensive spot so that my kids would be "separate" from my work in case of pesky feds, not pausing to ask for press passes, misunderstanding whose farm they were raiding. So much for that plan. After the Sonoma incident, incidentally, I unfailingly carried Sheriff Tom's business card, complete with cell phone number, in my wallet. I treasured that piece of cardboard like it was a literal Get Out of Jail card. In traffic, I practiced how fast I could pull it out of my wallet.

Call me naïve, but I never thought to interview my landlord, who owned both my cabin and my neighbors', about whether, you know, a tenant might be cultivating a federal Schedule I felony just off my front yard. I just didn't understand when I moved here how integrated cannabis is in Mendocino culture—having a cannabis plot is like having a grapevine or an apple orchard. Even a tomato plant. Who announces that to renters?

Heck, maybe it was even mentioned in my lease agreement's legalese! My attitude was different than if it had been an apple orchard, though, given my work, my Web surfing, and my phone

---

twenty-five plants, a law enforcement officer can determine that the resulting amount of medicine exceeds your immediate, personal "medical needs" as mandated by California's hysterically numbered SB 420 (420 used to be the police code for "marijuana smoking in progress," and 4:20 P.M. has become the established time across the nation for a medication break). That law, in 2004, codified and somewhat clarified the 1996 statewide Proposition 215, which itself provisionally exempted medicinal cannabis from state narcotics laws.

address book in 2011. Just as some families run fire drills, in the summer of 2011 mine ran "wrong address raid" drills. Men with guns bashing down your door, remember: not fun. And I had already been the target of mistaken anticannabis efforts once.

Some of those in the 5 percent "any cannabis at all is just too difficult for me to wrap my beliefs around" camp still like to argue, usually during Rodeo Weekend, that the "heritage" of Northern California lies in the timber extraction industry, and "these dirty hippies" ruined everything with their spotted owls and their orgasms.

True on the first "heritage" count, though only from about 1870 to 1940. Cannabis has now dominated nearly as long, with (in the case of outdoor cultivation) far less impact on the local salmon. I learned that in my own cabin's Brooktrails subdivision of Willits, the logging heritage lasted a whopping twenty-five years, from 1901 to 1926; two-hundred-foot-tall second-growth redwoods are springing up in a tree circle outside my office window as I type.

Of the hippie homesteaders, Sheriff Tom, who grew up in nearby Garberville as the class-president son of liquor store owners in the 1970s, says, "I was raised to believe they wrecked the county, now I believe they're helping us save it."

The fact is, the loggers-versus-hippies culture war is pretty much over in Mendocino County. The hippies won. Or rather they've crossbred with the "heritage" locals into a demographic known locally as the Redneck Hippie. Members of this demographic, known for mixing jacked-up monster trucks with tie-dies, comprise the typical Mendocino County teacher, the government clerk, the community radio station DJ, the organic–brew-pub owner, and the postman. Heading north on Highway 101, the second official volunteer highway cleanup sign you see after escaping Sonoma County credits the "Medical Marijuana Patients Union."

In public, the average Mendonesian sees little reason to disguise cannabis use. I've noticed that 4:20 P.M. at the farmers' market tends to be a bit of a ceremony. Even at the Frontier Days Fourth of July picnic in Willits, people passed small wooden pipes in full view—presumably group medical sessions with doctor referrals. It was like drinking a cup of tea. It didn't raise an eyebrow.

It's not meth. It's not alcohol. It's not violent. It's thus not a problem to Sheriff Tom, who was at the Fourth of July picnic, and who told me after our third interview that his view of cannabis is "Smoke it till your head caves in. I don't care. I just wish I could get it off the front pages so I could have more time to deal with the real problems in this county. This is my biggest dream." It's one shared by many of Allman's constituents: While it's by no means unanimous, I met no shortage of local cannabis activists who *want* to be a test case. They're ready for legitimacy. Sure makes life easy for a journalist.

And so this clueless newcomer finally adjusted to the casual, near-complete local acceptance of a plant considered felonious or even immoral elsewhere. Let me tell you, it was a relief once I finally woke to the fact that I needn't fear anything "green and leafy." Mainly because my own Sweetheart orders enough homeo-pathic herbs off the Internet to qualify us for kingpin status, by weight. She'd recently procured soap nuts from a website called iHerb.

My own backpack is never without a ball of small Baggies con-taining parsley and marjoram remnants, intended for sustainable refill at the food co-op bulk section.

And then there was my work: Every time a cannabis farmer pointed out a minute botanical detail on a plant in 2011, such as a single mite, or gender-revealing prebud, I'd end up with a sticky, THC-crystally finger that, on my ride home, filled my vehicle with a scent that would almost justify a Deputy Londo search. To this day my keyboard would knock an airport-sniffing dog uncon-scious. Thank goodness the sheriff told me not to worry—that Mendo simply doesn't care what the rest of the world thinks. Cer-tainly not the feds.

The depth of cannabis integration into life here reminds me of the time, waiting for a late flight to Seattle out of the Anchorage airport in 1993, that I saw a certified, beard-to-his-chest mountain man act surprised when his revolver set off the metal detector at the flimsy, pre-911, contractor-run security station.

"It's just my gun," he said with surprise, never imagining a place where it wouldn't be totally normal for him to be armed. That's how long some Mendonesians have been in them thar hills. They'd light up a joint in LaGuardia and then act apologetically surprised if anyone objected. I finally grokked that the home of such a mind-set is the obvious place for a post–Drug War experiment to unfold.

# SIX

## Setting Industry Standards for a Post–Drug War Craft Cannabis Market

> Chances are good that many of Cheech and Chong's fans have smoked pot. A 2007 federal survey found 42 percent of Americans 26 years of age or older admit—or recall—that they've smoked marijuana. Among 18- to 25-year-olds, 51 percent said they had used marijuana in their lifetimes.
>
> —Minnesota Public Radio, September 2011, upon ag giant General Mills hiring the comedy duo as part of its "High in Fiber" Fiber One brownie campaign

I found the principal farm I'd be researching for the 2011 growing season at a board meeting of a local cannabis trade group called MendoGrown. The meeting was held about a month after my family settled in on Valentine's Day, 2011, initially to a moldy cabin in the rutted hills near Ukiah along a daffodil-lined "road" called "Turn Around Now Lane,"* and then to our longer-term, even moldier cabin twenty-five miles north in the redwoods above Willits.

After being serenaded by steady overnight rain on the redwood eaves outside my cabin's window for the eighteenth straight night, I realized three things when I woke that March 15 morning.

The first thing I realized was that I had chosen well in settling in California's famous Emerald Triangle (the tri-county region

---

* I've changed the name to protect my landlord's privacy, but not by much: A lot of Mendo "subdivisions" have such "strongly consider camping or burgling elsewhere" street names. It's largely a self-policing county. My initial landlord, Greg, a non-permitted cannabis farmer, proudly told me that his canyon hadn't been visited by law enforcement of any kind since April 23, 1974. He knew the date. Everyone did, similar to the way that some factories measure consecutive days without a workplace injury.

that includes Mendocino), rather than in one of the other (at the time) fifteen medical cannabis states. I clearly was witness to the often literal emergence of cannabis from the closet and into the sunlight. I'd already met with a smiling sheriff not prone to "getting off his ass" to arrest cannabis fans outside his office. That was an important early clue. There are plenty of sheriffs, for one reason or another, who similarly wouldn't stress their gluteals. Few would admit it, though, and at that moment only one was willing to make it a key part of his codified law-enforcement platform.

The second mushily undeniable reality of Mendocino was that I had landed like a cork in the wettest spring in memory. That's another way of saying that before climate change, this would have been considered a perfectly normally wet spring. But everyone's forgotten this already. Most humans have terrible climate memories. Right after our arrival, my New Mexico–born sons saw their first, and, days later, their thousandth, newt. My oldest soon had a pet banana slug.

My first purchase in the county was rain boots for everyone in my family, except for the emergency hand-me-down pair featuring frog decals that my landlord's son passed to mine. In the gear store that February, folks were moping around in untucked sweatsuits and unlaced shoes, looking like they hadn't absorbed Vitamin D since the Bush administration. Day and night evolved into relative terms. The land basically become caramel.

The world was so soaked here that I felt I could fuel my vegetable-powered truck off whatever was growing on my bathroom wall. Persistent Mendocino mountain springs continued to do damage to dirt roads through June, and I don't recall switching out of four-wheel drive for three months. And I was covering a lot of ground. The MendoGrown cannabis trade, standards, and branding association had been founded by Matt Cohen in 2010, and the meeting I was attending was being held at his goat-and-cannabis farm—forty soaked minutes from my own cabin.

The third reality I was facing as a full-time cannabis journalist was this: I very much needed to find an actual plant to follow along its journey from four-inch cutting to doctor-referred patient. That was the narrative model that seemed to me to provide the most comprehensive route for examining the current and potential value of a nationwide regulated cannabis industry.

As it turned out, MendoGrown was not only the mechanism by which Matt Cohen was implementing a Napa-style cannabis branding plan—think microbrew versus Coors Light; an antidote to the common local prophesy that legalization of cannabis would mean a complete takeover by the big guys. It also provided the venue that allowed me to lock in plans with the farmer willing to have me tag along all season and trail one of his plants as it transformed, presumably, into medicine.

I had arrived safely enough at Cohen's soggy farm for that board meeting, parking in what seemed like a perfectly reasonable spot on the circular driveway near the flagpole and about thirty yards from his Northstone Organics Cooperative's ninety-nine plants. As soon as I arrived, Cohen, goateed with tightly pulled-back ponytail and in conservative (by Mendo standards) collared shirt, gave me a quick farm tour in the drizzle. He told me the tale of the exemplary service he received from the Mendo deputies when his alarms had sounded.

"We're no longer fighting the Man," Cohen said he realized as the law enforcers departed the second time. "We are the Man. If Rippers ever showed up here, the Sheriff's Department would be on them in a second."

Given that I was scratching a spotted goat between the ears when Cohen related the alarm anecdote and that he had given me his outer ranch gate's security code before we had even met, brazen theft seemed inconceivable to me. I kinda felt like I was on some remote ranch in Patagonia. But the truth is, the no-longer-wild weed he had growing within that small fenced area *was* worth more than its weight in gold until 2009. And will be again.

Life was good for Cohen that spring. A rural Mainer by upbringing (with stops on a New Mexico Native pueblo and in Boulder at the University of Colorado), he was newly married, to

an otherwise wonderful Alabama blueblood beauty named Courtenay who was an hour away from giving me some mechanically
disastrous but ultimately journalistically invaluable parking advice.
They appeared happy, though Matt had suffered a bout of gout on
his honeymoon that sent him to a Caribbean hospital.

"Did they prescribe medical cannabis?" I asked.

"Actually, no," Matt told me. "But I was allergic to whatever
they shot me up with, and nearly died."

Courtenay nodded studiously: He wasn't exaggerating. Still,
aside from any issues with the Barbadian health care system,
things were solid on all fronts: Cohen had been recently appointed
to the national board of the nascent D.C.-based cannabis lobbying
organization, the National Cannabis Industry Association (NCIA).
He was employing fifteen people year-round and ten more during
harvest time on the Northstone Organics side of things. The
cooperative had seventeen hundred patient/members.

The Northstone medicine was delivered directly from this
farm. Patients ordered off the cooperative's website, choosing
from among a dozen strains of flower, plus chocolate and other
edibles. In 2011, if you wanted to see how the Northstone cannabis
field looked at any time, you could just go to the collective's Facebook page. It was all right there: the glistening emerald medicine
waving in the Mendocino breeze.

"We have nothing to fear," Cohen said about Northstone
Organics medicine ending up on the black market. "We have
nothing to hide. Our harvest and distribution system is right out
in the open." In other words, the Redneck Hippies enthusiastically
welcome a journalistic examination of their industry without the
fog of a culture war lens.

While he nursed the crop, venture capitalists were starting to
ask Cohen to speak at investment conferences. He was glad for the
speaking fees, since he hadn't collected a salary during the first three
years of Northstone's operation. At the same time, he was the 9.31
Program poster child whom Sheriff Tom paraded in front of the
camera whenever national media descended on the sleepy county.

Cohen was happy to do it. The Green Rush Ganjapreneur world knows it's got a friend in Sheriff Tom. And, boy, what a well-connected world it is: listserves and blogs analyze the precedent embedded in every nuanced legal decision from Amsterdam to Montana in a Digital Age nanosecond, and "cannabis warrior" legal-defense-fund solicitations are common. Hundreds of cannabis activists hounded President Obama during his first two online town halls, forcing him to address—from their perspective, disappointingly—the issue by making "Will you end the Drug War?" the most asked question both times. It's just the latest version of It's the Economy, Stupid. This is the point Cohen and the new K Street cannabis lobbyists of the NCIA are trying to hammer home on Capitol Hill.

As a result, not too many of the permitted Mendocino County cannabis farmers I met were losing sleep over Big Brother. If they lost sleep, it was over what Bloomberg was saying interest rates might do to venture capital liquidity.

But for all his success, the endeavor of which Cohen, a produce farmer at heart, said he was most proud was MendoGrown, the trade group that was meeting that day. He believed this board's actions were, a decade down the road, going to define and (sustainably) enrich his beloved adopted county the way romantic getaways did Napa.

"We're endeavoring to make Mendocino synonymous with fine, sustainable cannabis and farm tours the way Napa is with fine wine and vineyard tours," he said. Often.

The MendoGrown mind-set is capitalism with an activist underpining. Cohen's belief in the legitimacy, indeed the prestige, of what he does for a living could be seen clearly in the fact that when he heard about an upcoming "Taste of Mendo" agricultural trade show booth at a San Francisco foodie convention, he got on the horn with its organizers that very day and asked that his niche not be omitted in future years.

That's how Cohen rolls. A little bit MLK, a little bit Mark Zuckerberg. Traditional hippies sometimes find him a little uptight.

He calls it "focused," an "eye on the prize" kind of mind. Like many in the Ganjapreneurial world, he is dedicated to cultivating a top-tier medical cooperative reputation while positioning himself for full legalization.

If statewide or federal reclassification of cannabis comes to pass—they both can be said to have some momentum as of November 2011, though the latter especially is no sure thing even in a second Obama administration—there were few people better situated to take advantage of it in the summer of 2011 than Matt Cohen. He'd studied his history.

"When alcohol prohibition ended on December fifth, 1933," he told me, "there were brewers and distillers ready to go the next day."

They, too, started as activist/entrepreneurs in individual states, even as Cohen and the other 9.31 permittees had. One day's bootleggers are the next day's San Francisco Giants billboard sponsors.

Or, as Cohen's Colorado colleague and fellow national cannabis lobbyist Aaron Bluse, independent franchise owner of a publicly traded, multistate cannabis dispensary chain called Altitude Organic Medicine, put it when we met in Denver, "I'd like my grandkids to know me as a legitimate, honest businessman. American from the ground up."

You can tell a lot about the ultimate aims of a budding ganjapreneur by asking what price he or she would like to see for a pound of cannabis in an ideal world. Mendo patient activist and grower Jim Hill says, "My farm would still be here if I wasn't getting paid a dime—it should be free, ideally," perhaps intending *free* as a synonym for *insured*. Matt Cohen's goal isn't free cannabis—he thinks that's crazy talk—but rather "highest quality, sustainable and affordable."

Official business at the March 15, 2011, MendoGrown board meeting, held at the kitchen table next to the Cohens' pool, was an illuminating phenomenon to observe. These people were on a mission.

To start, I feel it worth mentioning, what with cannabis still carrying for some, thanks to Messrs. Cheech and Chong, a lingering reputation for what might be summed up as "spaciness and lack of ambition," that this meeting, situated twenty minutes from the nearest town in a remote part of a remote county, started pretty dang close to on time.

This day the board's members were discussing the sister issues of standards and standardization. An example of the former is "How does the patient know how much THC and CBD (the two most-studied of the eighty known medicinal cannabinoids as of press time—it'll probably be close to a hundred by the time you're reading this) her medicine has, and that the medicine is free of pesticides and molds, and which testing method (liquid or gas) should we use?"

So that's standards. An example of standardization, which interests me both as a sustainability writer and as a rancher, is "How can we know that one farmer's Bubba Kush indica-dominant strain (commonly used for pain, MS, and as a sleep aid) in Boonville derives genetically from the same Bubba Kush indica-dominant strain another farmer grows in, say, Laytonville?" And that's just smokable cannabis. Cannabis edibles, particularly important for seniors and chemotherapy patients, also have food-grade regulatory issues to address.

I was fascinated by the board members' professionalism. When you've been an outlaw for your entire professional life, even discussing mundane issues like soliciting contractors for building ADA-compliant bathrooms (to meet California and OSHA workplace requirements) takes on an air of excitement.

This issue was actually discussed at a different board meeting, surrounding a proposed centralized county bud-trimming facility. In addition to providing local jobs, this facility would free the individual farmer from the time-consuming, smelly, raid-risking, and all-around worrisome harvest-time step. It would also promote medicine uniformity and thus a brand. Standards testing could be done at the facility, too, instead of at every farm. And payroll would be more official than the "toss some cash at the hitchhiker you picked up that afternoon outside Safeway" model sometimes used for bud trimming in the past.

At stake is a trademarked seal of approval, called, yes, "Mendo-Grown," the presence of which (on any agricultural package, not just cannabis) Cohen believes is worth many millions. Like a trade-marked "Fair Trade" and "Organic" all mixed into one. He and the other MendoGrown board members believe that the model will also provide the best, most consistent, and most reliable medicine for patients. Which is the ostensible focus, since all the growers are (for now) nonprofit, share-the-wealth collective members.

In an era of unsustainable (and thus teetering) genetically modified monoculture, Cohen believes MendoGrown's top-shelf craft cannabis model can even outperform the $7.6 billion that the American microbrew industry was worth in 2010, according to the Craft Bewers Association. It's not an accidental comparison: It was only a change in federal alcohol laws in 1978 that paved the way for the small breweries that started providing Americans with good beer. It happened slowly too: Fred Eckhardt wrote on allaboutbeer.com in January 2011 that by 1981, four of twelve microbrew efforts had failed. Today there are fifteen hundred microbreweries in the United States. For this reason, MendoGrown's board members do not fear Coors.

As I watched this discussion continue amid the clinking plates from the potluck at Cohen's kitchen table during the meeting's midway break, I felt for the first time that I was seeing a viable post–Drug War future. A meeting of the Continental Congress of cannabis.

# SEVEN

## Redneck Hippie Capitalism

Hemp is the standard fiber of the world. It has great tensile strength and durability. It is used to produce more than 5,000 textile products, ranging from rope to fine laces, and the woody "hurds" remaining after the fiber has been removed contain more than seventy-seven per cent cellulose, and can be used to produce more than 25,000 products, ranging from dynamite to Cellophane.

—1938 *Popular Mechanics* article entitled, "Billion Dollar Crop," published the year after the enactment of the Marihuana Tax Stamp Act initially criminalized cannabis on the federal level in the United States

The clear and pervading spirit among the MendoGrown board members—and I've since seen it manifest in other Ganjapreneurs in Colorado and elsewhere—combined advocacy and ambition. It was optimistic. It was having a good time. I find it hard to sum up this outdoor-farming, progressive, Digital Age Ganjapreneur mind-set in a headline, a catchphrase, a strain name, if you will, because it has at once elements of market savvy, compassion, humor, and activism. But I'll try. Maybe it's a future called Redneck Hippie Capitalism.

If so, it's one that will see a higher corporate tax rate than most businesses enjoy today. Every single 9.31 grower I spoke to during the 2011 season—of more than a dozen—said he is so delighted to be an open, law-abiding citizen that he is willingly paying even the unique taxes slapped on cannabis in California. This in an era where GE and ExxonMobil funnel billions in profits offshore, legally, and pay no federal corporate income tax.

The most obvious instance of special cannabis taxation, which is itself another indication of the maturation of and overall outlook for the industry, is the California Board of Equalization's ruling in 2011 that cannabis, while indeed a medicine as the voters said it was, is for some reason also going to be the only medicine for which the purchaser is required to pay state sales tax. In Willits, the rate is a small-fish-nipping 7.75 percent.

The cynical might say that these sustainably minded small fish are in the phase of their industry's development where it is to their advantage to present themselves as good corporate citizens. Market watchers of the burgeoning industry in California, Colorado, Maine, and elsewhere can be forgiven for sniping, "Sure, they're Hippie Capitalists now, but just wait until the consolidation phase. Wait until the real money starts moving in."

Maybe, but what I see, what feels like the dominant raison d'être for the Green Rush movement, is that enough grandchildren of the hippie generation have learned that "peace and love and fairly traded, local, organic" products are the goal; these represent the ideal way for humans to exchange goods. But—and this part is vital—if you pretend the market doesn't exist, you end up as a fifty-year-old seasonal bud trimmer living in his buddy's RV.

So this time these grandkids are out to make a living while saving the world. The MendoGrown model probably most closely follows the business MO of the Doctor Bronner's Magic Soap company. This is the Ivory soap of the American organic food co-op, distinguished by the label, which is covered in prophetic prayers. The grandson of the famously gifted if verbose founder, like all the company's executives, only makes five times more than the company's lowest-paid employee. He also makes sure the company buys some of its olive oil from an orchard worked jointly by Israelis and Palestinians.

Which is not to completely dismiss the cynics. In an industry that seems to be growing daily, there are a lot of ways this can play out, from more prohibition on the one hand to legally mandated cannabis medicating areas at public universities on the other. And there sure are bigger fish circling this pool: the venture capitalists.

A lot in this early stage is jostling—the company that gets the most buzz is the one that generates headlines and investors.

For instance, the aforementioned General Cannabis has an aggressive PR firm and is always in the news. And none other than Jim Hill woke up one morning in 2010 and switched on the plasma screen to find file footage of his plant-tending wife of twenty-six years, Trelanie, bursting forth from Bloomberg Television.

Hill day-trades in the mornings, usually garbed in tennis shirts and deck shoes. He's an eclectic character, if you couldn't already tell, who believes he's learned nearly everything he needs to know about cannabis genetics from his days breeding competitive greyhounds. But even he was surprised to watch the Bloomberg analysts discuss the promising cannabis market against the backdrop of his own greenhouse.

Another case in point: All of a sudden one day in July 2011, Matt Cohen gets a call from a man I'll call Kevin B. Smiley, staff attorney at an ultra-high-end international law firm. These guys have sixteen hundred lawyers on four continents and have advised banks you've heard of in multibillion-dollar mergers. This is the kind of law firm that makes judges and Bloomberg editors say, "Wow! Must be big."

This was in mid-2011. The U.S. credit rating had just been lowered and the markets were in the gutter. No one was investing in anything. Except, seemingly, in war and cannabis. Talk about hedging.

Seems Mr. Smiley wanted to represent everything Mendo-Grown stands for, pro bono. Intellectual property, litigation, marketing, the whole deal, including protection from creative infringement. "Like those who might want to ride on Mendo-Grown's coattails if we prove to be the branding trailblazers," Cohen told me—and there already are even in-county competitors, the result of the usual infighting so typical of the small-town *Homo sapiens.*

I shook hands with Smiley after a "Cannabis Cultivation Panel" at the Gaia Festival in the northern Mendo town of Laytonville on

August 7, 2011. This is one of the county's big gatherings, held at Wavy Gravy's farm. The panel itself, housed in a dolphin-themed, Playa-style geo-dome, was more of a "How to grow legally" panel than the "How to grow—period" seminars that essentially comprise the bat-guano section of any Mendocino County garden store between February and October. After the panel proper, the members took uncensored questions from an audience almost entirely comprised of cannabis farmers and their families.

I caught Smiley just before he began networking with the Mendocino County district attorney, who had been seated on the panel alongside Cohen and the sheriff. During the handshake, I asked him if he faced any stigma presenting the MendoGrown case to his firm's partners.

"It works on every level for us," he said without pause. "We'll gain experience in an important emerging market and we believe in what MendoGrown is doing. We think it's important."*

Or as Cohen put it when I asked him if he thought the VC honchos he saw circling the Marijuana Business Conference where he had presented on standardization the previous month were in it for activism or pure capitalism: "Pure capitalism." He said this in

---

* He was obviously only speaking for the West Coast office. When I confirmed the quote with Smiley at a public hearing a month later, he had a different message: "The pro bono committee here on the Coast loved it, but our partners at headquarters [back East] are a little worried about our Pharma clients. We'll see how it works out."

As we'll see later, in order to avoid a threat to his job once it became clear that his firm's out-of-state partners, explicitly concerned about their Big Pharma clients, didn't share the West Coast branch leadership's pro-cannabis bullishness, I honored the late-arriving request from Mr. "Smiley" to anonymize him and his firm.

The firm's Pharma clients should be worried. New Mexico, to name just one state, in 2010 added PTSD as a legitimate condition for which cannabis can be recommended in the Land of Enchantment. Of course, if the United States mimics Canada's recent efforts to limit cannabis production to a few government-authorized cultivators or biotech companies, well, this would be the Mendo-Grown board's worst fears realized. Cohen says he isn't worried because of the "even in a world of Coors, people want microbrews" argument.

his near-murmur of a monotone that makes him sound like the membership chairman of a restricted golf club.

I'm glad I had got my question in to Smiley when I did, because the coffee klatch outside the geo-dome quickly turned into a business conference. Seriously: a veritable networking session—the only thing missing was the nineteenth-hole clubhouse. I watched Smiley introduce himself to DA David Eyster, who briefly had trouble remembering into which pocket he had stuffed his own business cards.

The microscopic lesson was that Big Money and Big Law were prepared to bankroll Mendocino's idea of sustainable cannabis. The macroscopic revelation was that the topic is locally, top down, no longer a matter of stigma, and nationally it won't be for long. It's Smiley's distant partners who are out of touch. "The wrong side of history" is how Supervisor McCowen puts it.

When I looked at my photos from that day, featuring an American district attorney hobnobbing with cannabis farmers and their counsel, it occurred to me that perhaps it was time for me to get over my own lingering sense of culture war stigma surrounding this plant. Not only is it actually vital medicine for many, not only is it a potential source, through industrial biofuel, for America's energy needs, but it might be where I should be directing my broker, since it is clearly perceived to be an extremely profitable "investment space" to a lot of high-end venture capital. In the energy field and beyond.

True, for Wall Street, this kind of "emerging market," as Smiley put it, might very well lead to exactly the Coors-ization feared by many established black market cannabis farmers who oppose legalization, and implied in the Budweiser billboard that still haunts my dreams. At the Willits Food Bank, I met a cultivator doing community service who urged me to examine the "crazy complicated" red tape surrounding tobacco cultivation. "That's what'll happen to the small farmer," he told me of cannabis legalization as we stuffed grocery bags full of yogurt, nuts, and excess Safeway sponge cake. I did look it up and he's correct: Section 40 of Title 27 of the Alcohol and Tobacco Tax and Trade Bureau's regulations has 534 subsections, nearly all composed in legalese. No question the law favors big growers.

But for now, Cohen's MendoGrown movement was getting hundreds of thousands of dollars of free legal work, dropped unsolicited out of the sky and into its lap. Right before what might be the decisive battle, the D-day, or the Tet Offensive (depending on your view of cannabis) of the Drug War: federal rescheduling and decriminalization.

Though there is another front for the cannabis activists, especially east of the Mississippi and south of the Mason-Dixon Line. A perceptual one. Take it from a guy who grew up under the Cannabis Makes Your Head Explode educational model: MendoGrown and the rest of the Ganjapreneurs (even those on the industrial side) still have their work cut out for them when it comes to educating enough Americans raised under Just Say No.

I thought of this when a Northern California cannabis collective manager named Robert Jacob made this observation during a courtroom break, after a Sonoma County assistant district attorney babbled what even the judge seemed to recognize were outdated irrelevancies during the preliminary hearing in a 2011 medical cannabis delivery case: "Man. Some people are just gonna be carried into the future kicking and screaming."

Indeed, the public airing of personal prosecutorial opinion surrounding Drug War values (and budgets) is playing out in counties all over the state and in medical cannabis states all over the nation—with the specifics varying based on the nuances of each state's law. Safe to say that at the exact second Jacob made that comment in California, similar cases were in session in Michigan, Oregon, Montana, and Vermont. If a DA doesn't like cannabis—for, say, either religious or perceived professional advancement reasons, or perhaps because of a tricky in-house political tug-of-war between competing union interests—no legal trick is off-limits.

As a spiritual person myself, I'll point out to those who believe that the cannabis plant is somehow in conflict with their faith, that not just federal medical rescheduling but legislative decriminalizing of cannabis has a friend in televangelist Pat Robertson. The Christian Coalition founder said in 2010, "I just believe that criminalizing marijuana, criminalizing the possession of a few ounces of pot, [is] costing us a fortune and it's ruining young people. Young people go into prisons . . . as youths and come out as hardened criminals. That's not a good thing."

Even without the federal seal of approval, let alone the Evangelical one, the Mendocino County cannabis industry was only accelerating in 2011. Even the Ganja tourism avenue, with its grape, mushroom-picking, and redwood-frolicking templates profitably in place, has already begun. I saw it myself.

When I dashed off (with a wave to my stooped neighbor watering her cannabis garden with her dachshund) to an August 2011 herbalist talk about medicinal cannabis tinctures and recent cannabinoid research at an upscale coastal collective, I arrived at an event that was hopping: Locals and tourists alike were at the lecture, at least forty of them. I myself contributed more than a hundred real tourism dollars to the local economy that day, between my Thai lunch, my afternoon kayaking excursion, and the arrowroot my Sweetheart asked me to pick up at a local market for our younger son's diaper rash. I even grabbed a flyer from the town's real estate office.

The dream for the collective's manager, Gabriel Martin, is to broaden the appeal of the county's visitor brand. As I made my way home from that entertaining workday on the coast, I remembered how one farmer at the seminar had evangelized the nascent cannabis tourism market: "Let's get the word *wine* out of Mendocino's current slogan, 'America's Greenest Wine Region.'"

# EIGHT

## A Valuable Truck Burying

What MendoGrown issue is most important to you?
  Growing standards
  Politics
  Community involvement
  Tourism
  Job growth
  Local economy
  Sustainability
  All of the Above!

—Survey on MendoGrown locavore cannabis cultivation
trade group website, 2011

By the time Matt Cohen reconvened the MendoGrown meeting for its second half that March afternoon, it had already been a long, wet day. My plan was to catch the gist of the remaining discussion, then slip off to a haircut appointment in Ukiah. I didn't hear past the first item on the postbreak agenda, though, because it was at that moment that Courtenay Cohen glided in from the greenhouse. She found me on the high stool where I sat hunched and tapping notes, tapped me on the shoulder, and asked to speak with me in the living room.

"Listen," she said sweetly, cradling some freshly harvested shiitakes and wearing the scrunched-face expression of someone who hates to bother you. "I hate to bother you, but could you please move your, um, kind of large truck? Folks are having trouble getting around it and it's clogging up the straight part of the driveway."

She walked me outside to the porch in what I by now recognized was the downpour phase of the hourly spring cycle. Rainy season was predicted, I had read in the *Ukiah Daily Journal*, to end any month now.

I shivered to adjust. Then I examined my truck and its relationship to the Cohen farm topography. Maybe it was that we
journalists, as the chroniclers of the event, have come to expect a
sort of VIP access. I dunno. It looked like a fine spot to me. Plenty
of room for other vehicles to get by.

"See that patch of meadow there under the redwood?" Courtenay asked.

"The, um, that one with the standing water?"

"Yep, the little field there. That looks big enough for your
truck. That way people will be able to get by. And, hey"—chucking
my shoulder—"you won't get blocked in!"

At this point, I thought my initial spot had been well-chosen for
reasons of short-term geologic stability alone. But I mean, the lady
of the house asks me to move my rig. What was I gonna do? Say no?

Thank goodness not. Because that day, on account of my conveyance being buried axle deep in Earth's apparent first black hole,
I couldn't duck out of the MendoGrown meeting early, as I had
planned. Instead, forced to hang around after the meeting awaiting a tow, I got to speak at length with the cannabis farmer who
proved to be willing to let me follow a Mendocino County–
developed medicinal plant strain (called Cashmere Kush).

Yes, without Courtenay Cohen's questionable traffic-cop
work, I'd never have gotten stuck in the quickmud and this book
wouldn't be nearly as detailed.

I knew I was in for trouble before I'd even nudged into the
"field" very much like a kid scared to jump into a too-cold lake on
a dare. The moment I did edge my truck into Courtenay's potentially permanent parking spot, I experienced a second or three of
lateral "oh, no!" sliding that told me "eight-wheel-drive won't get
me out now." Not that I didn't try. Last time I checked, the tire
gashes were still commemorating the occasion that gobbled my
three-quarter-ton, four-wheel-drive pickup.

So I had to head back inside and sit through the entire rest of
the meeting, plus the gabbing and snacking afterward, before I
could enlist a good part of the MendoGrown board to tow me out.

For a little while, I grumbled to myself about missing my haircut. But until now I didn't rat Courtenay out.

And I'm glad I didn't. Because an hour after trapping my vehicle and badly overrevving its engine in an effort to extract it, while waiting patiently for the board members' feeding frenzy to break up and for Matt Cohen to throw his tow chain around some hopefully sturdy part of my left axle, I was able to have that crucial conversation with one of the meeting's attendees. He was thirty-three-year-old Tomas "Don't try to pronounce it: it's Hungarian" Balogh. He pronounced the Tomas like Thomas, though.

In my preliminary research for the project, we had spoken a couple of times, but one encouraging stance in particular he took this day convinced me that this was going to work: that I'd found the principal farmer whose crop I would cover for this book. He was a first-year Mendocino farmer, bringing his craft, and indeed his career, into the sunlight after a decade of urban indoor growing in the Bay Area.

Filling my own plate with a board member's home-smoked salmon in the Cohen kitchen, I was still early enough in my exposure to Mendocino cannabis culture's shocking openness to start Tomas off with my habitual "How do you feel about using your real name?" introduction.

Turned out Balogh, like nearly every 9.31 grower I met, was completely, almost compulsively, revealing about his work. A literal open book, when it came to his finances. His immediate reply was "I've thought a lot about it, and I keep coming back to the day I decided to be open about my career. It was a big decision. Have I told you?"

"No."

"Well, after I'd been growing quietly for eight years, I spoke in front of the Berkeley City Council in 2009—they were setting up dispensary regulations. And I instantly understood what people feel like when they come out of any closet. My knees were trembling at the podium, my palms were sweating. But I felt so much better afterwards."

Now the guy made "transparency" his business mantra. In addition to freely giving out both his MendoGrown and his nascent personal business cards—he had just decided to form an online medical cannabis delivery business he was calling the Kama Collective—to anyone who asked and some (like his 2011 farm neighbors) who didn't, Tomas didn't ask me for any privacy protections at all. No off-the-record guarantees, no name changes. No restrictions whatsoever.

I still find that incredibly courageous. There's no way Tomas could have known I wasn't another hack coming in to write a sinse-millionaire tabloid feature. Plus, it was conventional wisdom among cannabis players in 2011 that to open one's trap often drew a federal bead on a farmer. Stirred the wasp's nest.

"Sauron's eye," one grower told me. "As a small farmer with no legal budget, as long as federal prohibition is still in effect, well, it's just a little too early."

It's not an exaggeration to say that Tomas's freedom really is on the line until there's a change in federal drug policy. This is a man who paid his dispensary-supplying, indoor-crop taxes, even prior to going public. He did this, on the advice of his tax attorney, by checking the truthful if vague "direct marketing" career box on his tax forms. ("Contractor" and "carpenter" are two other common official answers to this ticklish "what's your line?" question for honest gray-market cannabis farmers nationwide.)

By sticking his neck out and revealing his line of work publicly, Tomas risked ending up in the new Mendota Federal Correctional Institution you and I recently built (for $110 million) outside of Fresno—for a ten-year medium-security detour. Like most people I met in Mendo, he was just going to ignore the little federal cannabis scheduling problem, which is in play in every medical cannabis state because of the pesky Supremacy Clause in Article VI of the U.S. Constitution.

Cannabis aside, Tomas was opening his whole cultivation and business plan to me, and he knew it. This is rare in the business world, and it's rare in the farming world. There was even a chance

I'd report on his more embarrassing traits, such as his unfailing and masochistic habit of rooting not just for the obvious San Francisco Giants, but for their hapless basketball cousins, the Golden State Warriors.

So why did Tomas so readily agree to allow one of his as-yet unborn plants to star in a book? I had to ask, to make sure *he* wasn't a federal agent—principally because my contract with my publisher mandated a genuine cannabis grower. So I did, near the end of our conversation that day. His answer was as simple and straightforward as that of any veteran activist on any issue. He gave it just after popping an organic cracker topped with homemade mushroom pâté.

"Prohibition must end," the UC Berkeley graduate said in the Cohens' kitchen, brushing his hands together in a crumbs-removing motion that I took to be both practical and metaphorical. "The Drug War [crunch] makes me a criminal, enriches real criminals in Mexico and elsewhere, and keeps patients from getting the best, most affordable medicine. It's a war [crunch] against America. Against my America. It's wrong [crunch crunch]."

Having just sat in on two hours' worth of MendoGrown rhetoric, I had my follow-up ready. "As wrong as other ills in the world? Ignoring climate change? Hunger in Africa?"

Tomas was ready too. This is a fellow who had experience banging on strangers' doors in conservative-leaning crannies in Florida and saying, "Yes, we can!"

"Connected to all of those," he said immediately. "What can I tell you? It's my issue. I think of myself as an American small farmer, providing jobs and a tax base, and now I'm returning to heal the land too. Did you know that I'm a second-generation freedom fighter?"

"I did not."

"My dad's a refugee from the Budapest rebellion in 1956. I'm educating *him* also."

I was both psyched and nearly convinced. Tomas definitely qualified in the openness category, which was crucial for me journalistically: He had absolutely nothing to hide. Maybe his mother would even give an "I'm so proud" or an "I'm so humiliated" quote. Actually, she didn't have to. This sixty-something woman, who had once personally seized her son's first crop—tucked behind the chimney during his high school years—in 2011 made a contribution to MendoGrown.

My next question was more technical. And it sealed things up for me. Just before I was summoned to my monster truck-pull, I asked Tomas, "Yeah, but will we actually be able to follow one plant's flowers all the way to one patient? Can you really know where every bud goes?"

Any can-do entrepreneur in any field of endeavor will recognize Tomas's reply. It gives a strong clue as to why America has always been, will always be, great. He said, knuckle-tapping Cohen's kitchen table twice, "We will, or we'll die trying."

Phew. I hadn't hired goat-sitters and relocated my entire family a thousand miles to the left for nothing. I would soon learn that this statement was typical Balogh: Make a decision—say, to be a proud, totally open American cannabis farmer—and stick with it.

I now had a plant to follow. Just then Matt Cohen told me he had rallied a crew to "rescue the writer." Mendonesians are used to giant vehicles in trouble. It was one of those things you allow for, like waiting in line at the DMV.

I found it notable even at the time—indicative of his agricultural roots—that Cohen, when he arrived on the disaster scene, didn't even look at my truck. Rather, facing a giant metal monstrosity only half visible near the trees across from his house, he stuck a finger into the muck and examined it closely. I thought he was going to lick it, but he only sniffed.

"Soft out here" was his typically succinct assessment of the situation in his yard. The guy was a farmer.

The muck that flew from about eighteen tires during the extraction (one MendoGrown board member, thank goodness, understood towline vectors) was black and fecund. With each "that do it?" inspection, my boot soles making hollow sucking sounds with every pace, I sidestepped orange-bellied newts, who did not in their pace appear to be rooting for this rainy season to end.

I, by contrast, was vehemently praying for such an abrupt change in conditions. I was wet, cold, late, and embarrassed, and my transmission was emitting menacingly inorganic smells. I didn't think this particular meadow could technically be considered solid ground, for real estate purposes.

Still, arms caked with mud in the seat of my freed truck, I was, within a few bumpy miles, caring less about the rain, my several more weeks of unshorn hair, and my pending mechanic's bill. I had a farmer and a plant to follow from birth (or clone-cutting) to patient! Tomas and I would soon agree to name the research plant Lucille after an initially belligerent neighbor of his: all harvestable medical cannabis plants are female.

I finally knew that all this Mendo openness had provided me the botanical access that this project demanded. At each stage of one Cashmere Kush plant's journey, if she made it horticulturally and seizure-free to a patient at all, I could chart her economic value, legal and social hurdles, and eventual role in a legal cannabis economic space. The present state of things in Mendocino enabled me to offer a view of how the future could look everywhere. Unless, of course, this Mendo zip tie experiment proved another wacky California flash in the pan.

Journalistically, I felt like my worries were over. True, this was Balogh's first outdoor crop after years of tuition-paying indoor medicine growing. And, well, I soon learned that he hadn't yet, as of the vernal equinox, quite lined up a property on which to grow his plants. But if he was willing to let me document the course of his optimistic business plan—and, incidentally, also his concurrent personal and professional organic awakening—I was willing to have a certain amount of faith that it would be worth reporting.

Whatever happened happened. If he failed, went broke, or got arrested, I'd document that. What I learned that rainy day in March is that Tomas, if he succeeded, did so because he believed what he was doing wasn't just a career choice. It was the right decision for his country. "I'm patriotic," he said. "I'm trying to help the economy and help patients."

It was a refrain I heard from a dozen farmers. Colorado cannabis dispensary operator Aaron Bluse told me this on September 26, 2011, on the day his bank, under federal pressure, reluctantly asked him to close out his Altitude Organic Medicine account. "My lawyer told me to get a shovel and store our money off-site. I'm not sure he was totally kidding. I'm a taxpayer trying to be aboveboard, and the absurdity of prohibition is turning mine into a cash-only business. That helps no one."

# NINE
## Intergenerational Neighborhood
## Relations in Cannabis Culture

Acreage and nice two bedroom home. Lots of water and elec-
tricity. Licensed for 99 plants (215 friendly). Looking for someone to manage and work out a fair agreement to both parties.
Email with questions. Ready to go now.

—Mendocino County Craigslist posting, March 19, 2011

**N**ot long after my truck had been repaired following its short
tenure as a boat in the Cohens' pasture, Lucille I,* the first
locally developed Cashmere Kush clone (four-inch cutting) of
Tomas's on whose economic, legal, medicinal, bureaucratic, and
highly scented coattails I was preparing to ride, was born. And
then, er, three days later, died. So did one of her backups. This
happened in the greenhouse of a friend of Tomas's named Leif.

Before her surviving identical triplet sister could be planted,
though, Tomas needed to find some Mendocino ground in which
to plant her.

True, the 9.31 ordinance pretty clearly states that any permitted grower who lives in a rural part of Mendocino County, pays
the program fees and inspection costs, and follows some fencing,
visibility, sustainability and distance-from-property-boundary
rules—plus submits to four inspections per season and can account
for where the medicine is going to end up—can grow ninety-nine
flowering cannabis plants without getting hassled locally. Yet in
early 2011 Tomas still had a hard time finding a "Zip-tie-friendly"
farm in climatically perfect Mendocino.

---

* She wasn't yet named, as Tomas hadn't yet found his property and had his
initial . . . encounters with the human Lucille.

Sometimes I accompanied him that spring as he ping-ponged around a mountainous county larger than Delaware, trying—and for two months failing—to find a safe, affordable, accessible spot to plant what turned out to be eighty-eight plants. Some others of his clones didn't make it from their birthing greenhouse, either, including Lucille II. I confess at times to wondering whether I should have been looking for a more . . . established Mendo farmer for my research.

It was always inspiring and beautiful, though, to take these windy rides around the county. Inspiring because of Tomas's unflagging entrepreneurial optimism ("maybe I could still lease that Potter Valley place if I could just get the Baptist guy and the outlaw grower neighbor to both come have a beer unarmed") and beautiful because of the scenery.

It was almost a routine for a few weeks: I'd leave my own gor-geously situated cabin, my nose already filled with the closest neighbors' terpenes, following the usual "have fun in the cannabis fields" kiss from my Sweetheart. More often than not this would happen just before my windshield wipers tried to disengage entire, needly redwood limbs blown off during a middle-of-the-night windstorm through which I, awakened by Doomsday sounds, watched constellations or shooting stars.

Then I'd drive, spilling tea as I made it down from the hills, to Highway 101 and then Ukiah's Oco Time Sushi, where Tomas and I sometimes met. On a typical morning, as I looked for parking in Ukiah, out of my speakers came the *Trading Time* call-in item swap show on community radio station KZYX. I listened as a three-thousand-gallon marine surplus water tank and a vintage bassinet were offered for barter in between underwriting spots for cannabis farm supply stores. KZYX and KMUD (in northern Mendo and Humboldt) are media outlets that provide the pulse of the community the way few radio stations can in the Digital Age.

Forty minutes later, in his Craigslist-purchased used Audi, Tomas and I would find ourselves entering ranch security codes in some rarely traversed-by-outsiders nook of the county and he'd fail yet again to line up a property. By proposing open, permitted cannabis farming, Tomas managed to ignite several already-festering neighborhood phone tree feuds before he even moved in anywhere. Black-marketeers often weren't fond of the idea. On the other side of the spectrum, the local Ned Flanderses generally preferred to ignore the major local industry.

Keeping me from fully enjoying these expeditions was the fact that Tomas the suburban-raised city dweller simply didn't yet know how to drive rurally. Trust me when I tell you that you don't want to be a passenger in these Mendo exploring situations. Especially when the actual driver is making his first foray into rural mountain traversing, in an Audi, no less. The open-toed sandals the former indoor farmer was still at this point sporting don't even provide the kind of support needed for what Hunter Thompson called the heel-to-toe work in these environs.

After this too-long search, Tomas finally landed at what might have been the Most Distressed Property in Mendocino County. Which, in a time of foreclosure abandonment and federal raids, is saying quite a lot. I was there when he first saw the trash heap of a spot. The litter scattered from porch to planting fields included everything from old pesticide bottles to exposed electrical wiring to bullet-riddled microwave ovens to several thousand flowerpots. He left that initial site visit scratching it off his diminishing list.

I was relieved: The place was an hour and a half from my cabin and I didn't relish a nauseating commute up and down the spine of three different mountain ranges. But to my dismay, he soon returned out of desperation and, in what I was to learn was typical Tomas fashion, intent on "restoring the karma, you know what I mean?" of the cliffy and admittedly spectacularly situated mountainside spot, of which at least one and possibly two of the previous occupants were at the moment in jail.

Call me crazy, but I believe it was the property's troubled history of multiple raids, middle-of-the-night, high-caliber target practice, and illicit tapping of the Pacific Gas and Electric power lines that might have left the neighbors on all sides about as anticannabis as is possible for former cannabis farmers to be. So anticannabis, in fact, that prior to Tomas's arrival, several of them had actually lobbied in favor of reducing Mendocino's even more liberal pre-9.31 plant numbers to the current ninety-nine.

You could accurately say that folks in these hills like to know their neighbors' business, but learning it is really not much of an investigation. Tomas's first job was to convince his neighbors that a youngster could "do it right." In fact, could help provide a template for the rest of his generation of farmers. Everyone already knew that the cannabis plant wasn't the problem, but rather the criminal bad apples who inevitably get lured to any industry facing prohibition. That's where the tax-free profits are. And this is why we know Al Capone's name.

In fact, one retiree neighbor, Loretta, told him skeptically when they first met for tea, "You seem well-groomed and civil, but so did [Mendo-connected 1980s 'King of Pot'] Bruce Perlowin." Loretta also took written notes during this meeting, asking Tomas about his upbringing, criminal record, and intentions. His non- (or not-currently) cultivating neighbors, in short, were expecting a very different kind of person from Tomas. Not, it's safe to say, a fellow taxpayer.

Tomas's problem was that he was being pegged as one of Those New Kind of Growers. The punks. He was thus confronted with that greatest of all Mendo conflicts: the generational one. Though I would soon learn from some iffy neighbors of my own that it has some basis in reality, Tomas was facing a hypocritical stereotype that shows that even former, true back-to-the-land hippies can calcify into curmudgeonly old farts.

Unaware of the backlash to come, Tomas paid his exorbitant first-month lease-to-own payment of $2,500 for the twenty-nine-acre spread (or what he thought was a lease-to-own payment) in a burst of vamped-up optimism. He also went off grid for his power to the moldy farmhouse, rather than forking over the $7,800 PG&E wanted in fines before declaring the past forgiven and turning on the juice.

Upon signing his lease, Tomas's first meeting with one of his neighbors was not auspicious. The fellow was a passable Hank Hill genotype, to use a botanical term cannabis farmers are always bandying about, whose cliff-burbling springwater was technically deeded to Tomas's land, though the line had been cut. He was not clutching a welcome basket.

Tomas sped up a few minutes late to the late-spring meeting in that, for Mendo, unfortunately chosen Audi. He in fact did emerge clutching an introductory bottle of wine, after creating the backwoods cloud of dust that is to the longtime rural Mendonesian's sophisticated language of dirt road etiquette roughly what a sex offender is to a suburbanite.

"I hadn't learned about Mendo Time yet," Tomas confesses now. "I didn't want to keep him waiting."

The neighbor, Chase Donnelly, refused to shake Tomas's hand. He did talk to the extended extremity, though. What he said was "I don't like you or what you're about."

After listening to five minutes of high-volume venting of the Abe Simpson school about disrespectful punk cannabis growers, why he had or had not retired here, the threat to America as a result of Hillary Clinton's State Department tenure, and liberalism in general, Tomas presented the winded Mr. Donnelly with the wine and his MendoGrown and Kama Collective business cards. He asked if there was a neighborhood watch he could join. Two weeks later Chase's spring was watering Lucille. Today even Donnelly's wife expresses surprise at the rapidity of the détente.

Mr. Donnelly simply didn't hate the idea of another cannabis farm back in the hood as much as Tomas loved it. In fact, an energetically unwavering but somehow humble belief in his calling was Tomas's MO. He appeared to draw bad luck like a vegetable-oil-powered truck draws Sonoma narcotics profilers, but he turned it into good luck. Part of it was his soft-spoken, good-humored demeanor, aided by such a trustworthy baby face you hardly notice the three-inch scar running across his left cheek. Most of it, though, was his clear stating of his intentions.

It's hard to say if he was any more successful with his neighbor and cannabis plant namesake Lucille, who was possibly possessed of a fantastically ironic backstory. A transplant from Southern California who'd married a neighborhood vintner and was known for vocal anticannabis views, she, too, had angrily rebuffed Tomas after his initial "here's my card and how do I join the neighborhood watch?" approach.

"I'm not sure she knows that if her husband weren't involved in the industry at some point, he would've been quite the exception in this county," Tomas said. "But she's really all right, maybe just a little lonely. She called me a few days later to explain where she was coming from. Sure, it was after ten P.M. and she sounded possibly a little tipsy, but her heart's in the right place."

Still, we agreed that we had a name for the plant I'd be following. Part of the karma restoration. Actually Lucille's not her real name—as with the rest of Tomas's 2011 neighbors, it seemed more respectful to maintain the canyon's privacy as much as possible. But the plant is named in her honor.

In soothing his remaining neighbors, Tomas's goal was both to ensure that no one placed a jittery call to the snitch line that the county still maintained, and, more generally, to be a legal ganja-preneur diplomat. And this was a mission that took considerable time away, at first, from, you know, little things like growing his actual crop.

A U-Haul was involved in that, filled with retail compost and the tiny cannabis cuttings that would call it their home. Diplomacy also took time away from Tomas's obtaining his yellow zip ties. Just when he thought he was ready, the sheriff's clerk reminded him that he had not yet registered his cannabis scale with the County Division of Weights and Measures as required in the cultivation ordinance. The 9.31 Program's drafters, many of whom had decades of evading the law under their belts, had thought of everything. Former criminals, it turns out, make great bureaucrats.

Tomas's overall business strategy, I realize now, was a sort of

Murphy's Law rope-a-dope. End goal in mind, he was resigned to losing battles, while remaining unwaveringly certain that he—he would say all of us freedom-loving, it's-the-economy-savvy, sustainability-minded Americans—would win the war.

At age thirty-three already well into the implementation phase of his dreams, I watched Tomas appear to keep his head the whole 2011 season despite suffering more setbacks than his injury-plagued San Francisco Giants.

His first and probably biggest hurdle, for example, was his new property itself. After hundreds of hours of old-fashioned elbow grease cleanup work at the trashed, oft-raided property,* he at last had a plausible home for his plants. Which by this point had been growing up in Leif's greenhouse for a month and a half.

Tomas estimates he removed more than two tons of trash from the property in his first week. And that was just the landscaping. He also capped the dangerous loose wires from the pirated electric lines and scrubbed off mold from the main house.

"Hey, if I'm going to be a boss I should be able to do every job," Tomas told me upon descending with a Jacques Cousteau–like thumbs-up into the former septic tank that was now one of the property's springwater tanks. He had to clean out the remnants of a rodent civilization.

Having journeyed these few, tiny baby steps closer to success—with *success* defined as patients receiving medicine nine months later—Tomas promptly named the place the Eagle's Nest, as it sat perched most of the way up a remote Mendocino hill.

The ride up to the property was bumpy. Motocross bumpy. Forget about texting or changing the radio station, I couldn't even *think* when I drove to the Eagle's Nest. One time I tried to make the ascent while carting my family's secondhand washing machine in my truck bed. Didn't really work out.

His neighbors parried, his lease paid, the first layers of trash at

---

* Someone had even ripped gratuitous holes in the property's giant outdoor greenhouse, which Tomas spun as "They air-conditioned it for me."

the dump, the greenhouse secured with new doors and one of the two outdoor fields cleared, I saw by my third visit that Tomas was apparently going to make it work, from a botanical standpoint, by the skin of his teeth.

Other farmers I was visiting already had plants in the ground when Tomas signed his lease. Had he arrived any later, his Kama Collective's crop wouldn't have had time to develop. And he knew it. He just wasn't the kind of fellow who dwelled on disaster narrowly averted. There was too much to get done today. Such as heading to pick up Lucille and "the rest of the girls" he had cloned six weeks earlier.

# TEN

## Replication of the Clones

This particular bill would help Kern County. It's a product that can be grown and used in agriculture. It's used in all different kinds of products right now.

—Kern County, California, sheriff Donny Youngblood, endorsing Senate bill 676, which would have created a pilot program allowing for the cultivation of industrial cannabis (hemp) in his conservative county and three other California counties, on Bakersfield, California, NBC affiliate KGET television, September 29, 2011

The door of Leif's greenhouse flapping closed behind me shut out both the effulgent sunlight and the elastic whopping of choppers in the low-horizon distance to the west. As the first sweat bubbles began to coalesce on my forehead, I sensed that any gaps in the structure's self-built frame—even the wood itself came from trees on the property and was hand-planed—wasn't going to keep the atmosphere any less humid than, say, midsummer in Equatorial Guinea.

But the tropical air itself was nothing compared to the wall of intensity that permeated my olfactory sense—and in fact a good part of my parasympathetic nervous system—the moment I entered the teeming greenhouse where Lucille and ninety-odd of her sisters and cousins were moments from being born. The smell, though not unpleasant, actually came pretty close to knocking me backward into the door.

These cuttings were going to be clipped, or "cloned," from their mother plants this April 21 morning. Tomas, at this point still in the midst of his frustrating property search, knew that wherever he ended up, this was the time of year to take cuttings. He was fortunate to have a local, trustworthy nursery. The litter would be safely babysat here in the maternity ward at Leif's farm for as long as necessary, but hopefully not more than a couple of weeks.

The scent was just shy of Totally Overwhelming. In a good, organic way. The term *contact high* barely begins to convey the palpable, pulsating sensations I was feeling within seconds, both corporeally and cerebrally. Let me put it in medicinal terms: I instantly forgot any notion of the carsickness I had been suffering following another missed teachable country-driving moment in Tomas's Audi.

With the wavering silhouette of the Mendocino Coastal Range visible outside, I felt like I was inside a Peter Tosh album cover photo. The man-size mother plants shimmered in the cross breeze, and the climatic conditions made me want to order a couple of Coronas from room service. Strangely, it couldn't have been much above fifty degrees outside in the early-morning direct sun. I suddenly understood why Outside Planting Day in these parts comes as late as mid-May.

"Wow," I observed to our tour guide Leif, who was leading the way through the bushy plant maze with Tomas one row to the side, "that is one green scent."

"What you're smelling are the terpenes," Leif informed me, chewing on a piece of straw under an oversize straw sun hat. "Sort of a resinous chemical component of the plant. They're hydrocarbons—more'n a hundred terpenes in cannabis. Lotta research going into the effects of the terpenes."*

---

* According to a 2010 article on the Berkeley Patients Care Collective website, *"Many plant terpenes act synergistically with other terpenes and some serve to either catalyze or inhibit formation of other compounds within a plant. For example, understanding the role of certain terpenes will allow scientists to manipulate cannabinoids to desired ratios. Some terpenes are said to modulate the physiological and psychoactive effects of cannabis.*

*"Cannabis usually contains a significant amount of a terpene called beta-caryophyllene (BCP), which contributes to the aroma and flavor. Studies show that this terpene, also found in other legal herbs, spices, and food plants (it contributes to the spiciness of black pepper), activates the CB2 receptor (a human cannabinoid receptor) and acts as a nonpsychoactive anti-inflammatory."*

"I'm undergoing some right now," I disclosed. "Is there some researcher who wants a report?"

"Yeah, the terpenes are probably strain-specific, just as the endocannabinoids are," Leif reported.

"So *that's* what this whole county smells like," I said. "Now I know. They should rename Mendocino Terpene County."

The research Leif was referring to seems to indicate that these terpenes might play a role in the plant's medicinal properties.

Meanwhile, I saw why, upon our arrival at his farm, Leif had said, "This way to the ladies," leading Tomas and me past horses and straw bales, through his hangar-size barn, and up a hill to the greenhouse. Since cannabis is a dioecious species (distinct male and female plants) and since only female plants produce medicinal flower buds, every cannabis field has what you might call strong feminine energy. This was thus the *Red Tent* of greenhouses I was in. Leif stroked a plant of the OG Kush strain and invited me to squeeze the main stem and smell.

Doing so with my right hand and both nostrils had two immediate effects. The first was that my fingers became too sticky with cannabinoid resin, for hours, to effectively type on my phone's text pad. This even with the lubricating effect of the near-constant faucet of sweat raining off my forehead. These were healthy ladies.

And powerful ones. So powerful that finding myself inside a 1970s reggae album cover photo was not the most astonishing part of the day. Leif told me casually, "I can take two thousand clones off these mother plants in a day." I was still processing that abundance when he added, "And then do it again two weeks later."

Cue *Star Wars* theme. That's nearly fifty thousand genetically identical plants per year, or up to a quarter million pounds of medicine, from one seven-dollar mother plant. Cloning from the same plant arguably doesn't work forever—there's a debate raging on genetic degradation and I've heard some interesting arguments on many sides. But it works for years. Hence no cannabis supply shortage on planet Earth.

The second effect of being invited by a plant kingdom farmer to interact with his crop was that the farmer in question seemed to me to be crazy. Beyond squeezing and fondling, Leif was constantly talking to, even singing to, the plants. As a goat rancher who has no problem sleeping in the corral, if necessary, in order to nurse a kid back to health or scare off yipping coyotes, I realized that I had previously, unconsciously, drawn the "we're all family" line at the border of the animal kingdom.

In other words, even though I'd read about the documented benefits of talking to plants, I'd always had a hard time inviting the sap-blooded, chlorophyll-producing organisms into what De Niro's Jack Byrnes in *Meet the Parents* calls "the Circle of Trust." I felt silly and insincere when I tried. Rabbits? Sure. Tomatoes? Not so much.

"Oh, aren't *you* thirsty?" I heard Leif ask a bushy Pineapple strain mother plant down the greenhouse corridor. Her long, thin, handlike leaves were indicative of a sativa phenotype, valued for appetite stimulation and possible tumor-reduction properties. I could see that Leif was tending this plant as much as I husband my goats. I watched him snip off a few yellowed leaves along her bottommost branches. An analogous process to my monthly goat hoof-trimming.

I tried to get a little oxygen in with the terpenes during my next few breaths. Results were mixed. Yet the terpenes themselves are not thought to be psychoactive as such, unless you consider Pavlovian effects.

Probably the best example of that phenomenon was provided late last millennium by my music-major college roommate. Forced by an unfulfilled science requirement to take Psychology 101 with four hundred freshmen when we were upperclassmen, he legendarily submitted the following response to a midterm short essay question, which had asked that he "give an example in your own life of a conditioned stimulus and a conditioned response, as made famous by Pavlov and his immortal dogs."

Concisely, in neat cursive, my roommate had written, as best as I remember it, "*When this exam is over, the thought of almost already being high on the Kind Sticky Green Bud waiting for me in my bong will cause me to salivate expectantly and even to smile. This is an example of a conditioned stimulus, since the bud itself isn't physically here with me in Miller Building Room 319. When I actually exhale that very Kind Sticky Green Bud's heavenly vapors back in my room, that will be an example of a conditioned response, since I am now experiencing the stimulus that is creating the response.*"

I saw the returned exam. Almost as notable as the answer itself was the manner of grading by a no doubt sleep-deprived, adrenaline-drained graduate student. The grader marked my roommate's answer with a NOTICEABLY LARGER check than he'd given all the other correct answers on the page. In fact, the passage of time might have me exaggerating, but I actually recall *two* large checks next to that answer.

When I think back on that essay now that I'm becoming a student of the economic history of cannabis, what strikes me is that as recently as the early 1990s, designer strain names, while in existence as far back as the 1920s, were far less ubiquitous than they are today. Back then, it was either fragrant, high quality ("Kind") California Green Bud (*sinsemilla*), or yucky, seedy, much less expensive Mexican weed.

There in Leif's greenhouse, by contrast, the strains were so varied and nuanced that some purport to provide fully opposite therapeutic effects than others: There's cannabis bred for energy-boosting needs (often pure sativas), and cannabis for sleep (usually a mind- and muscle-relaxing indica). And indeed I could see marked differences in the plants surrounding me at the moment: an indica-leaning Grand Daddy Purple was dark green and bushy, reflecting its high-elevation Hindu Kush roots, while a nearby sativa of the Casey Jones strain looked as though it would be comfortable dancing in a Hawaiian or Jamaican breeze.

Which was all very journalistically valuable, but the greenhouse cloning experience had me sweating enough to need a change of clothes. And perhaps a large pizza. Tomas and Leif seemed used to it. So I steeled myself for a wild ride and possible coma and listened to these two farmers, two colleagues, talk shop.

# ELEVEN

## Birth of the Lucille Triplets and Tomas's Crop Comes Home

Marijuana has been smoked for its medicinal properties for centuries. Preclinical, clinical, and anecdotal reports suggest numerous potential medical uses for marijuana. Although the indications for some conditions (e.g., HIV wasting and chemotherapy-induced nausea and vomiting) have been well documented, less information is available about other potential medical uses. Additional research is needed to clarify marijuana's therapeutic properties and determine standard and optimal doses and routes of delivery. Unfortunately, research expansion has been hindered by a complicated federal approval process, limited availability of research-grade marijuana, and the debate over legalization. Marijuana's categorization as a Schedule I controlled substance raises significant concerns for researchers, physicians, and patients.

—American College of Physicians 2008 position paper entitled "Supporting Research into the Therapeutic Role of Marijuana"

The Office of the General Counsel has determined that no VA physician shall complete any forms for the State of Michigan for medical marijuana. However, for patients whose treatment plan from a non-VA physician includes use of medical marijuana, presence of marijuana in a urine drug screen is acceptable.

—Suzanne Klinker, Medical Center director, Battle Creek, Virginia, in a letter dated June 19, 2009

Leif and Tomas were of similar age, and friends. Relatively new friends but good ones. Leif's wife Leah, too, was a skilled vegetable and cannabis farmer—and sheep herder: Leif being Jewish, their 2011 Passover shank bone came from their own herd. Later in the summer, while she was pregnant with her third child, I saw Leah administering an organic "compost tea" to the soil where their medicinal cuttings had been transplanted near the sheep meadow in the family's sublime central county spot. Leif's mother and stepfather were also gentleman cannabis growers, though more as a hobby—they started about the same time as their kids, following Proposition 215's passage in 1996.

Culturally, Leif and Leah didn't come from what you might call the Puritan tradition, but they were not hippies, not in the original sense of the word. They were taxpaying Bay Area refugees, a young couple in their late twenties. Yet Leif only charged Tomas some symbolic amount per clone that day in the greenhouse; seven dollars I think it was, for nearly a million dollars' worth of eventual medicine.

When I see how Leif and Leah conduct their lives, I realize that one of my favorite sayings, which asserts that "the sixties happened in the seventies," doesn't go far enough. The best part of the sixties, the idea that interaction with other humans can be comprised of cooperation and not merely of "it's a jungle out there" competition, is still active, even dominant in some parts of our planet. And nowhere more so than in Mendo. It's not a money-obsessed place. It's a contentment-obsessed place.

I once stepped outside of the Willits hardware store at sunset. It was a remarkable sunset, the sky dripping a grid of nectarine Q-tips over the horizon, and when I looked around to see if anyone else had noticed, the first three people I saw were taking photographs.

Back in Leif's greenhouse, I was still trying to unstick my index finger and thumb with my dampened handkerchief—temporarily removed from its job cooling my neck—and mulling the "call them what you will" properties of terpenes ten or fifteen minutes after I learned about them, when Leif's voice cut through the thick greenhouse atmosphere. "Wanna try to cut the clone you'll be tracking?"

He was extending a small garden clipper toward me.

"What?" I said, returning from some thoughts about how really far it is between galaxies.

"Wanna do a cutting?" he repeated.

"From the, ah, mother plant?" I asked. I was shocked by the question, because I thought the process would require an advanced degree in horticulture. But cannabis cloning turned out to be closer in difficulty to connecting Velcro.

"Nothing to it," Tomas said, I thought generously, since his livelihood and dreams depended on it being done right. "Watch us do a couple."

I watched them do about eighty, and then I gingerly snipped a four-inch Cashmere Kush baby in the diagonal manner that I had been observing from a plant about my height that looked to have equal parts sativa and indica characteristics. I dipped the newborn in some root-stimulating enzyme and into the middle of her temporary "oasis cube"* home, with a "good luck, baby girl" wish from Leif.

"Better take two, no, make it three cuttings from this lady," Leif said prophetically, stroking Lucille's mother plant, which in turn came from the genetic lab of another local farmer. "If you're writing a book about this strain, you want to make sure at least one of the cuttings survives. With three, you're probably good."

The Lucille triplets were born. Leif later assured me that the ensuing two fatalities weren't my fault. "At least one in three cuttings doesn't make it—that's just how it works," he consoled me after the first Lucille's passing a week later.

At the moment in the greenhouse, though, I couldn't believe that all of these tiny, Kelly green cuttings, now filling up rows and rows of seedling trays, would grow into the monster outdoor trees I'd heard about—and in a few short months. But Lucille's Cashmere Kush mother plant possessed particularly good prospects: Developed, as she had been, at the nearby seed lab, Leif felt she was ideally suited to this exact ecosystem. Judging from her potent burst of terpenes, I couldn't argue.

---

* An egg-size oasis cube is just a more nutritively sophisticated version of those tomato seedling peat pots you can pick up at the nursery.

Lucille's mother plant was really making the reproductive rounds too. She already had plenty of clipped junctions. I've since seen "Cashmere Kush" listed on plenty of collective and dispensary cannabis strain menus, and it placed fifth at the 2011 Emerald Cup medicinal cannabis competition. Her daughters Lucilles II and III and their eighty-seven cousins of twelve different strains (about 60 percent of them indica-dominant) lived in Leif's greenhouse for those six weeks while Tomas harangued potential neighbors and landlords in his open-toed sandals. When he returned to pick the girls up for transport to the tidied-up Eagle's Nest on June 13, I accompanied him. In a U-Haul.

Winding such a conveyance through a redwood-lined backroads part of the county whose "lanes" were of the width required by a large bicycle struck me as roughly equivalent to spray-painting CANNABIS TRANSPORT VEHICLE over the images from Vermont and Wisconsin the company usually favors on the sides of its trucks. There actually was a sticker on the dash suggesting that we "Keep it in the Green." But that, ostensibly, was about some kind of fuel efficiency setting.

Tomas and I had met in Ukiah for lunch that day after he finished some errands. We pulled back in front of Leif's greenhouse on what had turned into a blustery June midafternoon. When Tomas hopped down and threw open the sliding rear gate of the U-Haul, it appeared—and smelled—as if half of Mendocino County's manure was inside. I suddenly understood what his other "errands" in town had been that morning. The pile was steaming.

"Compost," Tomas explained. "And bat guano."

I had an immediate question. "Did the guy at the landscaping place think it was in any way odd to be adding—what is this?—four cubic yards of decomposed, you know, refuse, into the back of a rental truck?"

"Dude," Tomas replied with a laugh, "I don't think it was his first one of the day. He asked if I wanted a receipt and wished me happy planting."

Now lined up outside their birth greenhouse, I had a "my how you've grown" sensation when I saw Lucille II and III—hereafter simply Lucille; she was reborn twice, sort of like Bob Dylan. She was, like most of her friends, nearly eighteen inches tall. A deeper green than I remembered from their birthday and uniformly perky, the crop overall looked like a troop of young tomato plants ready to leave the nursery. Tomas and Leah used wheelbarrows to move and lovingly stick the future medicine into the U-Haul compost one by one, creating a very temporary bonsai garden.

Despite the care taken during loading, Tomas fretted about the safety of the plants, given the questionable stability inside the metal square of a rental truck. To this Leah proffered helpfully, "They say you want to simulate rough weather conditions with transplants. Seriously, you're supposed to create a windstorm with your mouth and arms. Makes 'em tough."

This was Tomas's first move from indoor botanist to outdoor farmer, and you could see the uncertainty on his face. We bumped the forty minutes back to the Eagle's Nest more slowly, I noticed, than we had come—so Tomas could begin the second of the 2011 season's three transplantings.

When we arrived at the farm, Tomas was vocally, fist-pumpingly relieved to see that most of the plants made it home from the nursery that day. Each one had a potential value of tens of thousands of dollars and could reach dozens of patients. At this point I felt like I was watching the moment in the documentary when the just-hatched Mexican turtles tentatively begin the arduous march down the wide beach to the shoreline.

Real life was about to begin for these young ladies. Summer's blessed sun would soon be upon them. They were, for the next six months, freely living, mountain-air-absorbing organisms.

In fact, before we left Leif and Leah's farm that day, Leah had correctly suggested that we'd never guess what she had on her deck. Turned out to be a pair of two-week-old barn owl chicks, which had come as an unintentional bonus gift with a recent hay delivery. Leah had a tweaked shoulder ("Have you considered medical cannabis for that?" I asked) and so invited me to reach into the cage myself, as though offering me a butterscotch candy. After having savage claws wrapped tourniquet-tight around my fingers for longer than I really needed, an eager-to-get-planting Tomas rescued me. He said to the caretakers of his crop, "Well, thanks for babysitting the girls."

"Sun's free," said Leah with a shrug, unpeeling the owl from my finger while the chick peered at me with what looked like hunger. And I think now that Leah's one statement sums up the pervading Mendocino cannabis farmer philosophy. The sun is free. And doesn't use petroleum or violate the Clean Water Act.

And so Lucille came home. She was a plant developed by a neighborhood agricultural scientist to thrive in this exact climate without a drop of glyphosate. She was a local, through and through.

# TWELVE
## Lucille's Gregor Mendel

The best gardeners of my generation.

—Michael Pollan on cannabis farmers, in a 2009 PBS
documentary based on his book *The Botany of Desire*

**B**efore following Lucille to one of her patients, I wanted to learn where she had come from. The horticultural Dr. Frankenstein who in his lab—in Mendo this is generally a peeling redwood barn—had devoted the good part of a decade to breeding Lucille's Cashmere Kush strain was a second-generation grower and general contractor named Rock. Rock was of the generation that invented Mendo Time. Which is to say, I arrived at our labside meeting first. By a while.

When the fifty-one-year-old rumbled up, back from a deck-building job, he struck me as a relaxed person. Friendly and generous but not feeling an urge to rush bonding. The farmer who had referred me to Rock had himself lived locally for more than a decade and had met him all of twice.

I had chosen to follow this new strain of Rock's in the first place for two reasons: First, I found through the Mendo Gossip Telegraph that I could actually meet its progenitor, its Gregor Mendel, the guy who developed her genetic line. Rock turned out to have heard of "that monk" who is the father of modern genetics, whose calling he shares and whose techniques he daily uses, though he didn't know his name.

"I learned the basics—you know, dominant and recessive genes, genotypes and phenotypes—from talking to other farmers when I was growing up," he told me. "I asked a lot of questions. Folks here are very generous with their knowledge."

And Rock, also a sculptor (his milieu is driftwood, often arranged with seascape backgrounds), had the classic Mendo back-to-the-land upbringing. *Dharma and Greg* didn't capture the extent of it. This was a lifestyle too weird for San Francisco. And, hey, it "worked," if you value things like "contentment," "self-awareness," and "closeness with one's parents."

But he sure had Mendo Wild West stories for me. Classic "sixties happened in the seventies" tales. Among the more memorable tidbits was Rock's casual, afterthoughty mention that he had "finished" using LSD at age twelve because "I'd learned what I needed to know."

The second reason I chose—or allowed locals to convince me to follow—Cashmere Kush is that Leif told me that the strain had, based on its lineage, a good chance of possessing a promising medical property that was at the cutting edge of cannabinoid research. This was a quality I wanted to analyze in a biochemical lab following harvest in the fall. Specifically, I was interested in the strain's level of the possibly cancer-fighting cannabinoid CBD.

THC/CBD ratios are the latest thing in the cannabis medical field and a number of researchers believe that they are seeing value in a particular combination of these two most well-known canna-binoids, much like the famous nutritive benefit of balanced omega fatty acids. I already knew that hemp seed oil possesses the ideal Omega 6/Omega 3 ratio, without fish oil's mercury risk—that's why I've drunk it every morning for years. The balanced medical properties of the plant are showing similar promise.

As I found out from Dr. Courtney, nearly all U.S. cannabis research is preliminary, because of the difficulty in obtaining fed-eral approval even to study the plant, for any reason. Given the kind of substances that *are* approved—not just for study, but for use by American consumers—by our federal regulating agencies, you'd think a cannabis bud would explode in your hands, instead of just making them fragrant and a little bit sticky.

Dupont's EPA-approved and much touted "green" herbicide Imprelis, for example, got recalled in August 2011 after slaughtering a swath of centuries-old pine and spruce in the Midwest. Cannabis has actually never killed another organism. Unless you count the chicken that gets roasted whenever a chemo patient pops a eucalyptus cannabis lozenge and gets a strong appetite boost.

When he showed up for our meeting at his small coastal farm on May 19, 2011, I first asked Rock why he'd chosen the name Cashmere Kush for his newest designer strain. Rock, barely stopping to pull weeds as we walked past his pond and through his early crop of salad greens, half-smiled and assessed my face, as if to see how in-depth an answer I really wanted.

"I have a very sensitive nose," he began, which was not what I'd expected him to say, but which I now know is a perfectly normal remark from, say, an expert vintner. I understand much better in light of something a Colorado cannabis farmer later told me: "In an evolved society, wine and cannabis tasting competitions will be held together."

"Once I knew I had it from the bouquet, that I had the new strain, I thought it carried an Asian mountain scent along with its Himalayan ancestry," Rock continued. "But I kinda felt with the turmoil over there [in Kashmir], I'd spell it like the soft wool—with a *C*. Because her medicine is gentle but effective. It's a Kush, but it doesn't give you the couch-lock you feel with many indica-dominant strains."

Sometimes, you know you're in the presence of a genius. It's in the tone. And the word choices. I'd never heard that term, *couch-lock*. I repeated it and laughed.

"Your sativas generally show the heady effects of the cannabis from the sixties," Rock explained. "Which was mainly from Mexico. Very social." He walked with the instinctive "step around the obstacles without really noticing them" gait of someone who had grown up where he was at the moment. I tried to make notes as I dodged watering cans and cacti and cats and sculpture. "Indicas have a reputation for being effective painkillers, but also of zonking you out a bit. You find yourself locked on the couch for a couple hours."

Most Americans under the age of seventy have probably noticed that there's been something of an indica, and specifically a

"Kush," fetish in the cannabis world in recent years. It seems half the strain names in a Bay Area or Colorado dispensary somehow incorporate the word *Kush*, which doesn't have a firm definition but is loosely an indica genetic line. Although by now, Internet-slang.com just defines it as "High grade marijuana."

Think of apple variety names. They tell a story. I'm describing a marketing literary genre that Michael Pollan calls "Supermarket Pastoral." Or in this case "Dispensary Pastoral." One day students will be able to major in these disciplines.

Why is the Kush brand such a favorite? One reason is that it grows well in prohibition-friendly indoor environs. Another, explained SoCal collective manager Raimondi, is "if it appears in a hip-hop song, it becomes a desirable strain." As in Dr. Dre and Snoop Dogg's 2010 song entitled, er, "Kush."

Sometimes, a Mendocino County naturopathic doctor told me, you *want* couch-lock, from a therapeutic standpoint. "That body high is what gives significant relief from chronic pain, especially for patients with rheumatoid arthritis, MS, or other pain issues that cause sleep problems. A Grand Daddy Purple or a Bubba Kush strain is often wonderfully effective for those needs. PTSD too."

Back in my botany seminar with Rock, I asked, "How did you know you 'had it' with Cashmere Kush?"

Rock gave a quiet laugh toward his boots. "Actually, I thought I had it four years ago: It seemed to have the quality and taste I was looking for, a heavenly—just really such a uniquely piney bouquet, and it held up to mold and mites just fine on the farm. So I gave the seeds to all my friends and it just melted into nothing out there—fell apart with mold all over the county. So I started over and now this is the second crop and she seems to be ideally adapted [to our climate and soil] up here. It's a really delightful little strain."

It's impossible to overstate the importance of this kind of field research to the Mendocino cannabis industry. A plant that's well-adapted to the regional microflora and -fauna and to its climate is simply going to produce more and better medicine. Even within Mendocino County, there are so many microclimates that a strain that thrives under the baking sun in Covelo might not do so well in dripping-wet Fort Bragg.

So, much of the early Green Rush had been fueled by cannabis strains that had one key quality: They grew well indoors. These are not always the strains that thrive in the outdoor-dominated sustainable cannabis world. Every time I asked someone, from Colorado dispensary owners to cannabis lawyers to growers, "Why did indoor growing start in the first place?" I got the same answer: "Folks needed a place that wasn't exposed from above."

Diesel generators kept electric bills from getting suspiciously high during the depth of cannabis prohibition, but massive petroleum use, obviously, isn't sustainable. The plants that will thrive in outdoor cultivation's renaissance will be like radio stars who could also make it in television: The lights are much brighter.

Labs like Rock's—there are dozens in Mendo—are where the next-generation strains are developed. Rock's farm was old-school, well-hidden and cozily low budget in a *Little House on the Prairie* kind of way. A nailed-together shade cloth and chicken-fencing kind of operation, with ducks waddling around and plants sunk into soil he and his family have been nurturing for decades. Rock is one of those farmers who believe "it's not how it looks, it's how it works." U-Haul compost was not necessary here.

Cannabis—still under greenhouse cover for part of the day at this early time of year—was mixed in with the vegetable crops; all of them thick with darting butterflies and bees. Plus the occasional chopper ripping the sky overhead. In spite of—or maybe because of—this native polyculture strategy, Rock's plants, at least this early in the season, appeared especially robust to me.

As we toured his farm, Rock described how he loved being "tricked" by an atypical genotypic trait in a more common phenotype, and having to reassess which strains he would crossbreed the next season. No clones for Rock. He's a seed-and-pollen guy. Sure, he's what you might call a "field geneticist" rather than a lab one. But for most of human history, all geneticists have also been farmers. The field *was* the lab. It's why we have corn, riding horses, and all the other incredible experimental breeding results we enjoyed pre-Monsanto and Syngenta.

Rock is a minute-detail-noticer. There was a time when he might have been called a Druid. Someday, at a putative cannabis-tasting competition, he'll be considered a judge-worthy connoisseur. His sense of smell will be insured by Lloyd's of London.

A half hour into our chatting and plant-sniffing, an elderly neighbor came over to buy a half-dozen personal-use seedlings for five dollars each. No one seemed too worried about the transaction unfolding in front of an on-the-record writer. Then, after a few more plant genealogy lessons from Rock, I hit the journalistic jackpot when Rock's John Muir-look-alike father, Joe, ambled over, wearing a leather vest and pouch. He hugged his son, shook my hand, and allowed me to ask him about the early days.

Nineteen seventy-three, the year Joe relocated to Mendocino County from Southern California and started growing cannabis with seeds from his own Mexican stash, was clearly a simpler time.

"When I first planted, we didn't know from buds," Joe told me. "Until probably '79, or '81 we cut the whole stalk at six feet, seeds and all, dried it on the roof, and called it good. *Sinsemilla* [the technique of growing only females for seedless flowers] came about the same time as the helicopters." He pointed into the sky. Today's artificial bird was far away. "One day a neighbor came back from another neighbor's farm and said, 'The flowers are where it's at.'"

Boy. You hear a lot of businesses described as homegrown, but you couldn't mean that much more literally than this. Standing at the R&D birthplace of a multibillion-dollar domestic industry, I was blown away. From rooftop ad hoc drying—sometimes harvested by horse and wagon from steep hillsides—to manicured bud-trimming facilities in only thirty years!

THC itself (delta-9-tetrahydrocannabinol) was only identified by Israeli researchers Raphael Mechoulam and Y. Gaoni in 1964.*

---

* Mechoulam wasn't a one-hit wonder. In 1993, he led a team that identified a new, endemic THC-like substance in the human brain that he named anandamide, from the Sanskrit word for inner joy.

In the time that I've been researching this book, the number of known cannabinoids has increased.

We're talking about a less-than-half-century botanical advance rarely seen in history and one, conventional wisdom has it, that is almost entirely the result of prohibition. In other words, if you're a cancer patient who can eat thanks to a potent sativa strain of cannabis, you might want to add, "Thank you, God, for President Nixon and the Drug War," to the evening prayers. And we American citizens, collectively, financed it.

Meaning cannabis quality had *better* be good, since we've invested a trillion big ones in it. Small farmer subsidies, you might say, though not from the Department of Agriculture budget (as yet).* This way of looking at the situation doesn't declare the Drug War a failure but rather a lucrative success for everyone, just as Nixon allegedly intended. The Northern California cannabis outlaw band Camo Cowboys puts it well in their song "Flower Police" (being a more peaceful version of the infamous Mexican *narcocorridos*):

> The way it works is kind of a trip,
> It's a symbiotic relationship,
> The fact that's shrouded in obscurity,
> Is that they need us for job security.
> They're the Flower Police,
> They doin' their job,
> That's all right with me,
> Long as they keep on,
> Supporting the local economy.†

---

* A California judge in 2011 issued a "What was *he* smoking?" ruling to the effect that cannabis is not a crop, since to admit otherwise might allow cultivation in areas zoned for agriculture.

† This is as true in the international Drug War as it is inside U.S. borders. A Mexican grower in Chihuahua State told me, three years before the current escalation in violence, that his cousin the state police officer would habitually schedule a raid to nab a token bale or two of contraband, while the real

Accordingly, Joe, tilting his head as he thought about it after the manner of a semiretired Bilbo Baggins, described Mendocino County Sheriff's Department personnel as "always pretty supportive" of cannabis farming. This reflects the will of the people: Mendocino County actually first voted to decriminalize cannabis for any purpose in a ballot initiative in 2000, though that was later repealed. Joe made his assessment in the tone that a Kansas farmer might use to explain that his senator was generally supportive of wheat subsidies.

After we'd spoken for a while, admiring the irises, Joe asked if Rock would be able to work on some cabinets at his house the following week, sniffed the plants we were sniffing, nodded and grunted in approval like a head chef giving the soup of the day a final taste, and pushed off.

Rock and I then headed inside his barn so I could see where the genetic alchemy happened. It all was amazingly potent and terpene-soaked to my amateur nostrils, but Rock kept opening mason jars under my nose and saying things like "Smell that? The hint of plum there at the finish? When I got that in the ninth generation, that's when I knew I was onto something."

To which I replied some form of "Ummm, sure. Of course. I think so. That, er, smell at the end, you mean?"

It smelled like high-quality cannabis to me. It smelled like Mendocino County. It smelled like the first smell to greet me on my deck each morning before my run, thanks to my neighbor's poorly kept secret of a garden inside the not-really-a-hot-tub fencing. But then this is exactly analogous to my reaction when a wine tour leader tries like a skilled psychic to lead me to experience "oak balances" or "pear depth."

Rock is not rich. One could argue that, along with his general contracting, agricultural R&D is a half-time gig for him. And yet he routinely achieves industry-benefiting results of which most lab

---

connection was happening at a boat three beaches away. "Everybody wins," he explained. Except the U.S. taxpayer.

technicians tinkering with synthetics can only dream. When, four months later, Tomas had Lucille's flowers tested at the Halent Lab, run by University of California at Davis chemistry professor Donald Land, the report came back that she contained 12 percent THC and 1 percent CBD. I watched as Halent reps actually came to the Eagle's Nest on October 6 and packed six samples of her flowers into sealed bags.

Those numbers were good news and bad news for Tomas. True, he would have loved, from his first plant tested, to be able to promote a balanced CBD plant on the Kama Collective online menu. So 3 or 4 percent CBD would have been ideal, though 1 percent isn't low. I knew that Buffy Madison would be delighted to hear of such a plant: Her doctor suggests she seek out strains with a balanced cannabinoid profile for her raw shakes. I'm personally interested to follow her results. One investor I spoke with predicted a billion-dollar American cannabis food industry within a decade after legalization. "No one has to get high in the food sector, which broadens its appeal even further," he told me.

As for Tomas Balogh and his Kama Collective, there were eleven more strains to harvest and test from the 2011 crop. And CBD is just one of scores of cannabinoids, all with potentially distinct medicinal properties. Halent in 2011 tested for fifteen. Lucille might be loaded with some valuable but barely isolated compound. Tomas says it'll be helpful for Kama Collective to have these baseline test results and revisit them in five or ten years. Most significantly for the moment, the hearty (but by today's standards not overwhelmingly intense) THC content indicated that Lucille would likely have immediate benefit to patients.

"A new strain is a big mystery," Tomas said. "I hope people try her and she helps someone in a way that no other medicine has been able to. No matter what they're suffering from. I don't care if she reverses a bone disease or gives a chemo patient an extra meal a day."

And yet for all her potency, Lucille didn't come from a gene-altering Big Biotech or Big Pharma lab. She came from a Mendocino

County barn. It's still meticulous selective breeding, but much more Mendel than Monsanto.

Cashmere Kush, I was seeing with my own eyes, was much better described as "bred" than "engineered." Now I was going to spend a summer and fall getting to know one of this strain's progeny. Hopefully, if Tomas and his crop beat the elements and avoided the feds, I'd watch Lucille mature from a four-inch, locally legal clone cutting into a nine-foot flowering medicinal cannabis bush whose buds would presumably help upward of two dozen patients for a year.

Or not. Maybe she'd be a dud. Maybe patients would reject Lucille. Maybe she'd expire a few weeks after planting in a fatal case of powdery mildew. These were the major concerns of Tomas Balogh's life. For the industry at large in Mendocino County, though, everything hinged on the success of the local permitting program that cultivators believed made concerns like Tomas's perfectly legal ones to have.

# THIRTEEN

## The Zip-Tie Program Comes of Age, Musically, Before My Eyes

The Humboldt County Board of Supervisors will hear from Mendocino officials Tuesday regarding our southern neighbor's seemingly successful medical marijuana ordinance. Mendocino County 2nd District Supervisor John McCowen, Mendocino Sheriff Tom Allman and Mendocino County Counsel Jeanine Nadel will make a presentation [on the 9.31 Zip-Tie Program] to the board at 1:30 P.M.

—Eureka (CA) *Times-Standard*, September 5, 2011

O n April 27, 2011, in the Willits Community Center—a cavernous, mural-adorned, airplane hangar of a municipal project with poor acoustics—I was a fairly stunned witness to what might have been the first-ever rendition of "Happy Birthday" sung by a roomful of seventy open cannabis farmers to a sergeant in their county's Sheriff's Department.

When the sincere if cacophonous rendition finished and twenty-seven-year law-enforcement veteran Sergeant Randy Johnson ate a slice of the cake brought by the third-party cannabis farm inspector with whom he has one of those workplace marriage relationships (think *Moonlighting*), Johnson brushed the crumbs from his mustache and, in a passable Dennis Franz impersonation, tried to call the 9.31 informational meeting to order. I was witnessing post–Drug War harmony.

Each of the monthly sessions during the 2011 growing season was more standing-room-only than the last, reflecting a Zip-Tie Program that was exploding in popularity as word spread along the grower cannabis-vine. In 2011, the program more than quintupled in membership, from eighteen permitted growers to ninety-five.

Even the third-party inspector glowed on her website about creating three local jobs as her business expanded with the program's success.

It helped that come August of 2011 no 9.31-permitted growers had been busted. County-wide, a record 725,000 plants were seized by law enforcement. Nationwide, too, the most recent available figures (for 2010), show historic highs in cannabis arrests (853,838), and for the first time, cannabis arrests now accounted for more than half of total "drug" arrests nationwide, according to the FBI. New York City was also at the moment embroiled in a scandal surrounding police profiling of minorities for small cannabis arrests. This actually had as much to do with funding as racism: more arrests mean more presents from Santa Drug War.

The view of those living inside the Bubble[3] is "Talk about heading in the wrong direction. Talk about fighting a war to lose. Close to a million Americans still got popped in 2011 for this ancient plant we grow." And it's not hard to see why they feel this way. These might be the final battles, but if you're taken down you're taken down. That's the ultimate message of *All Quiet on the Western Front*: the protagonist is killed in action on a day when the winning side was already known and the official report declared "all quiet." War sometimes runs on autopilot.

Accordingly, one message to take from these arrest-and-seizure numbers is that the Drug War is not likely to fizzle out on its own. It needs help. Someplace that can show the rest of America what legal, permitted cannabis growing might look like. If only somewhere in the United States a community was demonstrating what would happen if citizens demanded and legislated the Drug War's end! If only cops and cannabis growers could somehow become allies not just to mutual benefit, but to the economic and public-safety benefit of the community!

Oh, right. Mendocino County, California, where I was now living. The fellow I had in mind might have been inhaling a slice of birthday cake when I had this thought, but it nonetheless happens sometimes in history that the perfect person ends up in the perfect job at the ideal time. I shudder to think what the world would look like if the 49ers hadn't hired Bill Walsh as coach in 1978, and Joe Montana hadn't been drafted. Paunchy, gruff-like-a-teddy-bear Sergeant Randy Johnson was, similarly, probably the ideal human being on the planet to manage the burgeoning 9.31 Zip-Tie Program for Tom Allman's Sheriff's Department.

Allman had one shot: He pretty much had to choose well in appointing an administrator for an experimental and internally controversial law enforcement directive. He did. Almost no one believes Sergeant Randy is secretly a federal mole. Also few confuse him with his considerably more gangly All-Star pitcher namesake, baseball's "Big Unit."

For one thing, prior to being assigned to the then-tiny 9.31 Program by Sheriff Tom in 2010, Sergeant Randy had already been through a decade of skin-thickening training working in Internal Affairs. "So," as he put it on my first inspection ride-along, "I've already been off the department Christmas party list for some time."

But it's much more than his previous title that makes Johnson a strong choice. It's more even than his solid organizational right brain (he makes lots of lists on his clipboard), indefatigable work ethic (he can't remember the last time he wasn't on overtime), and flexible, feedback-oriented style of management. That quality allowed, for example, an on-the-fly increase in preflowering, pre-zip-tied plant numbers to two hundred for permitted growers midseason in 2011, to make space for the composting of any worthless male plants. This is another way of saying that cannabis farmers in the 9.31 Program now have more time to get their plant numbers down to the maximum ninety-nine before their final inspection each season.

No, Sergeant Randy is the perfect guy for the Zip-Tie Program because the program, as he calls it, allowed him to personally flower. That is to say, even though he didn't crack a smile when a roomful of potential federal felons sang him "Happy Birthday," I got the sense, from looking in his eyes, that Randy Johnson is a man who has not often been popular before.

He seems to like it. Actually, he told me as much. In his remarks to the 9.31 informational audience following the cake break (meetings in cannabis territory are nearly always exceptionally well-catered), he said, albeit in a Chris Farley security guard's I-need-*you*-to-move-*this*-over-*here* tone, "Two years ago I knew *two* things about marijuana: If I *found* it on you, it went to the *evidence room* and you got cuffed and went to *jail*. Today I see you guys are just *more farmers* in our community. Just like the people I see selling *vegetables* every week at the *farmers' market*."

Again the fact that this is a county with an identity figures in. Whenever he delved into 9.31 standards and practices, Randy's 2011 speeches were littered with "We" this and "We" that. This use of the first person plural is crucial. It's another example of the "Mendo is about Mendo" phenomenon. Who knows if Randy himself plants an organic vegetable garden—I'm pretty sure not, and more than pretty sure he'd never use cannabis himself—though in what I call the Carl Sagan Rule, who can ever be positive? He told me, as part of an "I'm still a cop" conversation at a farm inspection, that he can "tell by looking in his eyes if someone's smoked a lot of pot in his life."

Hmm. President Obama himself confessed to "inhaling, frequently." And a 2011 Australian National University study concluded that any "adverse impacts of cannabis use on cognitive functions either appear to be related to pre-existing factors or are reversible . . . even after potentially extended periods of use."

Yet despite the fact that cannabis is not his medication of choice (he joked, "Too bad I'm on duty!" when George Fredericks asked him if he'd like something to drink when we'd arrived for the June 15, 2011, inspection), Randy encouraged 9.31 permittees who attended his meetings to utilize the rare gathering of rugged individualists to network like any professionals. And they did.

"It's amazing to watch," Sergeant Randy told me. "Getting these people together is like herding cats."

The crowds, by July, were topping one hundred at the monthly informational meetings and had an increasingly backwoodsy look and smell as folks of both genders and all ages from twenty-one to apparently ninety-five emerged from the hills to ask the tough questions about inspection costs and privacy protection: Are even 9.31 informational e-mails encrypted? Is the 9.31 permittee list kept secret from unfriendly deputies and feds?* Most of all, understandably, they wanted raid-protection guarantees. Well, that, and a sense of whether Randy would make them get their self-built barn up to code.

Sergeant Randy answered all these questions as best he could, considering that the issue in 2011 was evolving, on every level, across the nation, in courtrooms and in governors' mansions, by the week.

Even more significantly than the enforcement protections, Randy emphatically endorsed the outdoor-friendly cultivation guidelines that are built into 9.31. This in a time when, on the federal level, the EPA as an entity was a target of polluter industry employees known as Republican Congress members. Cannabis can't be called "Organic," since that's a trademarked federal term that requires USDA approval, but the Mendocino players in the industry were at work crafting sustainability standards on their own. I saw once again that the local thinking was that a "green" brand was a lucrative aspiration.

An example is section 9.31.040B, which tries to mitigate planet-unfriendly indoor grows† with the wording *The indoor cultivation of marijuana plants shall be limited to no more than one hundred (100)*

---

\* In Michigan, your taxpayer-salaried federal prosecutors, in September 2011, were trying to subpoena medical cannabis patient records from state health officials. That should really hit the cartels where it hurts.

† Utilizing (free) sunlight, as opposed to grow lights, is both much cheaper and crucial, from a "humans continuing to live on planet Earth" perspective. According to a 2011 research paper by Nobel Laureate Evan Mills, indoor cannabis production in California produces four million tons of greenhouse gases annually, the equivalent of a million automobiles. Since not every cannabis patient or farmer lives in gorgeous, spacious Mendocino or Humboldt counties, there are also emerging technologies such as Digital Age LEDs which aim to make indoor growing, well, greener. Watch for this debate to unfold in a big way in coming years, especially vis-à-vis clean water regulations.

*contiguous square feet per legal parcel.*" The ordinance also addresses light use and water sourcing, and mandates conforming with under-negotiation sustainability standards.

The way Sergeant Randy saw it, he was simply reflecting Mendo values. And almost without fail, Randy likes the citizens he inspects. This is a fellow who's seen plenty of criminals in his day.

There's a reason that sustainable cultivation standards are as integral to 9.31 as cannabis itself. In a 2004 county-wide popular referendum, three quarters of a million biotech dollars couldn't buy a Genetically Modified Organism (GMO) election here.

"It wasn't even close," campaign co-coordinator Laura Hamburg told me on her Ukiah deck, of the "GMO-Free Mendocino" effort, surrounded by clippings about the Measure H ballot initiative. When it passed, it made Mendocino County the nation's first to explicitly ban the cultivation of genetically modified crops.

"Monsanto and Syngenta's front organizations outspent us seven to one and we got 57 percent of the vote," Hamburg said of Big Ag's effort to stifle Measure H. Instead of the genetically modified monoculture taking over much of the world's farmland, in Mendocino County, an eradication raid of a Roundup Ready (GMO) cornfield has been carried out. And in 2012, there's a state-wide California ballot initiative pending on GMO labeling. Talk about not being in Kansas or even New Mexico anymore. Mendo strikes first again. In the Measure H vote, Mendocino County voters were able to unite on two of their biggest issues: 1) sustainability and 2) not letting outsiders tell us what to do.

Such is the sustainability climate in which 9.31 operated by 2011. Which is not to say that the program was uniformly popular in the community. Especially the law enforcement community. In fact it is no accident that Randy unfailingly inveighed his 9.31 audiences and the farmers he inspected to be sure to cross every behavioral and bureaucratic T the ordinance called for, because "we're all in this together: Let's make this work. There are people who don't want it to. One diversion to black market, one sanitation slipup, could ruin it for everybody."

This is such a Randy refrain that I had it memorized by July. Always with "we" this and "us" that. I got to hear it and others of his favorite topics on my first inspection ride-along with him, to George Fredericks's farm, on June 15. On the forty-minute ride itself—everything in Mendocino County is about forty minutes from everything else: roughly twenty on the highway, twenty in the hills—Randy, grittily and with seeming genuine anger, trash-talked a questionable left-turner at a changing light—"should we git 'im?"—and then planned dinner with his real wife via handheld Blackberry (contravening a current CHP distracted-driving billboard campaign) as we wound through the hills in his soon-to-be-upgraded, official-issue gray Taurus. The most memorable moment of the actual inspection for me was when I heard him preach what I would learn is his core mantra.

"The first word in this program is *medical*," he lectured George when he found an empty juice bottle in the barn Fredericks was planning to use, months later, for drying, curing, and processing. "Think white coats. Think gloves. If our opponents can come in and find one little thing wrong with any farm, one stray mouse dropping, we're all screwed."

Among "the people who don't want" 9.31 to succeed, Sheriff Allman estimates, may only be 5 percent of the county's electorate, but is upward of 90 percent of his own department (Sergeant Randy confirms this estimate). What this means, I realize now, is that, statistically, those deputies who twice had to babysit Matt Cohen's cannabis plants in the summer of '10 might not have in fact left the farm and its eight-foot-tall plants with a sense of a "job well done." They were more likely raised and trained to think of the place as harboring "dangerous narcotics," with Cohen playing the role of potentially violent criminal. Let me tell you, the only dangerous thing on Cohen's farm was its mud and its goat horns. Even his employees' dogs would lick you to death.

Needless to say, the Matt Cohens of Mendocino County have handily elected Sheriff Allman, who was not the department rank-and-file choice for the post, twice.

Yes, Sheriff Tom's job is safe. His own hero, he told me by pointing out a framed portrait in his office lobby, is nineteenth-century Mendo Sheriff Doc Stanley, who chased some cattle rustlers for hundreds of miles, caught them, and then strung them up, before returning home to find most of his department had been laid off due to, you guessed it, budget cuts. You see why Tom relates.

Also not enthusiastic endorsers of the fledgling 9.31 Program, at least at first, were Allman's enemies on the County Board of Supervisors. As recently as April 2011, the overall body was skeptical, to say the least, about the program's capacity for raising the half-million dollars Allman predicted it would during the 2011 season. Supervisor Kendall Smith publicly deemed Allman's claim a desperate "funny money" pitch unreasonably, if understandably, aimed at protecting his staff from the budget ax every other county department was dealing with at the time (and still is).

Other opponents of the Zip-Tie Program I met included a Mendo store owner, who himself uses the plant. He griped to me, "I don't want this to be the economy that my kids grow up in, and take part in." The Ganjapreneur response to that argument I heard from Fredericks, Cohen, Balogh, et al is "Does everyone who lives in Napa County take part in the alcohol business? Does everyone in Southern California work in the nuclear weapons production business? No. Do everyone's kids in such places benefit from the tax base of an economy, in the case of Napa wine, worth eleven billion dollars annually? Yes. Cannabis growers haven't until now even been given the opportunity to pay taxes."

In a capitalist society, the Green Rush players maintain, it's hard to argue against the last safe cross-aisle reelection platform for any politician: building an economic base and luring jobs.

I should also mention criticism of the program I heard from the left. "The Zip-Tie permitting fees are essentially protection money," Jim Hill argues. "It's a civil ordinance purporting to protect you from criminal penalties." This is true, but 9.31 Program supporters like Tomas Balogh make this argument: "Politics is the art of compromise. We have a cannabis-friendly sheriff and district attorney willing to make our crop legitimate again. Most law enforcement administrators are so addicted to the Drug War that they'd rather die than acknowledge the plant has any value at all and can thus be cultivated by law-abiding citizens. You can work out the kinks as you go. One step at a time."

Furthermore, Mendocino County isn't creating a police state with 9.31 fees. Sheriff Tom points out that "the county has the same number of deputies now that it did in 1972."

And of course, once again, in listing 9.31's early presumed opponents, we're as usual leaving out the pesky feds, who were part of an interagency team coming to town in force in midsummer 2011, at Sheriff Tom's invitation, to clean out the Mendocino National Forest of illicit and often polluting public land grows. This "Operation Full Court Press" was fairly popular within Mendocino County, as it aimed to root out foreigners (or at least outsiders) growing on American soil using stream diversion and other unsustainable techniques. Two U.S. attorneys and a congressman were even expected to be on hand for the operation's wrap-up press conference.

No one, including Sheriff Allman, knew how the presence of federal law enforcers and legislators would affect the 9.31 Program, but Allman likes to take some kind of action every season to show that he's not, in his own words, "the Cheech and Chong sheriff." Supervisor McCowen whispered to me that it might be wise for me "not to talk about 9.31 too much" while Full Court Press was under way.

In fact, everyone was a little tense after the plants were in the ground in late spring 2011, because the U.S. Justice Department had apparently reversed its hands-off policy that began with a "we won't devote federal funds to messing with people abiding by state programs" memo a year after Barack Obama took office—this the famous October 2009 Ogden Memo.* In fact, after one particularly

---

* This is widely regarded as the Memo That Started the Green Rush: a 2009, since-contradicted note written by one (now ex-) Deputy Attorney General David Ogden that said federal resources should not be focused on "individuals

threatening letter sent by federal prosecutors to medicinal cannabis state governors in May 2011, Sheriff Tom jokingly (I think)
sent me this e-mail:

From:      sheriff@mendocino.com
Subject:   Follow-up
Date:      June 3, 2011 8:28:00 AM MDT
To:        fine@well.com

On Jun 3, 2011, at 8:28 AM,
Sheriff Allman wrote:

Doug-
    Thanks for the article. I have printed a copy for Randy Johnson.
When I get arrested, can I call you for bail?

Best Regards
—Tom—

Thus even law enforcers in Mendocino were part of the mass
(and risky) federal civil disobedience at play in California, Colorado, Montana, and the other medical cannabis states prior to
nationwide legalization. This determined flaunting of the Controlled Substances Act should be given a huge amount of the credit
when the taxpaying cannabis economy is finally allowed to take
off. Heck, I considered it an act of civil disobedience every time a
patient paid for her "Mendo Purps" strain delivery by credit card
on Matt Cohen's Northstone Organics website.

The best the Mendocino brain trust behind 9.31 could do was
to keep plant numbers at ninety-nine. As discussed, that is not an
accidentally chosen number. One hundred plants is the number at
which a federal sentencing minimum for conspiracy-to-distribute

---

whose actions are in clear and unambiguous compliance with existing state laws
providing for the medical use of marijuana."

kicks in. The coalition of supervisors and community members who drafted Ordinance 9.31 hoped that federal prosecutors would feel "respected" by the ninety-nine-plant limit.* This is a distinctly different approach than that of the Oakland, California, city planners who floated—then, terrified at federal threats to their personal freedom, withdrew—plans for indoor warehouses containing tens of thousands of municipally contracted plants.

By stark contrast, no one was backing down in Mendocino County. The people who *do* want 9.31 to succeed are ardent in their support. The woman who brought the birthday cake to that April 9.31 farmer meeting, third-party inspector Julia Carrera, for example, took a motherly attitude to the growers she inspected. She was active in seeking feedback for evolving sustainability standards for the program, and was by far the most media-suspicious person I met in the county. She later explained that this was because of a sense of protectiveness about the program. "I don't want exploitive coverage," she said of her unwillingness to return e-mails and phone calls, as national media began to descend on the county, salivating at the easy "legal pot" soundbite distillation.

Meanwhile, if the aboveground Mendocino cannabis community was comparatively stressed in the weeks before the Operation Full Court Press circus came to town, participant—and potential participant—paranoia about the Zip-Tie Program itself seemed to diminish by the day. Seemingly with good reason.

Sheriff Tom has a policy that any county law enforcer planning to "write paper" (draft and execute a search warrant) on a cannabis farm must first check with Randy, to see if the grower is in fact permitted by the program. Randy announced at a July 9.31 meeting that he'd already prevented three such raids in 2011, plus he'd fielded one inquiring call from a federal official with the Bureau of Land Management.

It should come as no surprise that, in a county rarely absent

---

* It was a big but reasonable assumption: A leaked internal Justice Department memo in 2011 suggested prosecutors ignore farms that grew fewer than a thousand plants.

the ominous *thwumpa thwumpa thwumpa* of helicopters overhead, this announcement was met with deafening applause in the Willits Community Center. For the 9.31 Program to work, a critical mass of Mendocino County cannabis farmers had to continue to trust Sergeant Randy Johnson and his boss. If Randy was actually some kind of a federal narc in local good cop's clothing, he sure was taking a long time to reveal himself. After having probably a dozen conversations and meetings with him, I'm pretty sure he isn't. Either that or the Academy would do well to institute a new Oscar category for "Best Supporting Narc Performance: Lifetime Deception Award."

# FOURTEEN

## The Mostly Volunteer Kama Karma Work Crew Arrives

Sustainably grown under the California sun.

—Tomas Balogh's Kama Collective motto

MendoGrown is a non-profit, member-based association of medical cannabis cultivators, business owners, and patients. Together, we promote California's locally farmed, sustainably grown medical cannabis, and advocate for a cannabis industry that benefits the community, the environment, and the California economy.

—MendoGrown sustainable cannabis trade organization website, 2011 (http://mendogrown.org/)

**B**ack on the farm, if Tomas Balogh thought that with plants in hand—or at least in U-Haul—and a place to plant them come dawn of summer, his problems were solved, he was disabused of that fantasy within a few weeks.

But what a few weeks they were. No sooner had he moved into the Eagle's Nest than he began what he considered his health-and-karma restoration effort at the property. Immediately—and this continued throughout the 2011 growing season—I watched Tomas and a parade of friends, some college buddies from the Bay Area or even older companions from his Sonoma County hometown of Rincon Valley, operate in a mode that from above probably looked more like an ant colony than any other type of organization.

I don't know where they all came from, or how he alerted them to a particular need, but they kept streaming in by ones and twos—right from the day he carted the girls home from Leif's greenhouse. Most of the volunteers had never worked in the cannabis industry before, and yet at the Eagle's Nest I always felt like I was entering a scene where everyone knew the task at hand. It made my own job seem so easy: just ask whatever questions came into my head while marveling how fast plants grow under the Mendocino sun.

Tomas had clearly built up a lot of good karma of his own in his pre-Mendo life, as these materializing friends seemed to come up to help him for nothing more than the clean air and evening potluck barbecues—a prototype for cannabis tourism, Tomas suggests. There was almost always someone there when I bumped up to the Eagle's Nest, presumably with medical-cannabis doctor's recommendation in hand, since that's a requirement of all even casual plant tenders in the 9.31 Program.

All eighty-eight plants were in fifteen-gallon pots within seventy-two hours of their arrival, which was also the fortieth anniversary of the modern War on Drugs as declared by Richard Nixon on June 17, 1971. A high school friend of Tomas's named Adam, fresh from the navy, was weed-whacking the edge of the newly cleared meadow near the Eagle's Nest fig trees when I arrived for my third visit. I couldn't believe it was the same place I had seen a few days earlier.

"Man," I said with an impressed whistle, "did you call the Park Service first? After fifty years even garbage becomes an artifact. I think you went down further than that."

Gone was the dump of a property, the grounds now visibly absent plastic water piping tangles, glass shards, and target-practice appliances. In their place was one of the more picturesque farms I'd ever visited. Tomas, assuming a successful debut season, was now certain he wanted to buy the place and run the Kama Collective from it.

The work, though, was just beginning and soon switched from reclamation and landscaping to farming proper. Muscles that were atrophied from indoor farming—or indoor careers in general—quickly became sore, audibly so even in the act of opening an evening beer bottle. A fellow Cal Bear friend-of-Tomas named Stella came into the picture in late June. She managed a high-end Italian restaurant in Oakland and discovered that she could double as a priceless, if amateur, massage therapist specializing in cannabis-farming-related musculoskeletal stress.

Thirty-one-year-old Stella was the Queen Ant of the operation. She made sure the Eagle's Nest had furniture, art, house plants, and a wet bar, which she tended. I'm not much of a drinker, but Stella continally provided top-notch media relations by pressing some frothy iced concoction into my hand after a tough day of cannabis research. I never imagined there were so many uses for Campari.

But she was much more than the Eagle's Nest hostess and a one-time judge at the *High Times* Cannabis Cup. In fact, the first person I saw in the unfenced planting area on one June visit was an—if you're talking about strict percentage of body covered—undressed Stella. Unless you count being covered in manure dust. She was proving nearly as strong as Adam in the fields.

In the same way that the universe is mostly empty space, Stella that day wore the kind of cutoffs/bikini top combo that only a Californian could possibly consider indicative of a nonsexual situation. Which is to say that Stella henceforth held few anatomical secrets from me or any observer. Like so many Californian women under the age of ninety, she not only hardly seemed to notice, she evidently expected everyone else not to as well. Alongside Adam, this Vitamin D-absorber was shoveling compost into wheelbarrows, which they dumped atop cannabis seedlings.

If beer commercials tend to feature women dressed like Stella playing beach volleyball and waterskiing, the cannabis commercials of the near future will have them shoveling organic fertilizer onto plants. I envision a female announcer pitching, "You're part of the Kama Kush Generation—get out there and work, so you can get out there and play. Now there's Kama Kush Light too. Always transfat- and GMO-free. Always medicate responsibly."

There were two plots at the Eagle's Nest: The dearth of level ground mandated this. Even though he considers himself a farmer, like most cannabis cultivators Tomas referred to each plot as a garden. When I asked him why, he said, "Because you can grow ninety-nine plants on a half-acre, if necessary."

"Wanna spray some neem?" was what Stella actually asked me by way of greeting at the upper garden that June day, holding up a flowerpot-size plastic atomizer for the organic, tree-derived anti-aphid application. "That way we don't have to stop transplanting."

Tomas and a friend named Jared were hand-watering plants nearby. They were doing this with a hose connected to a new, zaftig three-thousand-gallon water tank that collected the gravity-fed springwater to which Tomas had successfully negotiated rights from his neighbor Chase. Imagine if he had been five more minutes late for that meeting!

Jared had never been around a cannabis plant before meeting Tomas in 2008, but after some distillation and infusion courses at the nearby California School of Herbal Studies, he looked like a strong candidate for edible cannabis specialist for the nascent Kama Collective—this a vital product line for cancer and AIDS patients.

I heard Tomas directing, "Keep giving her water until the entire soil base is saturated and you start to see water standing on top."

Tomas left Jared to the watering and, having unloaded the rest of the U-Haul in the days since we bumped here from Leif's, pointed Lucille out to me from the multitude. This while I unsuccessfully tried to follow instructions to apply an even layer of neem to the underside of a few nearby plants. If it had been my farm, the plants wouldn't have lasted a month.

"I'm gonna give her a great final spot in the sun when she's in her big pot," he said with a "wink wink" jab to my ribs. "Give her every advantage." I think he was referring to the fact that two of the three plantings I had cut had not survived. The final transplanting was still several weeks away.

"But look," he said, pointing to a slight yellowing in one of Lucille's middle leaves. "I think she's already a little nitrogen starved." I was coming to learn that Tomas was always most at ease when he could talk botany.

"Can you fix it?" I asked, upset. For him, it was just ten or twenty thousand dollars bundled up in that plant. For me another mortality would mandate some serious self-examination regarding my own horticultural skills.

"I think I can," Tomas said uncertainly. "But everything's up in the air. I'm new to outdoor farming."

Examples, I was discovering, of cannabis botanical details that matter a lot include 1) the angle at which a superfluous non-budding branch is snipped, 2) when it's snipped, and 3) what its superfluousness says about the overall health of the plant. These are plants that have one purpose: make lots of flowers.

One thing I can say for sure: I finished that summer thinking about my tomato and lettuce crops on much deeper levels. Mendocino County was like a graduate organic farming seminar. On park strolls in 2011, my family heard me studiously saying things like, "These blackberries have a few more days ripening in them if this weather holds."

At this early season lecture, I asked Tomas, "Is there a formula for how much—what would you call it?—nutrition they need at every stage of the season?"

Tomas, in an Obama '08 T-shirt, picked up the atomizer and laughed. "Is there a formula for how much hay and grain all of your goats need?"

"Of course not," I said, still a little animal-kingdom-centric. "They're individuals."

"Exactly. Same with the plants on this farm.* Their needs are

---

* Same, too, with Mendocino County farmers. I've seen so many distinct versions of breeding, planting, fertilizing, watering, and harvesting by now that I could probably write a book entitled *Traditional Cannabis Cultivation Techniques of Mendocino County Redneck Hippies*. Often when I mentioned another farmer's method of, say, transferring plants into the direct sun, or aphid control, the second farmer would not be familiar with the technique. I thus sometimes felt like a bee, pollinating ideas between farms separated by two parts remoteness

as individual as any human child's. Even two plants of the same strain planted right next to each other might need a much different diet. Indoors, you have to check them several times a day, every day. One could be sick from lack of bat guano, and her sister next to her doesn't even get a sniffle. I might even have to back off that one so as not to burn the leaves. This girl," he said, expertly snapping a dead stem from Lucille's underbelly, "is just really thirsty for nitrogen right now. You don't want to see that yellow in the leaves. She should be more perky. Gonna triple down on the fish emulsion."

At that moment Stella reappeared to consult with Tomas to make sure a plant of the Casey Jones sativa dominant strain wasn't about to be planted too deeply. Wiping sweat from her brow with her forearm, she also announced that there was a chip-and-dip break waiting up at the house whenever Tomas wanted to call a break. I shot Tomas a "how could she be two places at once?" glance. The woman, I was discovering, was tireless. She was Radar, Jeeves, Friday, and Moneypenny all in one. Tomas's look said he'd known this since the Clinton administration.

"Whatever you're paying her, double it," I suggested.

My favorite Stella story, from roughly midseason: Finding the Eagle's Nest's newly erected garden gates locked after a three-hour drive from the Bay Area that started at six thirty A.M., she repeatedly scaled two fences and watered all eighty-eight plants, as promised, which took more than two hours. Tomas was at a funeral and had been off by a digit when passing on the lock combos.

Her explanation: "Hey, the girls were thirsty." She ascribed her work ethic to a high-achieving Korean-American upbringing, then added, "But it *was* a hundred and two out by the end. It was touch-and-go for a while. By the end of the day I had my watering system down. Then I napped, and after the sun set I had a lovely quiet evening reading. Big change from closing a restaurant on a

---

(in fact two mountain ranges), one part federal paranoia, and nine parts busy farmers' lives.

Saturday night. It was like therapy for me. Next time I'm going to make sure Tomas gives me the right gate combinations, though. Either that or he's going to have to start paying me."

"Welcome to the Digital Age entrepreneurial life" was the message I got when I heard that tale of beyond-the-call dedication based as much on friendship and activism as remuneration—at least until the venture is off the ground. "Welcome to Redneck Hippie Capitalism."

# FIFTEEN

## A Farmer Is a Farmer Is a Farmer

Last night the wind and rain together blew,
    The wall-curtains rustled in their autumn song.
The candle died, the water-clock was exhausted,
    I rose and sat, but could not be at peace.
Man's affairs are like the flow of floodwater,
    A life is just like floating in a dream.
I should more often go drunken through the country,
    For otherwise I could not bear to live.

—Li Yu, Chinese emperor, "Last Night the Wind and Rain
Together Blew," circa 970 C.E.

**B**efore delving into horticultural nuance, I want to make sure I adequately stress the importance of Tomas's cleanup of his farm. He quickly and undeniably achieved his goal of turning around the Eagle's Nest vibe. There are more than a few farmers out there—and not just your more obsessed devotees of the bio-dynamic method—who believe that this is as important to a successful harvest of any crop as sunlight, soil, and strong plant genetics. When he spoke of the Eagle's Nest, Tomas now did so with pride.

But when it comes to starting a business, even a not-for-profit one, Tomas made the inevitable discovery that it's Dreamer Beware. Not that a crystal ball would ever deter a true dreamer. That's why study after study is concluding that the best entrepreneurial skill set, which Tomas possessed in spades, is not a good head for numbers or even a willingness to cook the books, but blind optimisn.

Acccordingly, if you've ever tried to live your dream, you'll probably recognize why, after 2011 season setbacks #42 and #43 (losing a couple of young plant limbs to an unexpected windstorm and being turned down by the sixth bank* with which he proposed storing any eventual liquidity after informing the manager of his agribusiness niche), Tomas barely permitted a hint of negative thought to breach his affirmative armor.

"Remember when I told you at Matt's that we'd deliver Lucille to a patient or die trying?" he asked me over sushi in early July. I remembered. "Well, just so you're aware that die trying is on the table. I don't want Kama to be a cash operation. I want patients to be able to use checks and credit cards." Tomas shrugged and popped a piece of rainbow roll. Nowhere to go but forward.

Even beyond the routine rigors of small business management, what watching Tomas's first season travails taught me more than anything is that the first thing to remember about outdoor cannabis farmers is that they're farmers. That's probably the second and third thing to remember about most of them too.

The best ones, the ones who are going to survive recent federal posturing and price doldrums resulting from oversupply. They're not, for example, necessarily skilled real estate speculators or financial planners. Their calendar has to do with frontal cycles, phosphorus ratios, and chlorophyll. Not interest rates and escrow. Not over-the-counter public offerings.

Even the "natural cycles" part of farming was new to Tomas. During his previous ten years as an indoor farmer, he had always played the role, if not of God, then at least of the sun. If outdoor farming in general isn't always the Zen blood-pressure reducer the popular press assures us it is (these authors obviously don't have goats), indoor cultivation is obsession.

Tomas's way of phrasing his indoor mind-set was "I found my

---

* "There are good people in the industry, and smart people. Those are the kinds of customers banks want to have, and they will be the first ones banks go back to when the legal issues are resolved," John Whitten, senior vice president of Colorado Springs State Bank, said in the August 24, 2011, *Boulder Daily Camera*, after his bank announced it, the last one in Colorado to do business with the medical cannabis industry, would close all connected accounts. "I would hope that if it became legal on the federal level it would be like any other business and we would go back to them."

undiagnosed OCD was a useful trait." If he discovered one aphid on a plant, he would cancel camping trips to alter the atmosphere in his Berkeley grow room and fix the problem. He thought by the hour. Less humidity for a bit. Check the $CO_2$. Apply a little pesticide. Now he needed to think by the season. And nix the synthetic pesticides.

With plants in pots and ready for full outdoor living, Tomas discovered that he faced a learning curve steeper than you might expect for someone migrating from cannabis farming to . . . another kind of cannabis farming. Outdoor cannabis cultivation is a whole different botanical process. One best described as "The earth and a half-billion years of photosynthetic pigment evolution know what to do better than you do."

Though it would require less of Tomas's OCD, at least in terms of daily micromanagement, he would soon, he hoped, be dealing with ten-foot (or taller) trees, instead of three-foot plants: He had to leave more space *between* three plants than formerly contained his entire garden.

Before his first 9.31 inspection, which was scheduled for July Fourth (Sergeant Randy didn't take many days off), it dawned on Tomas that, like every farmer since the questionable human decision to stop hunting and gathering,* he was at the mercy of nature. "Can you believe that?" he asked me. "In the twenty-first century." Indeed, in an era when an application of Roundup is a hardware store visit away. The wake-up call was the fierce windstorm that damaged a couple of limbs on a plant in the Kama Collective's upper garden.

Once cannabis plants graduate fully outdoors from their preschool nurseries, incubators, and greenhouses in May or June—this,

---

* There's an anthropological line of thought that the cannabis plant, in being nutritional and spiritual and providing fiber good for yurt building, might have been a major cause of this development. Which could have been fine. It certainly would help explain why people get so passionate about the dang plant, the world over (I saw a headline about some recent "Indian hemp" arrests in Ghana, in September 2011). Unfortunately, once humans stayed put, government, lawyers, and Sean Hannity soon followed.

of course, varies not just by state but by microclimate—Leif told me, "you want sun, sun, and more sun." In fact, when the nutritive rains have (hopefully) ended each spring, you want sun for five months until the shorter days trigger hormonal "time to lure some pollen" thoughts in the female plants' fancy and cause their calyxes (flower clusters) to begin to form. You want sun, essentially, until harvest time in October and November.

Twelve hours of sunlight or more keeps the plants "vegetative." Fewer than twelve hours, the females start to worry about winter, and their biological clocks tick. To lure male DNA, they produce psychoactive resin. That resin is why we have a Drug War. Or at least a cannabis war. It lures us.

That's also why indoor growing is so much more intensive than outdoor: In a grow room, you're creating an environment stripped of nearly all characteristics of natural botany except the absolute necessary ones. Outdoors, you face that unreliable, uncontrollable, and helicopter-exposed duo of astronomy and meteorology. Indoor growers don't have to invent rain dances. They just turn a spigot.

Outdoor farmers have to be patient, or pray a lot, or both. What they get in return is much, much hardier plants. And, MendoGrown's members would say, much healthier medicine. All I can say to that is, as an organic rancher and consumer, if I went into my food co-op in New Mexico and learned that I had a choice between broccoli grown under the sun locally or broccoli grown under a diesel-powered grow light in a warehouse, um, well, do I need to even finish this sentence? It's the same with eggs from free versus captive chickens. I can taste it every morning in my ranch eggs: There's nothing like them in a supermarket.

The thing is, it's not just me. There wouldn't be artificially lit broccoli grown in my food co-op because no one would buy it. Once America's hundred million Friends of Cannabis become legal members of society, large numbers of them are going to demand the same growing standards in their cannabis as they would in their tomatoes or their corn.

Yes, you can stop reading between the lines: I'm saying people who shop at food co-ops and who only eat organic food are more likely to be Friends of Sustainably Grown Cannabis than those who gobble high-fructose corn syrup and drink Coors Light.

And this is why, from a business perspective, Tomas Balogh, Matt Cohen, George Fredericks, and the rest of the Mendocino 9.31 growers believe they are onto a good thing. A niche with a bright future.

As an experiment, I looked at 2010 season bud samples of similar Super Silver Haze strains from a Mendo crop and an indoor crop. If the robust dark green of the outdoor-grown medicine represented, say, Shakespeare, the grow-room bud, sporting a much lighter, almost sickly green tint with a far less dense bouquet, would be Grisham. Or, in food terms: organic-farmers'-market verses supermarket broccoli. And that's just the visual sense. When it comes to the presence of pesticides, the differences only increase.

Whether grown indoors or outdoors, that female cannabis plant facing sunlight deprivation really wants to reproduce. I've heard it said that a light-deprived cannabis plant surpasses the banana slug as the world's horniest creature. To really glue on that pollen, to make sure the male chromosomes hit the mark, the lady cannabis plant produces, in crystalline trichomes, the sticky, psychoactive substance that all the fuss is about. That has cost you and me a trillion bucks since 1971. That allowed Woodstock to happen, though the sticky crystals in question only needed 1 percent potency to keep the hippies so very impervious to the fact that they were dancing in cold mud. Today, cannabis with 17 percent THC is not uncommon. No wonder it's considered effective for chemo pain and arthritis.

But, oh, the risks of outdoor farming. If an unseasonal Pacific storm moves through in late July after the plants have been moved outdoors, a million dollars of crop can be destroyed in a blink. At Jim Hill's farm, I saw two-inch-thick green stalks that had snapped in overnight windstorms. So, no, despite the seventies slang, cannabis doesn't grow like a weed. Not at professional quality.

Outdoor cannabis farming is not just constant work, with as few days off as the goat herding with which I am all too familiar, it's hard work, some of the hardest I've ever seen, and I've known Republican press spokespeople. Before his first Sergeant Randy inspection, George Fredericks had been up all night planting. And I myself busted a gut—just a minor hernia, nothing to worry about—merely acceding to an offhanded request from another, Sharif Moye, that I give him a hand moving a hale Afwreck strain plant in a fifteen-gallon pot ten feet in June 2011.

And outdoor plants become, by any standards, gargantuan. Forget everything you've ever imagined about a cannabis plant, indeed about the boundaries of the words *plant* or *herb* in general, and start thinking *Little Shop of Horrors*. Think forest. Outdoor-grown California cannabis plants are the redwoods of the herbal kingdom.

The most robust individuals I've seen growing under the Mendocino County sun shocked me. They still shock me when I look at the pictures taken in September 2011. They look like special effects. Like a Cheech and Chong Nice Dream. Members of a home-developed sativa strain of Jim Hill's called Scarecrow, they were fourteen feet tall, as tall as adjacent mature apple trees, with nearly the same diameter trunk, and both required the same full-size ladder for harvesting. And the really funny thing is that Moye, the grower responsible—along with his boss Hill—for these Amazonian specimens, was apologizing for the trees' not having "fully filled out this season." This guy set the bar high. "Got to," he explained. "There's a lotta competition out there." Remember when Americans spoke like that?

Depending on the strain, a healthy outdoor cannabis plant will usually provide between one and ten pounds of medicine. Rock-bottom wholesale prices are $2,000 per pound ($3,000 is closer to reality for top-shelf cannabis), so Tomas, depending on his first season luck, stood to provide his Kama Collective with $880,000 gross, if he harvested an average of three pounds per tree, and patients utilized his entire inventory. The latter was not a big assumption, given demand for the best outdoor-grown Mendocino cannabis flowers.

By way of comparison, when I was in college in the infamous Campaign Against Marijuana Planting (CAMP) days of the 1990s, Rock told me, black market Emerald Triangle cannabis cost north of $6,000 per pound.

"Helicopters were everywhere, all the time," he said. "Supplies were down. Business was good."

Even though he spent easily hundreds of hours, often at night, doing research online, and was continually consulting with more experienced farmers at MendoGrown board meetings and on cannabis blogs, the indoor-to-outdoor transition wasn't at first a totally smooth one for Tomas. When I met him, Tomas was so green about rural life in general, let alone outdoor farming, that his very posture was glaring to locals. I recognized from my own life what you might call the suburban transitional embarrassments that Tomas was heaping upon himself as a Mendocino County immigrant.

First, there were those open-toed sandals I've brought up a few times, and which were noticed by any landowner when he toured prospective farm rentals in the spring. These made me cringe, for coyote-scat and barbed-wire reasons alone.

Even more conspicuous to this rural neo–Rugged Individualist was Tomas's Audi. Even though I had to admit it provided a better harvest time shield than my own conveyance from unfriendly law enforcement along the famously treacherous Highway 101 distribution corridor, the poor machine, intended for the Autobahn, endured more bottoming-out damage in the first weeks I knew Tomas than it had in its previous three years carrying him around his Bay Area haunts. It was largely a question of clearance and shocks. If Tomas wanted to become a Mendonesian, he needed to ditch the metrosexual ride.

In short, Mendo knew it was dealing with a product of the 'burbs. And Tomas did too. He found a more locally low-key used white Toyota truck by midseason. He also, I was delighted to see, got himself a pair of leather work boots.

These, of course, were just surface appearances, if telling ones. More vitally, Tomas the indoor specialist at first was smothering his plants with overprotectiveness. For example, within hours of the first (and fairly) typical June windstorm that had noncritically damaged those one or two limbs, half his plants suddenly had more bamboo supports than Thailand.* This was by all accounts an excessive response, somewhat akin to putting a champion skier with a strained wrist in a prophylactic body cast and then sending her down the racecourse.

"This is how you do it indoors," he told me later. "Your whole crop can go south in a day for so many reasons, since the ecosystem is so artificial and your grow cycle is maybe ninety days, instead of a hundred and eighty."

It was easy to imagine some Balogh in tribal Hungary two thousand years ago obsessively tending the village cannabis plants. It was obviously in his blood. But he'd taken it a bit too far for the comfort of the outdoor crop. He was suffocating. To his credit, he wound up shrewdly "scaling back the OCD." He knew enough about the biology of the cannabis plant to adjust his technique. Which is to say, if he was entering the Big League in his debut outdoor season, his indoor experience, in many ways, was a valuable time in the minors.

The proof was in the terpenes. Within a few weeks, my every visit to the Eagle's Nest had me uttering that "my, how they've grown!" exclamation. Tomas did make the transition. He worried less. He watched for a few days before he acted.

And he still had plenty to do every day in the fields, which he habitually patrolled dressed in a Warriors or Giants jersey under the tracksuit of an Eastern Bloc gangster. Though what he had to

---

* Where, by the way, his most popular indoor strain, Super Silver Haze, developed, from the Thai stick of the 1970s. Tomas's collective was growing a dozen Super Silver Haze plants in its inaugural outdoor season.

do now was invariably subtler than the cultivation he was used to: preparing a soil-enriching compost tea, or slightly increasing one plant's water.

"Wow, the sun really does do a lot of the work," he observed early in the season, in the tone of the grudging witness to a mystical experience, of plants that were growing upward of a foot per week.

Still, it would be an omission not to observe that Tomas coddled, fed, changed (transplanted, twice), and even serenaded (usually via Pandora) those eighty-eight plants unceasingly for nearly eight months, like an expectant parent. These were in fact some of the most well-supervised organisms I'd ever seen. Like so many Redneck Hippies before him, he got downright biodynamic on their asses. Another way of saying this is that Tomas, like most farmers worldwide since the dawn of commodity agriculture, was not inclined to leave a million dollars of crop, any crop, unattended for too long.

Let us not forget that the plant under discussion is America's Number One Cash Crop. By Far. ABC News says its $35.8 billion annual revenue already exceeds the combined value of corn ($23.3 billion) and wheat ($7.5 billion). That's now. Imagine if every delivery didn't inspire a potential ten-year prison sentence.

The upshot of this economic reality is you get some supremely dedicated farmers. They say the best thing you can do as a parent is spend time with your kids. Be there for them. If Tomas ever has a human daughter, I don't foresee any serious teenage problems. Only one plant died at the Eagle's Nest during the 2011 season—a Grand Daddy Purple strain, right in between two of her healthy sisters. But Lucille kept growing.

# SIXTEEN
## Emergence of a Sustainable Outdoor Cannabis Cultivator

Find yourself here.

—Slogan of California State ad campaign, 2011

Organic Dark Chocolate (Cocoa butter, sugar, vanilla, soy leci-
thin), Organic Powdered Sugar, Organic Shredded Coconut,
Organic Coconut Milk, Organic Cannabis Coconut Oil, Earth
Balance (palm oil, canola oil, olive oil, soy lecithin, soy protein,
non-dairy lactic acid, beta carotene), Organic Whole Roasted
Almond, Organic Coconut Extract, Organic Vanilla Extract,
Hash.

—Ingredients listing, Simply Pure Coconut Almond Cups, Denver,
Colorado (http://simplypure.com/edibles/coconut-almond-cups)

**M**onths later, during the hours of conversation around the
flower-trimming table, Tomas gave a lot of the credit for his
ability to transition to outdoor cultivation to his own evolution
into a sustainable consumer. In fact, trimming-clippers in latex
begloved hand, he said, "I don't think one could have happened
without the other."

My first long conversation with Tomas on the subject of sustainability occurred during a triple-digit, early-season reposition-
ing of more than half of the eighty-eight "girls" at the Eagles' Nest.
Beside us, childhood friend Adam, with the unsmiling silence of
Lurch, did 80 percent of the lifting.

Tomas asked me about the bar of goat-milk soap he'd noticed
in the bathroom after I'd crashed for the first of several times in
the Eagle's Nest guest room. My Sweetheart had packed this for

me in an oft-reused organic yogurt container labeled in Magic Marker, for some forgotten reason, "falafel."

"You travel with your own soap?" he asked.

"I'm trying to avoid sodium lauryl sulfate," I told him. "Isn't everybody?"

"Sodium lauryl what now?"

"It's the stuff that makes most commercial soaps and shampoos bubble. There's some evidence it might be bad for you. And it's certainly not necessary. I've come to a place where if a chemical in any product isn't necessary, I just avoid it. There've just been too many bad chemicals."

"You know, I'm getting interested in that," Tomas told me in a way he had of making you feel like you just caused him to have a stunning revelation. "When I grew indoors, I'd buy this Avid stuff for mite control. They sell it at grow shops in individual packaging without any directions. My guess is that very few growers know how much to use, or if it's safe. The more I learn, the more responsibility I feel to patients. I'm growing people's medicine."

Ditching toxins, Tomas was discovering, might be a good policy for someone branding himself as a sustainable farmer. I could almost see the lightbulb going off over his head. He began expressing regret for the coatings that were sometimes on the medicine with which he had supplied dispensaries in the past. And he soon became a compulsive label reader at the grocery store.

Over the course of the 2011 cannabis season, Tomas also became a regular at the Pesticide Action Network's Web Index, to make sure any antimildew application or nitrogen booster, whether or not the manufacturer declared it "organic," passed that organization's muster. He was learning about one new toxic acronym per week. "I've always been a studier," he told me, crediting his success in college to his study habits. At one point he considered digging up his water lines, having learned that PVC pipes can leach toxic BPA.

This all proved additionally valuable, Tomas said, for his standards research for MendoGrown. "We want to go far beyond USDA Organic, which we can't apply for anyway, since it's federal." The group was in talks with a Swiss company called IMO for a bundled range of services including quality testing and fair trade certification for MendoGrown-certified cannabis.

Tomas summed up his emerging education on the food-consumer and medicine-producer front concisely while weeding the weed one July afternoon. He asked me, "Have you ever noticed that we're not supposed to be eating poison?"

The Ukiah organic food co-op and the town's Safeway supermarket are across the street from one another. Tomas, by the time his San Francisco Giants were statistically eliminated from 2011 playoff contention, barely ever set foot in the Safeway anymore. He was an enthusiastic member of the food co-op, whose nonprofit business model his own Kama collective followed.

In fact, during the time I followed Lucille, he went from Doritos to "organic blue corn chips" when he wanted to watch one of his sports teams lose a game, and, equally importantly, from $169-a-gallon grow-shop Nitrozine to more effective $6.99 fish emulsion for the crop. In his words, "I'm liberated from grow-shop tyranny."

And unsustainability. During the summer of 2011, Tomas became almost a zealot in his belief in the potent, real-world correlation between farming methods and the medicine he hoped his eventual Kama patients would receive. Or as he was to put it at harvest time, "I've been a successful cannabis grower for ten years and this is my first real crop."

Even his sleep patterns changed. Soon after he first moved into the Eagle's Nest in May, Tomas confessed to great unease about the bobcat and wild-pig nighttime noises he kept hearing outside the farmhouse window. He even asked me if I recommended his getting a hunting rifle to at least "make some noise." I advised against it.* He was finding that the local deer, in particular, love

---

* The Drug War has a rhetorical front, manifest in press releases about busts: Because some growers are criminals (just like some software company executives are, and some dermatologists), the official version of a raid whenever possible mentions guns found on the premises: A hunting rifle will sometimes get photographed next to seized cannabis as evidence that a farmer was "armed." Similarly, farmers and attorneys tell me that some law enforcers have been

the cannabis plant, and he frequently had to storm outside yelling to keep a particular doe and her two fawns from dining without a vet's recommendation.

But by July he told me, "I can't sleep in the city anymore. I need to hear a deer or a hawk."

Eventually, perhaps inevitably, Tomas's overall perspective expansion reached the astronomical.

"I can't believe the stars," I heard him say one early autumn evening when his off-grid system failed in the middle of the Cal-Oregon football game he'd been watching.

"We live in a galaxy," I observed.

"Never been able to notice that before," Tomas said, pulling out his phone. "Which reminds me, I better check what the weather's supposed to do tomorrow: I'd like to get some fish emulsion into the roots in the next couple of days. If the girls aren't gonna be stressed by wind or anything else."

Given how much cannabis can be grown on a small farm, it's entirely feasible that the entire market for top-shelf medicinal cannabis can be satisfied by a network of individual, sustainable cultivators like Tomas. For our energy and food supply, textile production, and other business uses like car parts and home building, industrial cannabis will require much larger farming operations. But North Dakota is ready. So is central California and, if their leaders and farmers are smart, scores of other struggling agricultural communities in the United States.

---

known to weigh seized green, leafy material in its heavy glass storage jar to make a seizure appear weightier. During farm raids, the scale might be laden with the entire plant, branches, leaves, and even soil ball, for the same reason. Even the actual number of plants seized can be subject to a kind of midraid hanging-chad-type negotiation: Is that root ball all one plant? This matters a lot when a farmer is dancing close to that federal ninety-nine-plant conspiracy cutoff.

The cannabis activist side uses these psy-ops, too, of course. Every anticannabis legalization op-ed from Nebraska to Bakersfield is smacked down in a polite but withering letter from an executive at Americans for Safe Access, NORML, or one of the half-dozen other major Stop the Drug War organizations. Or better yet by a doctor or some other professional who is a member of one of these organizations.

# SEVENTEEN

## Collective Farming in the Time of Helicopters

The War on Drugs has been an utter failure. I think we need
to . . . decriminalize our medical marijuana laws.

—Barack Obama, 2004

In May 2008, the County Council for Hawaii County voted not
to accept federal . . . funding for state and local law enforcement's
aerial surveillance and eradication efforts, citing complaints
from many residents who reportedly opposed the program because
low-flying helicopter missions violated their privacy and
disrupted rural life. Consequently, law enforcement agencies
were constrained in their efforts to effectively monitor outdoor
and indoor grow activity in Hawaii County, where most of the
state's cannabis cultivation occurs.

—U.S. Department of Justice National Drug Intelligence Center's
2009 "Domestic Cannabis Cultivation Assessment"

A farmer like Tomas only gets to worry about things like the
weather and mites if all of the incessantly droning helicopters
overhead choose to honor the giant 9.31 permit banner affixed to
his fence. So far they had for two seasons, with one mostly recti-
fied exception in 2010. They'd landed somewhere else for the
"everyone down on the ground" routine.

That really happens, even in Mendo. Usually it's the feds or
County of Mendocino Marijuana Eradication Team (COMMET)
officers looking for excessive, non-9.31 grows. Of course, most of
these raids result in acquittals or dismissals. Still, at a 9.31 meeting, I heard Sergeant Randy advising growers facing a raid to "lie
down until the yelling and screaming stops and the guns are hol-
stered. Because they will be drawn. That's what these guys do."

Jim Hill described the raid "game" this way: "They come in,

they interrogate you for eight hours, you make them coffee, you call the lawyer, they punish you with the process a little bit, and it all goes away."

Hill even felt that the county's Child Protection Services (CPS) folks are in on the game. "They take your kids for a day," he said. "Feed them some processed food, you get them back. They get paid. The worst thing is when the mother screams and carries on during the raid. It scares the kids. If you're someone who's really worried about it, you should take your kids down to the CPS office in Ukiah today, to meet the folks there. Then it'll be Aunt Kim and Uncle Jeremy—a sleepover, instead of a scary experience. That's where they get you—frightening you that they'll take your kids away. Think of it as a short vacation. A free babysitter."

Only three words are needed to describe the chances of explaining *that* strategy to a woman like my own Sweetheart: "not bloody likely." That's why when I came here to learn about cannabis I tried, unsuccessfully, to find a spot in the county where there wasn't cultivation going on immediately around my family. Luckily we avoided any, you know, address mix-ups during raids. I lost a little sleep over it, though, once I had my neighborhood "Young Goodman Brown" reality check, and thanks to a jolting experience during an early July visit to the Eagle's Nest.

It was late on a sunny afternoon of the kind often frequented by pairs of DUI butterflies. Seeking some quiet to record a few thoughts regarding Tomas's level of preparation for his upcoming 9.31 inspection, I was making my way behind the farmhouse on the opposite side of the property from the fields. I recall observing that Adam, now wearing a weight belt since he was training for a triathlon,* was trimming the stone paths in a triangle between house, cannabis fields, and bench-lined pear and apple orchard. Beyond that was the stream.

I waved to Adam and a few minutes later found myself standing

---

* He wound up placing third, earning an invite to a national team event in New Zealand. He told me he did not mention his preferred training regimen to the team's coach.

in front of that Eagle's Nest's creek, tapping some notes into my trichome-sticky phone. I was trying to rally that last really important thought when an obese bumblebee startled me with an abrupt and very close-up hello. We were actually eye-to-eye for an instant, the equivalent of an interspecies handshake. It was at that potentially inspirational moment that the unmistakable bass drone of a helicopter ripped as strangely as an interstellar alien would through any sense of peace, well-being, and contentment I was feeling. It seemed very, very, close.

Needless to say, my heart leapt in an attempt to get not just out of my chest, but out of the country. My first thought was "Feds or COMMET?" This was because I wanted to discern the relative value of holding up Sheriff Tom's business card like a Red Cross first aid kit.

Food co-op and airline mile cards spilling precariously out of my shaking hands near the stream, I started to extract the proper card.

Then I thought, "Wait a minute. No need to panic here." Learning from my adventures in Sonoma County, I had my phone tree, including Sweetheart, editor, and literary agent, ready to call my lawyer anytime, day or night. He would SUV to the rescue like the hero so many attorneys are.

True, I had yet to call such a lawyer. I kept meaning to. I had permission from the entire phone tree membership to give their personal contact information. I just hadn't felt very threatened since steering north of the Mendocino County line. The truth is, one can get a little comfy about being around cannabis when the county sheriff, in your first interview, explains the lengths he will go *not* to arrest someone for positive feelings about the plant.

Still, how much control did Allman have over his men? COMMET's crew, one has to presume, is comprised of the 95 percent of Sheriff Tom's staff who actually consider cannabis cultivation a crime. I did try to contact the COMMET office once, to see if I could get on one of their plant-spotting overflights, but they didn't call me back.

Before I had too much time to worry about the attorney-on-retainer oversight, it became clear that the chopper was on its way to someone else's field today. And still so loud! Its existence at all seemed to me to be unconstitutionally invasive in a Land of the Free/fourth amendment kind of way. The fact that I was paying for it in a time of federal, state, and county debt crisis was an irony too sad to relish. Costs more than a thousand dollars an hour to operate, I'd read in a press report.

Now I had a moment to feel relief for Tomas, who would have been in the hole for close to a million dollars if that helicopter crew was coming for him. Even if it were true that COMMET's deciders (though not the feds) have to consult Randy before embarking on raids, Tomas's plants weren't yet wearing their zip-tie necklaces. The inspection that would, he hoped, allow that was just days away. Plants are routinely cut down during a raid, before any criminal charges are filed.

Cannabis farmers, until the end of prohibition, get used to overflights at their peril, not that there's much that they can do about them. At the brewpub or the world music concert, everyone talks big, weaving tales of waving to the choppers, mooning them, and displaying suggestive middle digits. But older, more established growers especially tell me they're best looked at as summer mosquitoes: You have to live with them, but if there are too many of them swarming, you might have to go inside. Or, if they swarm your farm while you're at the farmers' market, to Hawaii for a couple of weeks. Cheap summer fares on Expedia.

Mosquitoes, yes, but very expensive mosquitoes to you and me. American taxpayers shell out five hundred dollars per second to fight the Drug War; 858,408 people were arrested for cannabis in 2009. Instead of "to fight the Drug War," you could say "to help keep black market prices high, the prisons filled, and the cartels reaping their profits." When we could be following Tower of Power's advice and benefiting from billions in taxable legal revenue.

This bugged me, because I myself could never get used to living in a scene out of *Apocalypse Now*. Especially in light of how downright Pooh Corner everything in this remote county was when the helicopters weren't around. My three-year-old son, though, from our afternoon walks and like any not deaf person who steps outside in Mendocino County, quickly learned to point out "choppers!" Actually, he even more quickly tired of the game, preferring the quiet.

Take it or leave it, though, because for now helicopter noise is Mendocino County's summer soundtrack. Something you just have to deal with in warm weather, like the summer before tenth grade when it was "Born in the U.S.A."

Helicopter overflights are common enough, in fact, to serve as indication of the arrival of planting season. The noise begins as early as April, when Mendocino County law enforcement personnel—who better qualified?—run taxpayer-funded aerial cannabis-spotting classes for narcotics agents from around the country.

For his part, Tomas, like all Mendo growers who wished to remain sane, treated helicopters the way Robert Duvall's Colonel Bill Kilgore treated incoming artillery rounds in *Apocalypse Now*. He strolled confidently among them, sidestepped when necessary, and plotted the unemployment of their financiers.

Not all cannabis farmers dream of the end of the Drug War, though. Remember when old-time grower Joe told me times were good when prices were high thanks to comparatively massive seizures in the 1980s? This economic relationship is not lost on many of those who make their living on the production end. For-profit, black-market American growers commonly see themselves as existing in a symbiotic relationship with narcotics law enforcers: As the Camo Cowboys sing, they keep one another employed.

Farmers dedicated to the renegade economic model see it as a (sometimes literal) shotgun marriage. No one worries that a raid will hurt more than a mosquito bite. So they're happy to let a failed Drug War help them make their margin; pay their kid's tuition.

Cannabis prices were low in 2011, and without CAMP, COM-MET, the DEA, and the menacing string of memos and directives emerging from the Holder Justice Department, they would have been even lower. For a black market farmer of America's most profitable crop, it was business as usual.

Tomas Balogh didn't want to see the plant stay underground. Despite mechanical pterodactyls, historically low prices, and the challenge of starting a collective by harvest time, he remained unfailingly upbeat through the ups and downs of the 2011 season. Routine entrepreneurial growing pains, the seasoned businessperson will no doubt observe. Still, it's a real person's life.

Midseason, the guy learned that he couldn't even rely on his candidate—and boss, for six months, in 2008—President Obama to stop the War on Drugs, at least in his first term. What seemed at the time to be the climax of a series of vague but threatening federal letters to state officials, some of which temporarily halted implementations of state medical cannabis programs, including New Jersey's, came on July 22, 2011. That was when, dogged by the fact that "Why won't you end the Drug War?" was the most asked question asked in both of his online town halls, and that people had questioned the Drug War during several in-person Q&As, the president finally said, explicitly, at an event in Maryland: "Am I willing to pursue a decriminalization strategy as an approach? No."

I and about thirty of his friends jibed Tomas no end about Obama's utterance. My e-mail was accompanied by a subject reading simply, "Um." He took it with his usual good humor, claiming, as a door-to-door canvasser, absence from actual Oval Office decision making. But the message was clear to the medical cannabis business and activist community: the president had thrown them under the bus.

A few weeks after the president's rhetorical flip-flop on cannabis, Roseanne Barr—perhaps having heard the same soundbite—threw her hat in the 2012 presidential ring on the Conan show, declaring ending the Drug War as her number-one platform position.

"I'm not an election worker in 2012," Tomas told me just before harvest in October, not having issued an endorsement as of this writing, though he did start wearing Obama 2012 T-shirts in the fall. "This election, I plan on being a valued contributor."

Memo to candidates: There are thousands of Tomases out there. A National Organization for the Reform of Marijuana Laws (NORML) conference in Los Angeles is a hot ticket these days. People use it to network. And cannabis is their number-one business issue. This industry generates enough revenue to influence the entire Congress, if it ever gets organized on the national level.

These are people who will provide tens of thousands of jobs, potentially in every state. And this in addition to polls consistently showing that a majority of Americans want decriminalized medicinal cannabis. They want it more than any other kind of health reform. At the 2011 "Reform" Conference in L.A., sponsored by the Drug Policy Alliance, California's lieutenant governor, Gavin Newsom, opened the event in front of twelve hundred people, and he spent his entire address blasting the Drug War.

Tomas, as a member of the thirteen-billion-dollar California business community Newsom was pledging to defend, had more immediate fish to fry: he had eighty-eight plants to tend to professional standards. That is, if the helicopters continued to choose farms other than the Eagle's Nest for their flower-picking excursions.

# EIGHTEEN

## Punks in Paradise: Seeing the Behavior from Which the Human Lucille's Concerns Derive

A good neighbor is a fellow who smiles at you over the back fence, but doesn't climb over it.

—Arthur "Bugs" Baer

I got to meet Lucille's human namesake when I left the Eagle's Nest the same summer day I was scared by a helicopter beside a Mendocino stream. Frankly, the quality of that encounter made me doubt I'd ever come to understand, let alone in some small measure share, her overall attitude about having a commercial-cannabis-growing neighbor. Bumping home after dragging Tomas's rickety ranch gate closed behind me, I stopped in a precarious cliffside deathtrap of a loose-pebbled pullout halfway back down the five miles to pavement, the oxygen already thicker, to write down the words "Today I learned about the choppers and the bees."

I made the note, most of it, anyway, and then saw a spooked fox dart up a wildflower-covered hill a few feet in front of my windshield. Suddenly a solid rap on my passenger-side window startled me as much as any chopper could. Why were so many people trying to test my heart today?

The knuckle rapper turned out to be a woman on the youngish edge of middle age, attractive in a primped Southern California kind of way, asking in an "I don't mean this literally" tone if she could help me with anything. Though nearly hyperventilating, I gave her my standard "accosted on a public road by someone who thinks it's private because it's near her home" line, well-rehearsed from rural New Mexican back roads. "No, I always pull over when

I need to answer a phone call," I said self-righteously, waving my new smartphone. "It *is* the law."

I was also, at the moment, well out of cell range. But the aggressive parry worked, as it always does. The scary lady skulked off and soon after I saw a cloud of gravel dust expanding around me. When Tomas later told me from my description of her SUV, frosted hair, and tone that this was the human Lucille, I for the first time knew we had bestowed the correct name on our research plant. She had grit.

Not that Tomas needed motivation. He wound up charming pretty much all of his neighbors before midseason. Retired school-teacher Loretta, in particular, commented that she appreciated the absence of spelling errors in Tomas's thank-you note following their first meeting for tea and cookies.

By the time I learned of the midseason taming of Loretta, I had had occasion to see why she had asked the tough questions. As a father, I learned what puts the mudge in curmudgeon. Specifi-cally, around midsummer, the neighbor on the other side of my cabin's redwood grove rented a place to some kids from Missouri (judging by the Cardinals logos stenciled on their trucks). They were here, it quickly became clear, for the Green Rush and the accompanying party.

The cumulative effect of their habitually off-leash pitbull, their twenty-five-ish, "frequently sprayed with heaven knows what" cannabis plants visible from my deck, and their tendency to use swear words at top volume, at all hours, nearly forced me to implement complex plans to rein the punks in. I was prepared to bring them a local melon by way of housewarming while as gently as possible explaining to them that I was ready to do what-ever was necessary to keep my family safe and sleeping soundly through the night. Including calling law enforcement—which Loretta had done to another grower neighbor of Tomas's.

"I'm in the fucking woods!" I heard one of them yell into his cell phone from the driveway late one evening.

"No, you're in a neighborhood with kids," I mumbled on my deck.

But they got evicted or for some other reason disappeared before I pulled the trigger on the melon plan. Still, I found myself suddenly much more sympathetic to the Chase/Loretta/Lucille point of view.

Essentially what I was dealing with was not a cannabis problem, but a kids-raised-without-my-kind-of-values problem. A "kids who don't have any model for respectable neighborhood behavior" problem. If those punks hadn't come to Mendo to try their hand at the Green Rush for a few weeks, they'd be back in Missouri working at a Taco Bell. Probably are now. They won't be a problem after cannabis legalization any more than moonshiners are today.

Today they are a big problem. My neighbors were youngsters who hadn't been raised at home. They might have lived at home, but they weren't "brought up." Beavis and Butthead essentially. It is conceivable that over time, if they stayed, they could learn both neighborly manners and the kind of business acumen that Tomas calls Cannabis Diplomacy. It's a major part of the MendoGrown mission. Local education about things like tax returns. Worker's Comp. ADA-compliant restrooms. But the 9.31 Program and MendoGrown's outreach, in 2011, was to that educational effort what Kindergarten is to graduate school. A very, very preliminary step.

Because much education is needed in-county. I hiked with my three-year-old in the hilly redwoods right out the back of our cabin one Saturday in September and, within fifteen minutes, came to an illicit line that was siphoning the creek along which we hiked every day. Stealing public water hurts the ecosystem. At some point during the summer we started calling the fenced area on the other side of our cabin "the garden" instead of "the hot tub." At a public meeting in Ukiah on September 9, a tall woman in furry Uggs who identified herself as a third-generation grower said she couldn't recommend cannabis farming anymore because "there are people coming here and poisoning our county."

Tomas, too, had come to feel that he needed to be a visible role model for younger-generation Mendo growers. This was another way I could tell, over the course of the 2011 season, that he was growing into his position as chair of MendoGrown's Communication and Membership Committee. While he was not by nature a judgmental person, I saw him once or twice get riled at the young punk growers among whose ranks his neighbors had originally (wrongly) counted him. The undisciplined punks weren't, in his view, acting as ambassadors for the emergence of this new generation of sustainable, local American farmers. "Cannabis growers are the good guys," Tomas said. "Mainstream America needs to see that. There's no room for bad apples."

A memorable example of a time when Tomas's patience was tried was at an Eagle's Nest shindig on August 20. On his porch, I saw him barely succeeding at being diplomatic when a black market neighbor began bragging about the hundreds of plants a visiting deputy hadn't been able to find a few years back.

A few minutes later Tomas told me, "I figure this is how it was during the Gold Rush. Some good folks seeking their fortune, some Yosemite Sams. Prohibition, unfortunately, lures criminals. Simple as that. Creates 'em, even."

"You didn't say anything to Phil just now," I observed.

"Time and a place for everything," Tomas said. "Sometimes I just want to grab a guy by the scruff of the neck and say, 'It's our job to be the face of the cannabis industry. There's a hundred million Americans who need to be unbrainwashed about this plant. Bring your crap to the dump. Don't light M-eighties every other night. Grow up and act like any other businessman.' But I have to do it in a way where it'll be heard."

Again, extreme youth is often at the core of the problem. I recall an experience one afternoon in a Willits park not long after this party. I was seesawing in the playground with my sons. There I heard one member of a clique of what I would've considered— from the black garb and boots—to be high school goths, say to another, "If you're so sick of living with 'em, just use this year's harvest to buy an acre of land and you can have your own fucking place."

A third kid endorsed the thought. "You can do a lot on an acre."

"Wow," I thought. "That represents a full fifteen years before the phase in my life when I began even *thinking* about real estate." Part of me was impressed. It was entrepreneurial thinking. But somehow coming from a magenta-haired kid using foul language in a playground, it seemed premature.

Still, you see why the discussion was happening. We've already covered that Mendocino County's cannabis crop is worth, conservatively, an annual $8.1 billion to farmers. If you're a Willits High School graduate interested in agriculture, how does that stack up locally against the rest of the crops that love the Mediterranean climate?

Well, the most lucrative federally kosher crop in the county, wine, chalked in at $74.9 million in 2010, according to county agriculture commissioner Tony Linegar, a big part of whose job—until he took the same gig in neighboring Sonoma County late in 2011—was basically to ignore what Sheriff Tom calls the T-rex in the room.*

And that $8.1 billion, folks, derives from one plant in one county in one state. It completely omits industrial cannabis (which itself doesn't include value-added products like the hemp oil I and my family drink every morning in our shakes), whose twenty-five thousand acres in Canada comprised the most profitable crop north of the border in 2010, and still represented less than 10 percent of the world market. Biomass efficiency of cannabis fiber as a fuel source is also estimated in multiple studies—one out of Oregon State in 1998—at five tons per acre, or five hundred gallons of biofuel annually. Cue Tower of Power. The tax potential, indeed.

It's safe to say that the young Mendocino farmer is aware of

---

* A Mendocino County ag commissioner once, in 1979, did try to include cannabis in his annual report, and the statewide backlash prevented a sequel of the rare truly forthcoming report by a public official.

The Lucille triplets one minute after their "birth" from their Mendocino County–derived Cashmere Kush mother plant.

Lucille's Gregor Mendel, a second-generation cannabis farmer, says of his barn-side laboratory: "It's all about genetic diversity and experimentation in the field."

This is a new standard.

| | |
|---|---|
| Indica/Sativa: | 90%/10% |
| Finishes: | Mid Oct. |
| Yield: | High; Mid to large dense colas |
| Flavor: | Sweet and Kushy with a strong presence of Skunk. |
| High: | Up and clear |

"People want to know what cannabinoids are in their plant," testing company Halent Labs's Colleen Brand told me.

Mendocino County cannabis farmer Tomas Balogh prepares to transfer his Kama Collective's crop back to his mountainside farm, the Eagle's Nest.

Adopt-a-Highway cleanup sign, Mendocino County, California.

The impossibly ironic billboard near which I was briefly detained by Sonoma County deputies on April 4, 2011.

The namesake cannabis regulation zip ties themselves. These form a bracelet on every permitted cannabis plant's main stem.

Tomas Balogh's farm narrowly passes his first Sheriff's Department inspection, on Independence Day 2011.

ATTENTION LAW ENFORCEMENT

This medical garden has permit #E20110122 pending with the Mendocino County Sheriff's Office. For more information please contact

Thank you.

While federal cannabis prohabition exists, Kama's farm-side sign has only limited authority.

Cannabis farmer
Tomas Balogh buys
his zip ties from the
Sherrif's Department,
generating, this
August day, $4,400
for Mendocino
County, California.

A zip-tied Mendocino
County cannabis plant.

I inspect Lucille's terpenes and trichomes on August 12, 2011.

A flowering indica-dominant outdoor-grown cannabis plant, Mendocino County, California, 2011.

Outdoor cannabis flowers, Mendocino County, California, 2011.

Kama Collective medicine drying, October 2011.

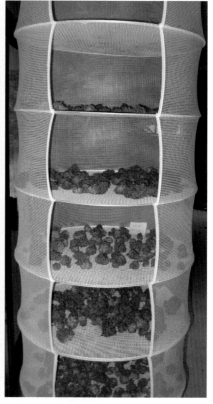

Left: Cannabinoid crystals on Lucille.

Bottom left: Trimming buds.

Bottom right: Trimmed buds awaiting packaging.

A sample from Lucille, ready for transport to the cannabinoid testing facility near Davis, California.

The 2011 Kama Collective harvest packaged and ready to reach patients.

Just another plant in the garden Mendocino. At center left are four cannabis plants. There's one more at center right—they have the darker-colored leaves. The rest of the plants in the garden are fruits and vegetables: watermelon, carrots, tomatoes, radishes.

Matt Cohen gives an October 23, 2011, interview to *The Sacramento Bee* in front of his federally chopped down, locally legal farm.

Cannabis farmer, activist, and would-be mainstream American Tomas Balogh protests the October 2011 federal cannabis crackdown in front of the Robert T. Matsui Federal Building in Sacramento, California, November, 9, 2011.

these figures: a well-tended five-plant garden makes a nice high school job. It's educational and you can save up your college spending money—maybe you'll major in sustainable agriculture or small-farm marketing. The problem comes when you're supplying your friends with black market cannabis.

When I mentioned the playground ganjapreneur discussion I'd overheard to Tomas, he sounded like his neighbor Chase Donnelly in suggesting such kids need a monthlong wilderness boot camp.

"They should learn how to treat the land, and that being a real farmer is not so easy," he told me.

"What, are you going to start growing grapes now?" I joked.

"Do I sound like an old fart?" he asked.

"You sound like you've put away the Mountain Dew in exchange for the Cabernet, bra."

Though not entirely. An obvious place to see the divide that exists even between a permitted, aspiring regular citizen grower like Tomas Balogh and the potential commercial American consumer market is in the realm of cannabis strain names. We're talking brand names, essentially. These matter in the kind of zeitgeist struggle in which Tomas and his industry are engaged. Only an urban indoor grower of the butt-crack-showing Red Bull generation would name any product, let alone a medical one, Chernobyl, Sour Diesel, or Satan's Pussy. Yet you see these and names like them on dispensary menus all over the nation.

Furthermore, I can say with some confidence that cannabis care providers are going to have some trouble getting even a friendly AMA executive committee to sign on to a medicine called "Green Crack."

Imagine the presentation: "Distinguished panel, this medicine is a cannabinoid-balanced cross of a Satan's Pussy mother with a Chernobyl father."

Tomas was in fact growing a half-dozen Chernobyl plants in 2011. It's popular as a powerful pain-reducing and anti-insomnia indica-sativa hybrid strain. And he understood what I meant when

I told him that if I were a patient, I wouldn't want to ingest nuclear waste.

"It's part of the fun-loving underground heritage of the industry," he at first defended. "Like NASCAR."

"You're the one who says the industry needs to grow up," I said. "That cannabis isn't an outlaw crop anymore. When I told her about Chernobyl, by the way, my Sweetheart suggested 'Puppy's Breath.'"

"How is that growing up?"

"At least it's not profane and doesn't convey . . . acute toxicity."

Tomas nodded and promised to rack his brain for a replacement name for Chernobyl. What he came up with at first kind of missed the point, I thought, when I got his e-mail two days later. He wrote, "How about Reggie Noble?"

Wikipedia told me that this is the given name of the Jersey-based rapper from the Def Squad and Wu-Tang Clan. "I was envisioning something more organic, conjuring more of a healing sentiment," I clarified in my reply. "Like 'Apple per Day' or 'Heavenly Recovery.' Maybe 'Redwood Serenity.'"

I was glad, though, that the exchange afforded me the opportunity to familiarize myself with a few of Reggie (working name "Redman") Noble's tracks: He's the real deal, as an MC. Tomas agreed to think about it some more, and I noticed some months later that a prelaunch version of the Kama Collective menu listing for the strain read "The Organic Cowboy." Which is my own online handle.

I suppose this is the modern equivalent of getting a Stage Deli sandwich named after you. Although research suggests that cannabis is probably less dangerous than a Stage corned beef on rye with slaw.

Even with the slow maturation of cannabis strain names in the industry, Tomas's neighbors had learned he was the kind of community member anyone would want. Nonetheless, the Eagle's Nest punk-troubled history would almost certainly loom over the property until Tomas brought in a few successful, taxpaying crops. That's about how long the modern California memory bank lasts.

Indeed Sergeant Randy, upon Tomas's first 9.31 inspection, said he considered it one of 2011's most likely 9.31 farms to be "tested." Which I think was meant to be synonymous with "potentially hassled by unfriendly elements within the department and/or by the feds."

I don't know if this concerned Tomas, but it worried me as much as Randy's Official Raid Response Duck-and-Cover Drill. With all due respect to Tomas's obviously genuine effort to comply with all nonfederal laws and be an aboveground contributor to society, I was at the Eagle's Nest a lot, and I really didn't want to be on hand for any misunderstandings that could result in weekly prison visits from my family.

In the final analysis, Tomas couldn't be responsible for what phone calls were or were not placed by his neighbors. He could only be responsible for his own behavior. And when it came to becoming a sustainable, outdoor-growing bona fide Mendocino cannabis farmer, his transformation appeared further along every time we met during the season. As someone who had himself recently made the journey from Value Meals to goat milking, I could safely declare that he was getting there. Fast. No longer a kid with an indoor green thumb, he was by midsummer an organic, Willie Nelson–listening gentleman farmer.

Tomas now had the field creds to evangelize outdoor-grown medicine outside the county. The MendoGrown board members had brought in a video crew and produced a DVD that sang the praises of sustainable cannabis farming. They wanted to see it playing on display tables at dispensaries everywhere, and they sent board vice-chair Tomas to make that happen. He recounted a San Francisco dispensary conversation from August for me.

Tomas: "What percentage of your medicine is sustainably grown outdoors?

Dispensary manager: "Ten percent, approximately."

Tomas: "Would you like to see that go up to 30 percent or

40 percent in the next year, with our MendoGrown DVD playing in a loop on this MendoGrown display?"

Dispensary manager: "Yes, I would."

It was a sales meeting that could have been held in the 1950s. All that was missing was the lounge where Larry Tate closed the deal. Different Happy Hour, frankly. Tomas doesn't dispute that the farmers for whom he is lobbying are businesspeople. "We're afraid to use the term *capitalism* because of the health care element, but MendoGrown is both a movement and an industry."

# NINETEEN

## A Modern Agricultural Businessman Prepares
## for a Fourth of July Regulatory Inspection

If the U.S. legalized marijuana today, the plant would be grown on big corporate farms, perhaps supported with unneeded federal subsidies and occasionally marred by scandals regarding exploitation of undocumented . . . farm workers. The liberal grandchildren of legalization advocates will grumble about the soulless marijuana corporations and the conservative grandchildren of antilegalization activists will play golf at the country club with marijuana inc. executives, toast George Soros at the nineteenth hole afterwards and discuss how they can get the damn liberals in Congress to stop blocking capital gains tax cuts.

—Keith Humphreys, PhD, Professor, Stanford Medical School,
from his Website http://www.samefacts.com/

**J**uly 1 through 4, 2011, was not a relaxed time at the Eagle's Nest. Actually, the hectic phase lasted longer than that—those days were simply comprised of nonstop, instead of the usual seldom-stop, work. Looking back on it, the time between Tomas's spring move-in and the looming Fourth of July 9.31 law-enforcement inspection was essentially one long work party.

Perhaps understandably, perhaps like any start-up businessman regardless of whether a couple billion tax dollars are devoted every year to interfering with his business model, Tomas didn't sleep a lot in the spring and summer of 2011. Which is par for the course for him, a fellow with two gears—fifth and park. He described hardly sleeping for six months in 2008 ("I basically lived at the Port Charlotte campaign office") helping win Florida for a loudly pro-medical-cannabis candidate, Barack Obama.

That experience caused a recurrence of his childhood migraines, which he had been successfully treating since adolescence with cannabis—that Super Silver Haze sativa strain, in fact. "I had no medical access in Florida, that's for sure," he told me. He resumed medicating (not often) after a migraine left him temporarily blind and sent him to the emergency room in 2009. He hasn't had a migraine since.

Turns out Tomas was on the right track: A study out of Vanderbilt University and reported in *Nature Chemical Biology* in 2011 found that ibuprofen and the rest of the nonsteroidal anti-inflammatory drugs (NSAID) in fact activate cannabinoid receptors. Too bad he had to do the research on his own.

By the eve of this initial inspection, the Eagle's Nest farm itself had already become Terpene Central, just like the rest of the county. They clung to doorposts as the cultural badge, like a hanging *ristra* in New Mexico. I could smell Tomas's property well before I reached it, in fact while still in full view of Lucille's husband's grapes. I later had to douse off in springwater just to get back into my truck. I'd frankly arrest myself if I pulled myself over smelling like that—and I *was* heading the next day to a Fourth of July picnic with the sheriff in attendance.

I wondered what human Lucille thought of the bouquet. Some people consider the smell quite a nuisance. But does Gilroy complain about the smell of garlic? It's just a plant. I personally didn't think the smell was offensive. No more so than any other farm odor is.

The whole panoramic tableau of the Kama Collective's planting areas, in fact, bespoke botanical health. When I'd arrived and entered the lower garden fairly late on the afternoon of July 3, I'd blurted my usual "My, how they've grown!" as I now did anytime I'd been away from Tomas's farm for more than twenty-four hours.

The work party was particularly intense during this period because, to put it bluntly, Tomas wasn't ready for his inspection. Specifically and most pressingly, the plants were in the ground before their fencing was built. That would be roughly like drafting your first year's New York Yankee squad without having yet built Yankee Stadium. And with only a one-year lease for the lot. The ladies needed somewhere enclosed to play, and fast. By dawn on the Fourth of July, specifically.

Tomas is a one-step-at-a-time-is-the-route-to-sanity kind of guy and thus, having just leapt his first couple of Code Red logistical hurdles, perhaps hadn't yet read the latest 9.31 regulations in enough detail to know until the last minute that he had two football-field-size fences to build. The Eagle's Nest was clean and planted, now it had to be up to code.

I *had* read the regs, and as the last chopper of the day was rudely returning to the Ukiah airport, I did wonder what possible plans Tomas had to ready the Eagle's Nest for its first Sheriff's Department inspection. Which, in an indication of how popular the 9.31 Program was becoming, was scheduled for eight thirty A.M. on the national holiday.

The patriot Tomas Balogh, child of a Hungarian freedom fighter immigrant, eager taxpayer, local nonprofit business owner, and potential employer, told me when he learned of the scheduling, "I gotta get me a flag. If I can find one made in the USA. I just can't think of a more appropriate day to come aboveground."

His civic pride was dialed in, at least, if not his fencing. Truly, even sixteen hours later as I watched the approaching dust cloud as Sergeant Randy and the third-party inspector bounced up to the Eagle's Nest in Randy's newly upgraded SUV (Budget crisis? Not in this program) right on time for the postsunrise inspection, the jury was decidedly out on whether Tomas'd be able to comply. For one thing, in the minutes before the inspection, he had asked me, "Do you have any padlocks in your [truck's] toolbox?" The 9.31 ordinance mandated that the gated part of his garden fences, which were now mostly erected, had to be locked.

In retrospect, I realize Tomas's whole first season as a legal grower was one really long game of catch-up. In fact, he started the season believing he would be a contracted farmer with Matt

Cohen's Northstone Organics, before he decided to forge out on his own with Kama: That had just been settled when we met. The two remain friends and Tomas attended Matt's wedding.

Tomas stood with his hands on his hips and we could see the silhouettes inside the sheriff's vehicle launching toward the interior dome lights on the rough final approach.

"Any advice from other inspections you've seen?" Tomas asked me nervously.

"Tell him your bud trimmers will be wearing white lab coats, hair nets, and latex gloves," I advised. "Better yet, call them 'processing technicians.'"

Sure enough, the Big Unit gave the "first word in medical marijuana is *medical*" spiel within fifteen minutes of his arrival— sounding like *South Park*'s Mr. Mackey addressing a full, if distracted, high school auditorium about the Dangers of Sniffing Glue.

To the extent that Tomas pulled off the July Fourth inspection by the epidural skin on the very outside of his teeth, he did it almost entirely with a little help from his friends—manifest in some serious all-night fencing work. Soon after I arrived on July 3 to witness this marathon segment of the perpetual work party, I found, in addition to some of the usual suspects (Stella now addressed Tomas as "boss," I noticed), a lineman-size, tattooed Honduran-American named Carlos bashing ten-foot fence posts through the alluvial Mendocino soil with a manual hole-digger.

Turns out he's a longtime friend of Tomas's with two kids about my own kids' age. I briefly got enlisted to hold the ladder steady on steep, uneven hillsides for Carlos, who outweighed me by perhaps 80 pounds. He told me that he and Tomas had learned how to build fences a few hours earlier from a "crash course on YouTube."

"Just trying to help out my bro," Carlos, a congenitally cheerful giant, said. "Got any earplugs? This is gonna be loud."

Tomas was in a blissful state of mind this evening, because he could unleash his OCD full bore and still not get everything done. "I'm inspired," he said during a break several hours later above the subsequent E-flat gong that was poinging around my tympanic membrane. "I'm hopeful about the future."

He and Carlos approached midnight on July 3 in sore-muscle agony that not even Stella's triceps pounding could have fully remedied. The budding ganjapreneur worked through it. At seven A.M. on Independence Day, over some kind of Hungarian ranch potato breakfast and on almost no sleep, he told me, "I feel like I can announce what I do to the whole world. My parents are thinking of investing in Kama."

At eight, with his crew having departed, Tomas was still on a ladder, tying baling wire. It was as Randy's vehicle rounded the final few switchbacks that Tomas smacked his forehead, rifled his pockets, and asked about my padlock collection. At the next 9.31 informational meeting, I noticed Randy had slightly modified his "I wanna make it work for all of us" speech to include, "But work with me, people: Have some basic prep work—like fencing—done before your inspection."

Though on the Fourth, Randy was visibly unsurprised by what he was seeing. Huffing and grumbling like Grouchy Smurf about all the confounded walking his new gig necessitates—Sergeant Randy makes a lot of jokes about his own paunch—he had no problem with my taking a smiling photo of him and Tomas posing side by side in front of, you know, a big field of federal contraband.

Then he hitched up his pants, grabbed his clipboard, and handed Tomas a list of everything that needed to be ready and/or fixed by the time the third-party inspector returned in a few weeks. In most cases, Randy will only show up to each farm once, plus a possible pop-in inspection during the season. It was a significant list that included sections of first, second, and third priorities. Safe to say locked fencing was at the top.

Sergeant Randy has a reputation for being tough but fair on inspections—for trying to make things work. One farmer had already told me, "On many of these Mendo farms, there's a lot he could say about building code violations alone. He usually picks one or two of the most glaring problems and mentions those."

When Randy had taken off, an ebullient Tomas gave me a detailed update on Lucille. Close-up, it was easy to see that things were going well. This was a plant living the photosynthetic good life. In addition to her dark green, palm-size leaves, she'd had another solar-powered growth spurt since I'd last seen her and her relatives. At nearly four feet, she looked bushy and stunningly healthy as she grooved in the breeze to a 1977 version of "Uncle John's Band" coming from Tomas's music player.

"She's already taller than any plant I've grown indoors," Tomas told me of the chosen Cashmere Kush. "I think she's one of the most beautiful plants in the garden."

I sure was relieved to hear that, after how worried Tomas had been about her on that earlier visit when she'd had the drooping leaves. No nitrogen deficiency this day. That Dr. Rock Frankenstein had really come through. Judging by scent alone, this plant's genetics clearly loved the spot.

"Overall, are you happy with how things are going horticulturally?" I asked. Tomas, not Lucille.

He was hand-trimming leaves from a Fire OG plant. "I can turn my OCD down a notch now," he said. "Or at least once the girls are all in their big pots."

"Yeah, right," I proffered.

"No, really." And this time he meant it. "Check out the grape bouquet on these Super Silver Hazes." He invited me to engage in the sticky-finger terpene routine. I'd never smelled anything like that before.

"I've never smelled anything like that before in all my years of growing," Tomas said, reading my mind. "The trichomes glisten— look at that. I don't know how I didn't see it earlier. Indoor is bullshit."

It really smelled like fresh grape. And my phone keypad still does.

It was a pivotal moment for Tomas, and a short-lived one. His phone sang what sounded like a fortissimo jazz xylophone solo there in the garden, and I could tell that it was Murphy's Law calling, from the way his "I'm outdoors growing medicine and talking shop with a million-dollar mountain view" smile faded as he listened.

Turns out it was his landlord's Realtor. Tomas's Easy Street fantasy was beginning to come apart almost as soon as it'd coalesced. I was soon very glad I wasn't researching the career of a whiner.

In recent weeks and with increased distress, Tomas hadn't heard back from the Eagle's Nest owner about receiving the vital "owner approval" form necessary for participation in the 9.31 Program. What I was witnessing at the moment was this fellow finally returning Tomas's increasingly urgent calls, saying he'd sign the form if Tomas agreed to relinquish his right of first refusal on buying the place. This even though the lease-to-own carrot had provided a lot of the motivation for Tomas's astoundingly comprehensive, often disgusting, time-consuming, and expensive cleanup of the Eagle's Nest.

Tomas had little choice but to agree. Three weeks later the place had been sold out from under him. To another grower, no less. Starting at the end of the year when Tomas's lease was up. Then that deal fell through, and Tomas was back in the hunt. But only if his collective had any money left over for real estate following the harvest.

As of this writing, Tomas is still looking for a farm on which to grow medicine in 2012 for however many members the Kama Collective by then has. When we met for a fact-checking session in November 2011, he told me, "I should start scanning Craigslist now, but I have a website to launch and a patient base to build." Another day in the life of a small American farmer and businessman.

# TWENTY

## The Zip-Tie Program Survives the Federal Eye

Mark your Calendar: Americans for Safe Access (ASA) is visiting cities all over California throughout the month of August to train and mobilize the grassroots base of support for safe access to medical cannabis! ASA will be hosting Raid Preparedness Trainings and Stakeholders Meetings in eleven cities hoping to get supporters active in their local, state, and federal campaigns for safe access. These meetings are a great way for patients, [dispensary] operators and staff, caregivers, activists, and others to plug in and make a difference! Be a part of this exciting statewide tour—and invite your friends and loved ones.

—Drug Policy Forum of California mailing list, August 18, 2011

MENDOCINO GENERATIONS (Coming Together for Healing) invites you to a Neighborhood Meet & Greet Tuesday, September 6 from 6 to 8 P.M. Come early, and shop and eat in downtown Boonville! Are you excited, curious or concerned about the opening of a cannabis dispensary in Anderson Valley? Please come meet dispensary managers Jamie Beatty, Chiah Rodriques and Laura Hamburg and enjoy delicious local food and beverages, learn about medical cannabis, ask questions or register to become a member. . . . Please do NOT park in front of the next door Valley Bible Fellowship.

—Invitation to Mendocino County cannabis collective opening, September 2011

Luckily for Tomas Balogh, the "movement" side of the cannabis industry he refers to was already two or three generations old when he arrived. A lot went into making Mendocino County such a War on Drugs safe haven. In an incident that's illustrative of an earlier phase in what Tom Allman calls his professional evolution from Drug Warrior to the Sheriff Who Helped Usher In the Post–Drug War Era, some three years after the GMO-Free Mendocino

Measure H initiative was passed, the redheaded single-mom scion of a Mendocino Redneck Hippie political family and the Measure H campaign activist, Laura Hamburg, saw her medicinal cannabis farm raided on October 25, 2007.

Fourteen (of the county's forty-three) deputies descended on her farm to charge her with three felonies. "I welcomed them at first," Laura said. "I couldn't imagine there would be any problem."

As Tom Allman was already the (if newly) elected sheriff at the time, and even though the pre-9.31 charges, as usual, were dropped—in this case due to a faulty warrant—Laura's father, Dan Hamburg, the former U.S. congressman for the district encompassing Mendocino, was and is not pleased by his daughter's treatment.

"If she'd been home at the time," Dan Hamburg told me angrily, "they would have taken her daughter away. My granddaughter. We were growing for my wife's stage-four cancer treatments."

Cue Typical Small Town Hatfield/McCoy saga. I've seen dozens of these in my Alaska and New Mexico life. Three years later still, Dan Hamburg is the current Mendocino Board of Supervisors member who for a long time simply wasn't inclined to let any Sheriff Allman–connected initiative proceed without a struggle.

When we first spoke, back in March 2011, Hamburg railed against several of the provisions in 9.31. It's safe to say there was more bad blood between Hamburg and Allman than in a mad cow. If Allman liked it, Hamburg didn't. Their quarrel has included red-faced shouting matches during public meetings, ostensibly over the sheriff's budget.

But after some early stumbles and much legislative skepticism, 9.31 in 2011 actually banked the half-million dollars in permitting fees that Sheriff Tom predicted it would. So the Supes had to issue a tail-between-the-legs mea culpa vis-à-vis the Zip-Tie Program, from the "funny money" nadir to a pipe dream that actually came true: It saved the department having to let seven deputies go, as Sheriff Tom publicly staked his reputation that it would.

At its June 2011 meeting, the Mendocino County Board of Supervisors called off (they called it "delayed") their Sheriff's Department layoff demands. One of humankind's oldest cultivated plants had directly saved the department from having to lay off nearly 20 percent of its field staff. These are actual, public safety, on-patrol deputies, the ones that Sheriff Tom ceaselessly "prays" can be used to fight meth and domestic violence.

Thanks to some expensive yellow zip ties, everybody (except for DEA budget drafters, lawyers, and anyone else who depends on the Drug War's multibillion-dollar largesse) won. It gets better, if you're a venture capitalist following the cannabis market. By late in the 2011 growing season, Sheriff Tom was leading 9.31 evangelical delegations to other California counties. His September 6 presentation before the Humboldt County Board of Supervisors, for example, carried the aura of a media swirl following a celebrity promoting an upcoming film. Regionally it was big news.

People here want a Northern California cultivation NAFTA. Nasty interdiction was happening in other counties even as Sheriff Tom spoke before the Humboldt supes. To use alcohol prohibition terms, a "wet and dry" county model appeared to be forming.

In a sign of how big the Allman intercounty hajj was, Mendocino grower Jim Hill and his botanist, Sharif Moye, opponents of 9.31's restrictions, took a day off from farming and flew up in Jim's Cessna to attend the Humboldt hearing in person.

Even more telling, five years after deputies working under Allman raided her own cannabis farm, the same Sheriff Tom was now helping the daughter of his nemesis, Dan Hamburg, design the security for the fledgling in-county closed-loop medicinal cannabis collective, Mendocino Generations, that she founded and was managing.

"We're using only in-county, 9.31 certified medicine," Laura Hamburg told me. "You know who grew it, where it's from, and what's in it."

The younger Hamburg said she views the permitting process as "a route to healing: not just for Tom and me, but for the whole community. When you actually see people from the other side in any debate, you realize they're human. And then you can usually find a middle ground."

Evolution, indeed. In the end, Mendo doesn't let its personal vendettas get in the way of what is widely regarded as good policy. Or, as Leslie at the food bank pointed out to me when we saw a fellow—a senior citizen, in fact—wearing a cannabis-leaf-logoed ball cap during a produce run, "Yep. People like to root for the home team."

There was more good news to come for 9.31 in the summer of 2011. Sealing the deal for the program's apparent success was something Sheriff Tom told me during the Gaia Festival on August 7, 2011. While working with federal authorities on the big national-forest raid of undocumented polluters for the previous two weeks (the aforementioned Operation Full Court Press), he'd flown twice every day directly over an "unmissable" twelve-foot-long, ten-digit, two-color official 9.31 permittee identification banner near the town of Covelo, very close to the Full Court Press landing pad.

"Not one" of his federal law enforcement colleagues, Tom informed me proudly, "said a word about it."

These banners are supposed to let aerial state and county law enforcers know when a farmer is in compliance with local growing regulations. Each banner is synced with GPS coordinates so that no one can simply print a banner without joining the program. Conceivably, though, it could be like catnip to a DEA team leader already funded and on a raid where "plant seizure" numbers were sure to (and did) make headlines.

This was the kind of thing that kept Tom Allman up at night. Some backwoods county could pass any ordinance its Redneck Hippies wanted to, the nightmare goes. Technically, federal law was being broken. Trying to explain the nuances to a reporter in Wichita might not be so easy. Much of Middle America is still trained in a forty-year-old mantra: "Drugs! Could be a stalker! Maybe even a terrorist!"

Under the dolphin murals in the festival geo-dome where he

had just completed the Cannabis Cultivation Panel, with some kind of Caribbean calypso jam seeping in from a nearby stage, I asked Sheriff Tom if he took that silence to indicate acceptance of the program. I wanted to know if surviving the federal "eye" was a sort of turning point for 9.31.

Allman, white shock of hair framing purple polo shirt and, yep, there they were: the kind of white tennis shoes that would have any cannabis farmer in America screaming, "Cop trying to look casual!" smiled at me. "Yes," he said.

Overall there were a lot more smiles at the Gaia Festival panel than the previous week's Full Court Press press conference in Ukiah, at which Allman did not dress in purple, and some of his colleagues were armed. In fact, it was hard to avoid the impression that on Wavy Gravy's farm Sheriff Tom was back among his peeps. He certainly seemed more at ease than he had when the Napa-based U.S. congressman for Mendocino, Mike Thompson, conferenced in from D.C. on the eve of a debt ceiling vote, had praised him with hands-down the operation's best unintentional double entendre: "Tom, we all know, has been living and breathing this issue for years."

Even at a time President Obama was signaling no inclination to end the Drug War, the 9.31 Program had held up under close federal scrutiny. The ninety-nine-plant limit, combined with (what seemed at the time) a slightly less fervid drug warrior at the helm of the Department of Justice's Northern District U.S. Attorney's Office than the one the poor Eastern District of California got stuck with next door,* Sheriff Tom felt, had proven an effective strategy.

U.S. Attorney for Northern California Melinda Haag, whom I briefly met during Full Court Press, and the rest of the federal

---

* This where—to a legitimate farmer like Matt Cohen—ugly busts of small farms and intimidation of local municipalities that were even considering cannabis permitting were unfolding weekly. The city of Chico's council members, for example, were threatened with federal prosecution by Eastern District of California U.S. attorney Benjamin Wagner, because of pending dispensary ordinance plans, according to a July 21, 2011 article in the Contra Costa Times.

deciders, Mendo thinking went, must've felt "respected." Although even Ms. Haag threatened the Humboldt County city of Eureka in September 2011, when the city attorney there was foolish enough to solicit her opinion on its new dispensary ordinance. After all, when asked, it's her job to enforce the Controlled Substances Act, which contends that cannabis is more dangerous than meth or even alcohol. Mendocino doesn't ask. Not publicly. It's the "better to apologize later than ask now" school of policy implementation.

The Full Court Press show left town after reclaiming Forest Service land from three dozen toxic illegal grows and seizing 632,058 plants and at least twelve foreign nationals. That left only comfortably smaller, nonmilitary-looking choppers echoing across the Mendocino hills, and you could almost hear the county's residents, including the sheriff who had organized the operation, emit a collective sigh.

And, oh, by the way, in what many in the cannabis community took as a sign of things to come, on the same day as the 2011 Full Court Press press conference, California governor Jerry Brown canceled state funding for the legendary CAMP (Campaign Against Marijuana Planting) program of annual cannabis raids. Indeed, I found this out via text while sipping federally funded Mendocino wine and listening to a U.S. attorney tout those "at least twelve" foreigner arrests at the press conference.

What was increasingly locally considered the economic miracle of the Zip-Tie Program had endured a major game of chicken in what was still, federally, the Just Say No Era. The feds came, they saw, they ignored; 9.31 was now, in many farmers' minds, over the hump.

It turned out to be a premature assessment. Still, if this book is being read ten years following publication and federal cannabis prohibition is over, 9.31 can be looked at as a Declaration of Independence, and 2011's Operation Full Court Press can be seen as a sort of Lexington. There are, Mendocino's sheriff is saying publicly, Good cannabis farmers and Bad cannabis farmers. Many people, Sheriff Allman included, never thought they'd see the day.

The fact is, in economic times as desperate as 2011, *any* home-grown industry that provided half a million in municipal revenue would be understandably grasped upon, rather like a life vest presented to a drowning swimmer. Cannabis is simply an obvious natural fit, in every way, for a county suffering as much as Mendocino. It's here, for one thing. The home team. Someone just needs to OK the agricultural commissioner to talk about it.

This is how harsh the economic situation was as 9.31 hit its stride in 2011: Librarians were looking for second jobs as bud trimmers—cannabis farmers being about the only folks hiring documented Americans. The Sheriff's Department sure wasn't. A March 17, 2011, headline in *The Willits News* pretty much summed up many headlines that spring and summer: "County Employment Drops Again."

I myself felt the fiscal pain when the actual Willits Library hours didn't match its website's: Budget cuts had it down to three days per week, and I had to explain to my disappointed, Dr. Seuss–seeking three-year-old about the national debt. I found it tough to coordinate budget cutback hours with my busy cannabis-field-visiting schedule. Same with a family visit to the coast: On a late summer Friday night, only 25 percent of one state park's campgrounds were open (at thirty-five dollars for a tent site) and our choices were limited to camping beside some kind of Harley-Davidson-based human sacrifice or finding a hotel.

The rhetoric behind the Zip-Tie Program's endurance and maturation is powerful in itself. But let's examine what it means, in bottom line value, that the 9.31 Program grew by fivefold in 2011. If most of the other 98 percent of Mendocino cannabis farmers similarly chose to "get permitted" in 2012 or 2013 (let's say there's a conservative five thousand of them here), the permitting fees alone would generate in the neighborhood of twenty million dollars for the county. And that's not counting law enforcement savings in incarceration costs, and deputy hours freed for Sheriff Allman's "real problems."

That twenty million dollars represents public safety revenues alone for one rural county on the medicinal production side. Not even sales tax and other revenue sources that fund roads, schools, and librarian hours. Map those kinds of numbers from a regional medicinal/social crop onto a nationwide industrial core, add on revitalized domestic hemp textile and biofuel arms, tourism legs, and food market head, and you start to see why some legitimate calculations put the value to the American economy of ending the Drug War at $80 billion, annually.

To put it another way, cannabis can play a significant role in helping America recover its financial footing, healing it in every area from trade deficit to national debt to agricultural productivity to foreign aid. That's one definition of *medicinal*. Perhaps Marvin Gaye wouldn't have had a hit if he crooned about "Fiscal Healing," but it's healing nonetheless.

# TWENTY-ONE

## How a Plastic Zip Tie Undergoes a 50,000 Percent Markup and Becomes an Insurance Policy

The amount of marijuana available for distribution in the United States is unknown; an accurate estimate regarding the amount of marijuana available in the United States is not feasible. Despite record-setting eradication efforts in the United States, the availability of marijuana remains relatively high, with limited disruption in supply or price.

—U.S. Department of Justice National Drug Intelligence Center's 2009 "Domestic Cannabis Cultivation Assessment"

It's a slippery slope. If it's not careful, the United States could end up helping the bad guys more than hurting them.

—Morris Panner, former assistant United States attorney, in the January 9, 2012, *New York Times*, commenting on a report that U.S. Drug Enforcement Administration agents have, over several years, laundered millions of dollars for Mexican drug cartels into banks including a Dallas Bank of America branch, in efforts to reach criminal leaders

Fiscal healing is terrific for municipalities. But what it means for any legitimate entrepreneur, especially in California, is government bureaucracy. Accordingly, August 12, 2011, was a big day in the ganjapreneurial career of Tomas Balogh. It was the day he was finally heading to Mendocino County Sheriff's Department headquarters in Ukiah. Why was he doing this? So he could pull out and badly dent his checkbook. Why was he doing that? For the right to openly announce, "I grow cannabis, officers. Lots of it."

In other words, zip-tie pickup day. I planned on joining. Starting a typically long day in my tough job this year, I kissed my Sweetheart and kids good-bye while ensconced in planet-erasing fog, and was soon touring Tomas's gardens under triple-digit sun. It was already another "the shade is too hot" summer day in Mendo.

This was an Eagle's Nest visit Tomas had inspired by announcing that Lucille had "reached puberty." That is to say, the days were getting short enough that the earliest-flowering indicas, unlike some of their tropical sativa cousins, were starting to bud. Powerful medicinal chemicals were at that moment developing as the fertile plants yearned to reproduce. The process lasted nearly two months in some varieties, amid the bees and the helicopters and the Pandora. The garden was now one big flower-making machine.

All Tomas had to do before we headed into the twenty-first century (that is, "town"), was water the eighty-eight ladies. And holy gazoley, on the sustainability front, I couldn't help noticing that cannabis sure can be a thirsty plant. The plants were now in their final two-hundred-gallon Smart Pot homes and immense to a one.* Some were pushing ten feet tall and eighteen feet around the widest leaf span.

Having seen other farmers using significantly more efficient watering methods than a daily hose soaking, and still somewhat shocked a couple of hours later by how water-demanding Tomas's putative sustainable crop was at the moment—up to eight gallons per day, per plant—the desert water-conserver in me decided to broach the topic. I had to—we're talking about more water than my young fruit trees drink back in the New Mexico high desert. And this all was going down while some parts of Mendocino County were in official water shortage conditions.

While we were en route to the sheriff's offices, I told Tomas about the Willits-based Dripworks irrigation company, which I patronized for my New Mexico ranching needs before I even knew

---

* "Smart Pots" are simply the brand name for sturdy, feltlike, foldable containers that, given the farm's proximity to Silicon Valley, didn't have the beeping automatic nutritive sensors I assumed they would from their name.

Willits was in Mendocino County, let alone which crop 90 percent of Dripworks' customers grow.

"Uses eighty percent less water than hoses or sprinklers and gives a lot more effective distribution," I lobbied. "You know, in case you're in pursuit of water neutrality on your farm."

"Next year," Tomas said, adding another item to the mental to-do list. Now that he was booted from the Eagle's Nest (or so he thought), he was through adding improvements to the place. Tomas also said that in future seasons he plans to implement the more biodynamic, in-the-local-soil method of planting that I'd seen at other Mendocino farms. He'd been reading up on native soil biology.

It was a good thing Lucille had already found her promised prime slice of local real estate on the east side of the upper garden. There was no lifting these plants anymore. Lucille herself was a small tree, and she was a mere child compared to the Super Silver Hazes, Sour Diesels (another strain in need of a name change), and (more aptly named) Skywalker women. More than one of these looked ready for transfer to Rockefeller Plaza. Indeed, when I saw the eight-foot spacing Lucille and friends were given back in June, it had seemed ridiculously excessive. Today it was revealed as barely enough.

I asked Tomas, now that I could see where much of the crop's flowers would be developing, if he had a prediction as to the final dry weight of the Eagle's Nest/Kama Collective harvest for 2011. Like all farmers everywhere for the past five millennia, he was loath to broach the topic. It ventures so far into Tempting Fate that people who work the land treat such questions as though someone's prying into their sex life. "Too early to say," Tomas said unusually brusquely. "This is the baseline year. Plus I'm going for quality, not quantity."

And so off to town. Always a mind readjustment for the rural American. Stop signs. Perfume. Headlines. The zip-tie-collection expedition itself was predictably friendly and surreal. Louise (call me "Lou"), the kindly, tiny, senior-citizen sheriff's office receptionist, thanked Tomas for being part of the program, while he filled out his $4,400 check for program registration and zip-tie fees.

"Thank you for *having* the program," Tomas the cannabis diplomat said.

"You bet," Lou chirped.

"Looks like it's really taking off."

He was referring to the fact that while we were waiting our turn, a man who had arrived before us asked for the county's landowner liability policy, since a renter of his wanted to join the program. "I think that's OK, but let me get you Randy's phone number," Lou had said.

All of us were surrounded by graphic antimeth posters, portraits of every Mendocino sheriff since the county's 1850 incorporation, and a valorious deputy photographed alongside George W. Bush after doing something heroic.

"It *is* taking off," Lou said to Tomas. "But, you know, you remind me of the initial farmer who came in here for his zip ties."

Lou shook her head and laughed at the recollection. "'First customer!' I shouted to the sheriff. My cousins were on vacation in Thailand and they saw the photo of me from the online version of the [*Ukiah Daily Journal*] newspaper. The whole family was calling me and asking me if it was true we were in business with pot growers. Ha, ha! They never let me forget it. Here's your receipt, dear."

"You should've told 'em you'd been undercover since the seventies," I suggested.

"I thought of that," Lou said, still laughing. This was the best-vibed sheriff's office you could ever hope to see.

Tomas was a customer, indeed. Seeing a check that substantial—only part of his official 9.31 investment—and the expensive packet of zip ties themselves reminded me of something Sheriff Tom had said just prior to one of our interviews five weeks earlier. Herding me into his secretary's office annex, he'd excitedly shown me a boxful of the zip ties. They were the kind people are always fixing old trucks like mine with.

So there they were. The famous, blinding yellow, fourteen-inch 9.31 necklaces that must collar every permitted plant's main stem. At $50 a pop, not counting an initial $1,005 registration fee and close to $2,500 in inspection fees.

While I pulled out my camera, Sheriff Tom said, "The guy in Jersey who makes these teases me. He says, 'How come I charge you nine cents for each one and you sell 'em for fifty bucks?'"

I looked up from the sea of zip ties and noticed the sheriff absolutely glowing with his revenue stream. His arms were extended like a game show host's displaying the grand prize. Or maybe just a creative administrator explaining his tactics in a time of budget crisis.

Then, sensing that I was doing some math as I looked at easily five thousand individual zip ties—what was clear was that the profit on zip ties was far greater than the wholesale price a cannabis farmer receives for a pound of medicine—the sheriff added, "I always like to remember what happened when we had a public hearing surrounding the fee increases for the program this year. Only two people spoke (holding up two fingers for me to watch in silence for a couple of long seconds). Both were in favor of even higher fees. Also veterans get a fifty percent discount."

Sheriff Tom really didn't have to protest so much. It struck me as credible to argue that a roughly $8,500 raid-insurance policy per farmer for a million-dollar crop wasn't too much to ask. If it worked. Most Mendocino County industry observers were saying by 2011 that 9.31 is far from a perfect ordinance, but that a lot of growers, who'd never even admitted what they do to anyone outside their families, believe it's a positive first step toward legitimacy. People were by now watching it from around the nation, thanks to a *Frontline* piece on PBS and other media attention.

Zip tie laden, Tomas and I returned to the Eagle's Nest to attach the eighty-eight labels, each with a unique plant identification number. Not the most rigorous of dexterous tasks, but someone immediately managed to misconnect a zip tie to an ancillary limb instead of to the main plant trunk on a Casey Jones hybrid.

OK, it was me, feeling superior journalism would result if I saw how a zip tie worked. But Tomas was buoyant all afternoon, and not just because he was finally zip tied, but because as we left the sheriff's office, yet another supportive friend, this one a graphic designer, had helped the cause by e-mailing him the logo for his Kama Collective's website.

Tomas called it up for me on his phone as we leaned on Sheriff Tom's SUV. It was best described as a wise female's inscrutable but blissful face—the name "Kama" is a Sanskrit word for one of the four essentials of life, encompassing wise wishes. Tomas said that after reading some business books about Internet marketing, he got the inspiration from "Nike," a Greek goddess of victory before she became a Swoosh. "You want something that stands on its own," he told me.

But to call the Kama model a woman was a stretch. She looked a little young to me, but, you know, I'm no hipster marketing whiz. I was still shouting "whazzup!" in 2010.

Maybe I should've said something then (I later did). Because mainstream cannabis legitimacy is central to Tomas's life mission. He prattled the whole bumpy way back to the Eagle's Nest about how dedicated he was to launching the collective endeavor with a sense of mission and "doing it right."

"I really want this to be a true collective," he was still saying during the zip-tying, which was timed perfectly for the purposes of mother mosquitoes trying to feed their families. "Get the patients involved, rent buses for field trips to the farm to trim their own medicine. Let the more mobile members get sicker ones to doctors' appointments. The senior Village Movement. That kind of thing."

Early ideas for the eventual Kama Collective website featured a button that read, "Take collective cultivation as far as you like." Click that and you'd be at a page explaining that you can reimburse for your own medicine as you do with tomatoes at the food co-op. Or you can come and water, or trim, or help fellow-collective members.

Tomas, overall, was at the "everything's going to work out fine after all" phase of the cycle, and I let him revel in it before the next logistical or meteorological disaster inevitably struck. Before I left that day to go blackberry picking with my family, Tomas said, "I feel something. Something that I think . . . I think it's lack of stress."

"Have you considered medicinal cannabis for that?" I asked.

His timing was good, when it came to taking a breath. The next part of the summer was known locally as the Lull: that beautiful week in August when the Full Court Press choppers were gone, the plants were in the ground, and much of Mendocino County was able to momentarily stop babysitting its plants twenty hours a day. That is, until the sleepless insanity of harvest and trimming began.

Additionally, Mercury was in retrograde, which gets noticed in a place where the bumper stickers tend to make me feel conservative. This meant that many of the more biodynamically inclined folks were of the considered agricultural opinion that caution was called for until the twenty-sixth of the month. A few thousand even took a day (mostly) off to actually leave the farm and attend, as I and my family did, the Gaia Festival in Laytonville. There they listened to India Arie on the main stage and the Cannabis Cultivation Panel in the dolphin-themed geo-dome.

This was an inside-the-bubble event. If you could handle a few alternative wardrobe choices and some open cannabis-medicating, it was also a child-friendly one. I watched one weeping kid get walked by a stranger to his not-quite-frantic mother, who was looking for him on the other side of the organic concession area.

At one point in between music sets, I identified myself as a journalist writing about the cannabis economy and asked one of the two deputies I found at the festival if his was a hard or an easy gig. "Oh, easy," he shouted without a pause, while a puppet parade noisily clamored by. "These folks police themselves."

That reminded me of something Mendo's district attorney Eyster had told me after the cultivation panel earlier in the day.

"When I fly over the county this year," the perspiring and smiling DA had told me outside the dolphin dome under some Tibetan prayer flags, "I see fewer large illegal grows within our borders than in the surrounding counties. I believe that's because more and more farmers know about 9.31 and are either growing within its numbers already to avoid attention, or are planning to join, or have already joined."

"Oh, yeah," I said. "I heard you've been giving busted growers the option to join 9.31 instead of being prosecuted. How's that going?"

"Great," he said, while a bare-breasted young woman meandered by eating a slice of watermelon. "I think the program's over the ninety-permittee mark now, and we're glad to be funneling some qualifying folks into it. Saves the county tens of thousands of dollars."

When I got an aerial view of Mendocino County the October morning Tomas and I chartered a plane for an hour and a half, it sure seemed like there were a lot of gardens down there. A lot more than you see or even smell driving past the U-turn advisory signs in the hills. Like, a plot of Smart Pots in pretty much every yard in some neighborhoods. "Ever been this high?" Sandy, the pilot, joked. She was actually anticannabis for religious reasons but favored legalization to end black market violence.

After ten minutes in the air we lost count of how many cannabis farms we'd seen—very few of which had 9.31 banners. But then Sandy knew where to look. In truth, though, you have a good chance of seeing obvious gardens and almost individual plants on Google Earth's higher resolutions when looking at any given swath of Mendocino County. I got some great aerial photos of the Eagle's Nest that day.

But Eyster was absolutely correct—we didn't spot very many farms larger than a hundred plants, and most were under Mendo's "we won't hassle you even *without* a permit" limit of twenty-five. Keep in mind twenty-five plants can still bring in more than 150 pounds, or five hundred thousand dollars. Still, pilot Sandy had noticed the change too. "It used to be like Kansas down there—rows and rows of plants. Now it's a lot of smaller farms."

Back at the Gaia Festival and judging by the line of people waiting to speak with him, David Eyster seemed that sunny August day to be a very popular DA.

And why shouldn't he be? The legal, permitted cannabis industry had already, midseason, provided close to half a million dollars to the Mendocino County coffers in 9.31 fees alone, saving seven deputy jobs. That was on top of state sales taxes, subsidiary contributions to the U-Haul, Smart Pot, and compost industries, and jobs for trimmers and couriers. Not to mention prosecution and jail cost savings for those steered toward legality rather than Punished with the Process.

What I was seeing outside that dome, alongside the painted sea nymphs and the giant soap bubbles someone was blowing, was more than the sight of a prosecutor networking with cannabis farmers. I was seeing the template for a workable, post–Drug War economy. The Gaia Festival's performances, seminars, and locavore concession stands made me begin to wonder if maybe my family'd be able to resume patronizing my favorite New Mexico Italian restaurant once the rest of the continent caught up.

It was around this time that the term *Drug Peace* started entering my head. I was seeing it in practice. It seemed to be working.

# TWENTY-TWO

## In Which I Discover That I Had Already Run the Gauntlet— and Learn of the Northstone Two

In light of California's decision to remove the use and cultivation of physician-recommended marijuana from the scope of the state's drug laws, this Office recommends that state and local law enforcement officers not arrest individuals or seize marijuana under federal law when the officer determines from the facts available that the cultivation, possession, or transportation is permitted under California's medical marijuana laws.

> —2008 California attorney general's Guidelines for the Security and Non-Diversion of Marijuana Grown for Medical Use. The then–state attorney general who drafted those guidelines is current California governor Jerry Brown.

If what they're doing isn't legal, no collective or cooperative is legal.

> —John McCowen, elected Mendocino County supervisor, on the "Northstone Two," the employees of 9.31 Program permittee Northstone Organics, who in 2011 were facing felony charges and ten years in prison in Sonoma County for trying to deliver labeled medicine to patients there

**T**he Drug Peace was working in the Bubble³. But the federal mis-scheduling of cannabis has resulted in a downright schizophrenic legal situation in large swaths of the now-eighteen medical cannabis states (sure to be more by 2014). To give one example, on September 29, 2011, Rhode Island's governor, Lincoln Chafee, announced that after five months of discussion, he was canceling plans to open three medical cannabis dispensaries in the Ocean State because he had "received communications from . . . the United States Department of Justice . . . that large-scale commercial operations such as Rhode Island's compassion centers will be potential targets of 'vigorous' criminal and civil enforcement efforts by the federal government."

And yet, the governor said in the same statement, "I remain committed to improving the existing medical marijuana cultivation and distribution system in Rhode Island. I am hopeful that the General Assembly will introduce new legislation in the upcoming session that will . . . not trigger federal enforcement actions."

For cannabis activists, eventually this "One Step Forward, One Step Back" syndrome results in a de facto sideways shuffling in place—sort of like a Deadhead dancing in a crowded coliseum. Even months prior to Rhode Island's latest shuffle, the constant teeter-totter situation was hammered home for me before a 9.31 meeting. In the parking lot of the Willits Community Center, I got an unexpected response upon telling Matt Cohen of my recent adventures with the Sonoma County Sheriff's Department.

Cohen's response there in the drizzle was to blink. He kept blinking, very occasionally, when I told him the part of the story where I found myself sitting in Deputy Londo's car wondering if Sonoma County's jails permit conjugal visits.

"If they were going to lie about smelling cannabis, what else would they lie about?" I inveighed with profound self-pity.

When I finished, Cohen blinked three more times, I think it was, before he noticed that I seemed to expect some kind of reaction. Along the lines of "Holy Shit! How much in civil rights damages are you suing for?"

Instead he checked that he didn't have to take an incoming call and then said, evenly, "Dude. You're bumping in a big, rambling truck across the Sonoma line? Let me guess. Bob Marley's blasting out of the speakers?"

"It was Steel Pulse," I corrected defensively. "And my tires aren't as knobby or as jacked up as you generally see around here." I had already noticed the perpetual monster-truck show that passes for normal traffic in the Mendocino hills.

"Of *course* you got profiled," Cohen continued, undeterred. "Ever take a gander at yourself? You look like just another grower. I've got two delivery guys facing felony charges from running that stretch of the Gauntlet right now. [Shrugging] Cost of doing business."

"The Gauntlet?"

"Highway 101 from the Sonoma County line to the Bay Area. When you're not in Kansas anymore."

I suppose it was true. Same scruffy beard.* Same (seasonally) muddy Carhartts. Same vaguely hircine smell. There were three other trucks from my model year in the lot with mine right then. Granted, on my own Funky Butte Ranch, back in New Mexico, I grew tomatoes, not a (however ridiculously classified) federal Schedule I controlled substance. But Cohen's point was that the Sonoma County Narcotics Squad didn't so much pinpoint that I'd gone native, as that I'd arrived already native.

"Your veggie-oil exhaust probably gave them the munchies," Cohen suggested waggishly while I was thinking it all over.

I heard endorsing laughter from behind me as more farmers who could play me in the movie arrived at the meeting. Well, if the Redneck Hippie description fits. It's easier to laugh now, a year later. It wasn't so funny at the time. In fact, my encounter with the employees of the Sonoma County Sheriff's Department was so decidedly unfunny when it was unfolding that those who have experienced the phenomenon tell me that it qualifies as a viable if mild example of that criminal justice phenomenon cannabis entrepreneurs and providers call Punished with the Process.

I thought back on Jim Hill's description of the practice as a game. "My advice to other farmers is, the sooner you recognize the rules, the better off you'll be," the twice-raided, never-convicted Hill says often of cannabis's bumpy progression toward legality on

---

* Charles Hill, Mendocino County medicine deliveryman for his brother Jim's two Southern California collectives, told me, "I don't have facial hair and I'm eighty percent of the way there," when it comes to avoiding law-enforcement profiling in unfriendly counties. Matt Cohen's attorney told me he'd advise "avoiding rental cars." My guess is that being female would help, too, but I personally wouldn't be willing to go that far if I were in the business.

all levels. "If you're raided, you'll understand what's happening and you won't be scared."

Now that it had happened to me, in the form of a brief police car imprisonment and implied threats of further incarceration, I understood that the Punished with the Process strategy is this: Anticannabis law enforcers and district attorneys might know quite well that they haven't a prayer of winning a jury conviction in increasing swaths of the procannabis U.S. (Sonoma County voters supported the full cannabis legalizing Proposition 19 in 2010 55 percent–45 percent, for example), but they can (and do) separate kids from parents for a day or two, seize seldom-returned cash and assets, and otherwise act in a constitutionally questionable manner. This before dropping cases weeks, months, or even more than a year later. "That's the game," Hill says. "Learn the rules."

I now know at least a dozen people who have experienced Punishing with the Process in unambiguously legitimate state medical cannabis cases. One sixty-one-year-old patient named Diane Fortier, of Santa Rosa, California, wept to me when she described her partner's missed delivery of his pancreatic cancer pain medicine in October 2010.

"It's night and day: The effects of radiation are hugely reduced by his cannabis regimen. It eases the pain and increases his appetite. He has good days when he has cannabis. It is criminal that they would stop that delivery—and it happened to us twice."

Fortier was referring to what I was calling the Northstone Two, a case in which two of Matt Cohen's Northstone Organics Co-op delivery drivers were being prosecuted in Sonoma County. These were the felony indictments that he had called part of the "cost of doing business" during a hectic period in humanity's relationship with the cannabis plant.

"I've known about the properties of cannabis because I worked for hospice for a number of years," Fortier said from her senior community. "It hands-down helped. I saw it right in front of my eyes. So I had been using it to treat my own severe arthritis, and I felt good about it for [partner] Bill [Harney, fifty-eight]."

Those are two patients Punished with the Process. The Northstone Organics Co-op, remember, has seventeen hundred patient members. California has between two hundred thousand and a million medical cannabis patients, depending upon whether you believe a 2011 UC Santa Cruz study or NBC Los Angeles. The Santa Cruz study, published in *Journal of Psychoactive Drugs*, also found 80 percent of participants said they had tried prescription medication before seeking cannabis recommendations. Participants also reported lower rates of alcohol, cocaine, and methamphetamine use than noncannabis patient rates.

Even Sonoma's own Santa Rosa *Press Democrat* coverage conveyed outrage at the treatment of the Northstone Two, whose medicine was packaged and labeled with the names and addresses of every patient, and included credit card receipts. Here is the lede from a May 21, 2011, article:

## Mendocino County pot club deliveries run afoul of Sonoma County deputies

Northstone Organics, a medical marijuana cooperative based in Mendocino County, appears to be about as legitimate as such an organization can be.

It has a Mendocino County Sheriff's permit to grow medical marijuana as a cooperative, undergoes county inspections, and its plants are tagged with Sheriff's Office zip ties, a measure aimed at protecting them from being seized by law enforcement.

"If what Northstone Organics is doing isn't legal, no collective or cooperative is legal," said Mendocino County Supervisor John McCowen, who spearheaded the county's medical marijuana permit program.

But the legal precautions, which cost the cooperative about $8,500 a year, could not guarantee safe passage of marijuana through Sonoma County.

> Daniel Harwood, 33, of Willits, and Timothy
> Tangney, 29, of Lucerne, were twice stopped by
> Sonoma County Sheriff's deputies in October
> while driving through Sonoma County on their
> way to deliver medicinal pot to co-op members
> in the Bay Area. Both are members of the cooper-
> ative.
>
> The two, who were stopped on consecutive
> days, were told they were pulled over for traffic
> violations: speeding in one case and not using a
> turn signal in the second instance. Deputies said
> the smell of pot led them to search the vehicles,
> confiscate the marijuana, and issue citations to the
> alleged offenders.

Felony citations. In other words, tickets. That stood out to me. Harwood and Tangney's crimes were serious enough to be felonies but not serious enough to warrant arrest? Kinda undermines the Merriam-Webster definition of *felony*, which is, in part, "a grave crime formerly differing from a misdemeanor under English common law by involving forfeiture in addition to any other punishment."

The Northstone Organics Co-op was handling legal costs for the Northstone Two, and it's safe to say there would be no settling. Minor "Process" hassles of his own aside, Cohen, a fellow working his dream job, had the forbearance to patiently hear and comment on my own Sonoma sob story that day before the 9.31 meeting. And I'm glad I heard his take. I'm particularly grateful that he gave me his shrugging "cost of doing business" assessment of twenty of the least pleasant minutes of my life—and I'm a fellow who once had to review a Paula Abdul concert.

Because as I slid home from that spring 9.31 meeting, the usual wedding cake girdle of muck-glued local flora drying like detailing on my truck's exterior, Cohen's acceptance of what seemed (no matter what one's views of the plant) cannabis's outlandishly subjective legal limbo left me wanting to understand something. Something even more than the answer to a simple question like "How common is the 'we smelled marijuana coming out of your truck' ploy?" in Sonoma County or other counties operating with a similarly antiquated anticannabis MO.

I was thinking bigger picture. I was wondering how it was possible that in one county a group of people could be considered patriotic, hardworking, and taxpaying agricultural professionals, and in another, just to the south, profiling targets. Felons. Not federal felons, but felons right here in medical-cannabis-approved California.

Given MendoGrown's dollars-and-cents focus, given poll numbers showing a solid majority of Americans supporting medical cannabis, given even the American Medical Association's support of research into same, given flipping FDA patents for same, for crying out loud, why did old-school Drug War Punishing with the Process still exist in 2011, especially in California? The voters were quite clear in 1996's election: medical cannabis is legal in the Golden State. How the heck are cultivators supposed to get the crop to patients?

There had to be a concrete reason roadblocks like the Northstone Two's charges were still being thrown up even in a county like Sonoma, where the electorate went 73 percent for Obama in 2008. To get to the bottom of that, I had to revisit those twenty less-than-fun minutes of unintentional Sonoma tourism. I didn't get much help from Sonoma County district attorney Jill Ravitch, whose assistant told me she can't comment on cases currently in litigation.

But the answer, of course, like most policies, lies in the do-re-mi. In other words (and let me know if you've heard this before): Follow the money. Federal asset forfeiture alone was worth more than a billion dollars in 2009, according to the *Sourcebook of Criminal Justice Statistics*, and the state of California took in $28,789,945 in seized property in 2009, according to a state attorney general's report.

These figures presume all seized cannabis and other banned materials are disposed of as mandated by law. And why wouldn't they be? Drug law enforcers are people and people are generally honest.

Sticking just with the state numbers, that means this innocent taxpayer's twenty minutes' property search near the Grab Some Buds billboard cost the seizure gravy train just under eleven hundred dollars.

Because that's what the Gauntlet is, as long as cannabis prohibition endures: a gravy train for Narcotics Officer Cash's crew and others like it all over the state. If they find cannabis and seize vehicles, or later seize boats and homes, ka-ching! If the accused in a case like the Northstone Two choose to plea and pay a fine, ka-ching! If arrest numbers are impressively high and the federal and state Drug War money keeps pouring in, double ka-ching! In California, 24 percent of seizure assets go to the state's general fund, and under what's usually described as "a complex distribution formula," the rest is distributed to local law enforcement agencies. On the federal level, U.S. Attorney Benjamin Wagner unilaterally "awarded" Stanislaus County law enforcers $154,875 following one raid, according to *The Modesto Bee*. Federal asset seizure doesn't even mandate returning property if no criminal charges are ever filed.

The premise of profiling was familiar to me from my fishing days in Alaska: Throw a net at the right place and time and you'll probably catch salmon. Along the Gauntlet, I was the odd jellyfish. After all, a lot of dented, oversize trucks rumbling through Detective Cash's jurisdiction come not just from Mendocino, but from Humboldt and Trinity counties (those other two points in the famous Emerald Triangle). And that doesn't include Oregon, Washington, and British Columbia.

It also doesn't include the U.S. Mail. I'll never forget my green, leafy moment at the Ukiah Post Office soon after arriving in Mendocino County. Extracting the postage payment from my pocket,

I carried with my quarters some shards of hay from a final New Mexico goat milking.

"Yeah, alfalfa, right," the Mendo postal clerk said of my apologetic counter swipe in March of 2011. "Baaah. Do you want insurance on that . . . package?"

Sonoma County—which has cannabis collectives and dispensaries of its own, and parts of which in 2011 were far friendlier to medical cannabis than many California counties one could name, for fairly transparent reasons including voter demographics and proximity to the Bay Area—hasn't yet made the decision to focus on raising revenue in a regulatory, zip-tie-esque manner. Though cannabis being ubiquitous everywhere except Antarctica, it could, easily, and areas of the county that do allow dispensaries sure benefit from the tax proceeds. It instead still mainly profits from the other, older Drug War model—the leading model since the Reagan Era asset forfeiture laws began: pleas, fines, and property seizure prior to conviction or even indictment. Punishing with the Process.

To this day, former drug agents have told me, the real addicts in the Drug War are law enforcement agencies, hooked on the value of cars and boats and homes—plus the cash—that belong to the citizens they are supposed to be serving and protecting. Sometimes, one former federal contractor told me, the law enforcement discussion during a raid sounds like the winner's circle in *Wheel of Fortune:* "Looks like we got us a boat, Lieutenant."

That's fine, all but the most intense anti–Drug War activists say, but seize from criminals: from meth manufacturers, say. Not from taxpaying Californians honestly doing everything they possibly can to follow state law, like Cohen and his employees. The Northstone Two, Harwood and Tangney, have been Punished with the Process, as of this writing, for more than a year. They are facing a possible ten years in prison, for doing their twenty-dollar-an-hour job, legally.

So the obvious explanation is that this "Less Than Zero Tolerance, tell everyone who meets the profile that their vehicle smells like marijuana" procedure is the quickest way to keep the Gauntlet gravy train running. Or to at least justify one's departmental budget. But it can't be good PR for elected Sonoma DA Ravitch. McCowen, also an elected official, embarrassed prosecutors by testifying *for the defense* in the Northstone Two case on September 15, 2011. So did Sergeant Randy. I was there.

Believe it or not, that wasn't the high moment in the preliminary hearing that day. That came when the prosecution's expert witness, none other than my compadre, Sonoma narcotics detective Andy Cash, testified that Northstone's medicinal prices, "if the quality was really A Grade Super Silver Haze," was actually a little on the low end of average, from what he'd seen from his undercover work.

When McCowen's turn came, assistant DA Scott Jamar, the poor sap who got this case, tried to paint the supervisor as a clone of his much more procannabis board of supervisors rival Dan Hamburg. Hamburg has cultivated the plant for his ill wife and I've heard him refer to it as "a blessing."

McCowen, by contrast, is a guy who wanted Ordinance 9.31 in the first place because "my Ukiah constituents felt that indoor growing in town was out of control." He told this under oath to a wilting Jamar from the stand during that September 15 hearing. He in fact has built a career out of *restricting* cannabis—reasonably allowing its Mendocino legality, but restricting nonetheless. In Mendo, that's a Reaganite. He puts the "devil" in *devil's advocate* for many Mendocino County farmers.

Because John McCowen is not an advocate of unregulated cannabis growing, those who are find him much, much too conservative. "I know some [Mendocino farmers] think I'm Satan," he told me. Jim Hill detests him.

Well, in the Green Rush Era in Northern California, a local conservative made the cross-county journey to testify for two questionably arrested cannabis medicine deliverymen in 2011. He said, "If Northstone is not legal, no one is."

As the amused courtroom audience filed out for the lunch

break, defendant Tim Tangney emerged and asked the world at large, "Did it sound to you guys like Cash was testifying for us?"

Everyone, including Northstone Two attorney Bill Panzer, nodded vigorously. "It was like you guys were working jointly," I couldn't resist observing.

Panzer said that the case, which was contentious that day, with lots of objections from both attorneys seemingly for breathing wrong, was hurting his friendship with prosecutor Jamar. "Scott asked me why I'm being so aggressive in front of the judge and I told him, 'I'm offended that you're bringing this case. You know you shouldn't be bringing it.'"

The Northstone Two case is still tying up Sonoma County courts. They're still, in fact, in preliminary hearings. The next hearing is in January 2012. In the period since the original traffic stops, 26,000 Americans have overdosed on prescription medicine, according to the Centers for Disease Control and Prevention, 500 have died from meth, and 23,199 have died of alcohol-related causes. None has died from cannabis.

It's hard to say exactly how much the Northstone Two farce is costing taxpayers—do we figure in the DA's salary? What about the real crimes going unprosecuted until this one is inevitably dropped or dismissed? One stat that is available comes from a California Justice Department budget analysis that says the state of California saved upward of a billion dollars while the plant was decriminalized between 1976 and 1985.

Cannabis continues to be medicinally understudied and only sometimes available from a safe, known source to Bill Harney, the Northstone patient battling pancreatic cancer. Pain and appetite are his biggest problems. "He's a trooper, though," Fortier told me. "Nearly always upbeat." As he waits for often agonizing episodes to pass, sometimes Harney is forced to take prescription painkillers for what relief they bring. And the American economy suffers too.

# TWENTY-THREE

## Panzer's Paradox

In the last decade, 6.5 million Americans have been arrested on marijuana charges, a greater number than the entire populations of Alaska, Delaware, the District of Columbia, Montana, North Dakota, South Dakota, Vermont, and Wyoming combined. In 2010, state and local law enforcement arrested 853,838 people for marijuana violations. Annual marijuana arrests have nearly tripled since the early 1990s, and is the highest number ever recorded by the FBI.

As has been the case throughout the 1990s, the overwhelming majority of those charged with marijuana violations in 2010—758,593 Americans (88 percent)—were for simple possession. The remaining 99,815 individuals were for "sale/manufacture," an FBI category which includes marijuana grown for personal use or purely medical purposes. These new FBI statistics indicate that one marijuana smoker is arrested every thirty-seven seconds in America. Taken together, the total number of marijuana arrests for 2000 far exceeded the combined number of arrests for violent crimes, including murder, manslaughter, forcible rape, robbery, and aggravated assault.

—NORML.org

... besides causing thousands of deaths worldwide and costing billions of taxpayer dollars, the drug war's most serious collateral damage has been to undermine the role of civilian law enforcement in our free society.

—Norm Stamper, thirty-four-year police veteran and
former Seattle chief of police, in the *Huffington Post*, on
November 15, 2011

Another effect of the Gauntlet method of keeping the peace—and similar selective farm and dispensary raids all over cannabis-cultivation country—is that they make noncriminals feel like criminals. Like, say, me, a law enforcement supporter, on April 4, 2011. Such traffic stops often involve, as in my case, profiling by hardworking law enforcement professionals that is under the best of circumstances highly subjective. In my case, this happened with Deputy Londo's questionable statement that my truck smelled like cannabis. From my own troubling, if admittedly short, experience on the Gauntlet, the memory of which for a while had me scared anytime I saw a police car, I learned how quickly my own sense of my position vis-à-vis the law can prove decidedly subjective.

One minute I was signaling to exit Highway 101 in my truck, a little late for a phone meeting with a television executive, but— other than working with Hollywood—an innocent man, the next I was being marched, with my hands behind my back and my pockets emptied, into the back of a sheriff's car and wondering if Sonoma County's prison gym had treadmills or just free weights.

I remember that when Deputy Londo approached my passenger window and made the cannabis-smell comment, I was initially more mad than scared. This was Northern California, 2011, not Moscow, 1970. I'm a taxpaying, law-abiding father of two, damn it. I didn't say this, of course. In practice, I tend to use a lot of "sir"s when addressing people with guns.

Before I knew it, I was decidedly not a free man. In custody, I was, frankly, petrified—and continued to be for the good part of a half hour, never having actually seen the business side of a sheriff's car. No one asked permission to search my vehicle, let alone read me any rights I might still possess in the Patriot Act Era. So I guess I wasn't under arrest, but what, really, was the difference?

Then another idea frightened me further. I didn't think anyone had transported cannabis in my truck, but I *did* now reside in Mendocino County: What if one of my contacts or interviewees had left a nugget or a brick of medicine in my truck, which, desensitized to terpenes from my food bank runs alone, I simply hadn't noticed when I left that morning after a kite-flying session in the park with my family? If so, I hoped the cultivator also had left one of Mendocino's particularly distinctive yellow zip ties on the plant. Yikes! I'd just picked up a hitchhiker the previous day.

After ten minutes of this treatment, cooling my heels while watching my truck get pilfered, my thoughts were getting more nuanced. What if I confessed that I was on my way to an interview at a medical cannabis dispensary in the East Bay? Surely *thinking* about the plant wasn't illegal.

I mean, heck, at this point in my research, as the first leaves were unfolding on that distant second of a Mendocino crop, the grape, I was still kind of afraid to click on cannabis-related websites, for crying out loud.*

There were far too many unknowns here for my comfort. All I knew for certain was that I was apparently busted for nothing, and nobody who cared about me was aware of this. That and I owed my paranoid landlord an apology.

Yes, even at the time, even while feeling the beginnings of a minor trembling fit coming on, I sensed that I was receiving a bit of karmic payback that April morning. That's because for the entire month plus of my Mendocino County residency to that point, I had been telling my landlord, a longtime cannabis farmer of what you might call the old-school, helicopter-cursing, cash-economy school, whose cabin I had found on Craigslist, that he was being "so last millennium" when he insisted that such sketchy searches as the one I was experiencing were still happening.

Boring me and even seeming a little crazy, he had insisted repeatedly, almost daily, that kids of friends of his had recently been taken from their parents, and that assets had been seized,

---

* These days my Google ads tend to hawk heirloom Canadian cannabis seeds or DUI attorneys. I hadn't yet learned, when I had my Sonoma incident, that I had nothing to fear from small quantities of cannabis in California. That California highway patrolmen in Mendocino County had in fact been routinely letting documented medical cannabis patients off with cannabis in their vehicles, and that, even without the famous "doctor's recommendation," the California vehicle code said that as long as an ounce or less had spilled into my truck's crevices, I wasn't "guilty," anywhere in California, of more than an infraction like speeding. One local told me that when Detective Cash asked if I had a little or a lot of cannabis, "he meant twenty or five hundred pounds."

especially when people tried to transport medicine out of the county. He kept pulling rank on me because he'd been a farmer in the county since—gasp—'96.

"Oh, c'mon, Greg, this is *California*" had been my condescending refrain. "I saw a couple sharing a joint on the running trail this morning. You probably grow few enough plants to be legal in this county. Where I live, my closest neighbor got something like a seven-agency, airborne bust for thirteen plants that really were for personal medicinal use. You guys don't realize how easy you have it."

Instantly, that April morning, I began to understand why Stephen Stills sang, "Paranoia strikes deep." Having one's hands behind one's back will do that. "They" clearly *were* out to get bearded, battered-truck-driving Mendonesians. I suddenly grasped the depth of what I would later dub Panzer's Paradox, named for something prominent cannabis attorney Panzer had told me. Panzer was not just Northstone's lawyer but also one of the drafters of California's landmark Proposition 215, which started the Golden State's medical cannabis train in 1996.

"When it comes to distribution, there is no uniformity in cannabis legal interpretation now," Panzer said. "It's a free-for-all. Whether what you're doing as a medical provider is legal or not is still a matter for a judge or jury to decide, unless the legislature clarifies. Good luck there. In the short term, before federal reclassification, I believe it's going to come down to the voters again. So today a cooperative courier might believe what he's doing follows state law, but a deputy or a prosecutor might not."

In other words, it's a good time to be a cannabis attorney. And for the past forty years, it's been a good time to be a narcotics officer. The Drug War as fought since 1971 is essentially law enforcement welfare. A subsidy as much as agricultural subsidies are, although ag subsidies at least provide food. If you want to know what the Drug War has provided, well, ask a Mexican citizen in 2012. Or ask yourself if the fact that you can, on any given day, smell terpenes in much of Northern California indicates a winning strategy.

Not that cannabis deserves, in its effects, benefits, and level of addictiveness, to be lumped with dangerous drugs like cocaine and alcohol, but most estimates call overall drug-use rates about the same as they were two decades ago. Not a lot to show for our trillion dollars. And this is not the fault of our hardworking law enforcement professionals any more than the result of the Vietnam War was the fault of a corporal slogging it out on point in a rice paddy. If a war is ill-conceived at its core, as Sun Tzu realized twenty-five hundred years ago, it can't be won. In other words, millions of Americans don't believe that "less cannabis used" should be a national goal any more than "fewer bottles of fine wine drunk" should be.

Yet the Drug War profits continue to be spread around. Its beneficiaries don't want to lose the cash. When it comes to economic impact, in fact, an influential 2010 Cato Institute report titled "The Budgetary Impact of Ending Drug Prohibition" argues that the end of the Drug War will shift incarceration budgets and cartel profits into private, tax*paying* industries (instead of tax-absorbing ones) and their subsidiaries (worth eighty-eight billion dollars annually) that go far beyond Willits's clothing boutiques and garden shops.

For instance, there's the website and graphic design companies Tomas Balogh was in the process of hiring to design the public face of his Kama cannabis delivery collective. There are the chemical analysis companies he'd be contracting in order to let patients know which cannabinoids were in each strain of the medicine he grew. Heck, even the Sergeant Randy–recommended Ukiah Sign shop (Crawford's), which makes the twelve-by-four-foot 9.31 permit banner intended to ward off helicopters the way citronella does skeeters, is part of the Green Rush economy (cost per permit display: two hundred dollars). These are like apps to the cannabis plant smartphone: entire niches springing up in an open-source, entrepreneurial marketplace. The fellow I spoke to at Crawford's said the 9.31 traffic "brought in a lot of business for us."

And those garden shops sure are thriving: Mendocino County's eighty-six thousand residents have twenty-two serving them. Nowhere is this more obvious than on Main Street in the Mendo "wine" town of Hopland. It lost its hardware store in 2010 but gained a downtown cannabis club called Collective Conscious Apothecary and a hydroponic supply shop called Emerald Garden Organic, with both, some think not coincidentally, located a few doors down from Sunny's donut shop. Nearly all the local garden stores, incidentally, feature a 1.5-cubic-foot soil bag called Mendo Mix, a sack of which I tried out on my tomatoes in 2011. Worked well.

Sitting there in custody along the Gauntlet while my truck got professionally trashed, I now had clear evidence that my landlord had been correct. Someone in the Sonoma District Attorney's Office was of the opinon that the Drug War was still on.

My freedom (but not my driver's license)* returned, I wondered, isn't there meth and alcohol violence to deal with in Sonoma

---

* This I realized when I tried to fly to New York for a speaking gig the next day. That my driver's license wasn't returned was undoubtedly an honest mistake on everyone's part, even if you have to figure the law enforcers had been through this drill a few times before. Still, for eleven days, I couldn't even get a call returned from the Sonoma County Sheriff's Department evidence room, dispatcher, deputies, or detectives. Then I mentioned the Punished with the Process experience to Sheriff Tom during an interview back in post–Drug War Mendocino.

He asked me, "Who was it?" and then said with a chuckle, "Londo and Cash? They both used to work for me." He whipped out his cell phone, pressed speed dial, and I had an apologetic Andy Cash calling my own line before I left the sheriff's parking lot.

Seems he (Cash) had mailed the license back promptly. And for that I am truly appreciative—as I say, I don't think he's a bad guy or even a bad cop. Only, he used my New Mexico ranch's "physical location" as an address. It's not even close to my mailing address. Luckily, my postman knows me. I got it back weeks after the incident.

Not having my license for a few weeks wound up further helping this book's research. In fact, I was actually grateful to have to talk my way through Oakland International Airport's security with only a credit card and a shredded photocopy of my passport smelling like my last meal in Chile. That's because I learned from the Transportation Safety Administration (TSA) manager there (a federal official, remember) that medical cannabis patients can fly with their medicine—indeed even with their living plants—through the airport.

County? No wonder some folks call the Mendocino-Sonoma border the Cannabis Mason-Dixon Line.

For a few weeks after my incident, I thought that part of the answer might have to do with turf protection: Drug squads need illicit cannabis to fight unemployment. Their own. But in my first, windy ride with Sergent Randy, he disabused me of that Camo Cowboys notion. "Oh, no, law enforcement is a steady gig. You've always got a job somewhere."

In other words, if the Drug War ends, or at least if the War on Cannabis ends, there'll still be alcohol. There'll still be meth and massive prescription drug abuse, unfortunately, and, even worse, there'll still be domestic violence. The realization reminded me of something I once heard a Louisiana prison poet tell NPR: "Most folks are good. But you spend time here and you realize there's a reason some people are in prison."

In truth, the difference between a friendly county and an unfriendly county has a lot to do with the career ambitions or personal cannabis views of the local DA and sheriff. If you're a guy like Charles Hill, who has to get medicine to patients five counties away in Southern California, it can be confusing. You have to know the politics of each county you enter and plot your course accordingly.

That's because California in 2011 was pockmarked with dueling schools of Proposition 215 interpretation* that were working

---

"We ask that they lay it out in the container along with their doctor's referral," the officer told me, adding frankly, "I always worry if they're flying to a state that doesn't have medical marijuana."

Illustrating that Panzer's Paradox extends even up into the friendly skies, this is decidedly not the policy, as signs about every ten feet make clear, seventy-five miles north at Charles M. Schulz Sonoma County Airport. California in 2011 had cannabis-friendly and -unfriendly counties, and it had friendly and unfriendly airports.

* Another important and oft-scrutinized document is the 2008 California attorney general's *Guidelines for the Security and Non-Diversion of Marijuana Grown for Medical Use*. There will probably be an updated version of this released by the time of this book's publication. The document is important because it reflects the state's top prosecutor's recommendation to everyone else how to handle cannabis in the Golden State. The wording of Mendocino's zip-tie ordinance mandates compliance with these guidelines.

their way up the California courts: The same was also happening in Michigan, Arizona, Oregon, and other medical cannabis states. In fact, Panzer says, the Los Angeles County district attorney, Steve Cooley, who lost the 2008 state attorney general's race both statewide and in his own county, is so ideologically opposed to cannabis that he has participated in workshops propounding his "if cash is exchanged, it violates state law" argument. The medical cannabis law that followed Prop. 215, SB 420, actually says nothing about payment for medicine, but it does discuss "collective cultivation." That's vague enough to allow anticannabis prosecutors to test out whether they can bust legitimate providers like the Northstone Two for accepting payment.

It's thus probably not an accident, Panzer believes, that officers involved in the Northstone Two case called up several shocked and frightened patients to ask if they paid money for their medicine. The Northstone Two themselves, Harwood and Tangney, who told me they are terrified at the prospect of doing time but are unwilling to plea, routinely travel with what they regard as confidential patient records.

Cooley's premise is absurd: I pay money to the Ukiah Food Co-op for carrots just as I do at Safeway. The money is applied differently. At the Co-op it's used to support a nonprofit budget rather than to benefit Safeway's shareholders. But to me, the consumer, the transactions look the same. Cash for carrots. Same receipt. If I choose, I can volunteer at the co-op to get discounts on carrots. So, too, with medicine at many California cannabis cooperatives and collectives. The big hole in Cooley Think is easiest to see with hospice issues: How can a bedridden end-of-life patient possibly help grow the plants on the farm? Of course she has to pay with money. That's her contribution to the collective cultivation of the organization. Others might trim buds or deliver medicine.

In the case of the Northstone Two, one Sonoma County cannabis activist who worked closely with county DA Ravitch on her campaign said that she is "walking a tightrope" between powerful law enforcement unions on one side, and that feistily progressive

Northern California electorate on the other. You know, "the people" that Assistant DA Jamar speaks for in pursuing the Northstone Two case.

Panzer's Paradox is a problem that will have to be overcome, Matt Cohen asserted, from the venture capital perspective, if the industry is going to thrive. This is one reason why the George Soroses of the world donate so much money to ending cannabis prohibition once and for all. It's bad for business.

As seventy-eight-year-old Progressive Insurance chairman Peter Lewis put it in *Forbes* on October 10, 2011, "I'm supporting innovative ideas to move toward a system that would regulate, control, and tax marijuana. I'm [treating] it with the same seriousness that I treated my former work running a large corporation. . . . I deeply believe that we'll have a better country and a better world if marijuana is treated more or less like alcohol."

# TWENTY-FOUR

## Redirecting Prison, Inc.

As someone who has spent their entire career in law enforcement, I know we cannot arrest our way out of the drug problem.

—Office of National Drug Control Policy director ("Drug Czar") Gil Kerlikowske, 2011

The total number of federal cases has almost tripled from . . . 1990. . . . The Bureau of Prisons is operating at 37 percent over rated . . . capacity system wide, with high security institutions operating at 51 percent over capacity and medium security institutions operating at 46 percent over capacity.

—United States Sentencing Commission's Report to the Congress: Mandatory Minimum Penalties in the Federal Criminal Justice System, October 2011

**C**annabis prohibition might be bad for many conventional Wall Street–model businesses. But someone's going to have to explain one important thing to the immensely politically connected private prison industry and its sometime competitor, the rich, if hardworking, prison guards' union—bless 'em—even at a seventy-three-thousand-dollar average salary in California, it's not a job I'd want. What these folks are going to have to grasp is that they'll have to redirect their ambitions in the event of a legal cannabis industry.

Because the huge numbers of incarcerated Americans represent another significant slice of the Drug War's vast pie. California alone spends nine billion dollars a year locking people up, most commonly young men with relatively dark skin. Even Pat Robertson doesn't think this is the route to a stronger America. Prison spending today eats up 11 percent of California's general fund. Higher education? Six percent.

Reordering the incarceration industry's priorities won't be easy, though. Some—not me, I have faith—would say, "Good luck." The California Correctional Peace Officers Association (CCPOA), one of the nation's most powerful, spent more than two million dollars in support of Governor Jerry Brown's 2010 election—just 25 percent of its annual lobbying budget—and has since been rewarded with a new contract that includes unlimited vacation days. Not that I blame them for asking. It can't be relaxing working in a prison all day. And I support unions.

It's safe to say that, as with the DEA and Office of National Drug Control Policy (ONDCP) "education" budgets, some of the rest of that war chest goes to making sure jails stay full.* Prison guards need prisoners. Unless their role is somehow reimagined. I dunno, perhaps those not needed to supervise prisoners who have committed real crimes can help in non-incarceration industries. Moving the nation's grid to solar and wind? Prescription drug abuse and fraud control?

It's fun to dream, but no matter how the facts look on paper, any journalist who's done enough public sector work knows that to expect an administrator of a bureaucracy who has a mortgage and two car payments to consider abandoning the multibillion-dollar budget he's worked his way up to managing is to live in a Homer Simpson "Land of Chocolate"–scale fantasy. Change in drug policy is going to take citizen demand. A tipping point.

Still, I was surprised by the candor in DC-based DEA public affairs officer Rusty Payne's quote to me on October 14, 2011. I asked, "Does the DEA have a plan if cannabis is reclassified out of Schedule One?"

---

* In fairness, while the CCPOA did spend a million dollars fighting a 2008 California initiative that aimed to reduce prison overcrowding by giving non-violent drug users the option of treatment instead of incarceration, it stayed neutral on the state's 2010 effort to legalize cannabis. This gives some activists hope, and several told me it's that the lobby groups they'd also like to see change their approach include the California Narcotics Officers' Association, the California Peace Officers Association, and the California District Attorneys Association.

He said, "Our job is to enforce the Controlled Substances Act. That's what we do. People want to knock on our door. But they forget that Congress makes the laws. Congress can change the Controlled Substances Act anytime it wants. We don't pick and choose what laws are good. We enforce the CSA, whatever it is. If it changes it changes."

That was refreshing to hear coming from DEA headquarters, but it also involves a certain washing of hands of the situation. A "we're just following orders" mentality. The Drug War is not grounded in reality. It is grounded in inertia. I once saw a documentary in which a Rastafarian priest said, "You can try to pull the truth closer to your view and I can try to pull it closer to mine, but the truth is stubborn: it just stays where it is."

Probably a good person to consult about the, you know, actual facts on the ground is a cop. Better yet, a prison guard. Better still, someone who's both. Chad Padgett is a former corrections and youth services officer from Walton, Indiana, and a member of the national anti–Drug War group Law Enforcement Against Prohibition (LEAP). He's been on both sides of the Drug War.

"Marijuana prohibition does not work and never has," Padgett says on the LEAP website. "As alcohol prohibition showed, making a drug illegal is the single most effective way to put it in control of violent gangs and drug cartels. By prohibiting marijuana, government gives up the right to control and regulate its production, distribution, and consumption. If marijuana was brought aboveground as a legal industry, we could regain control over it. We can have safe streets or marijuana prohibition, but not both. We can prioritize violent crime and reserve horribly expensive and limited prison space for those who injure, kill, steal, and cheat others, or we can continue to prioritize a war on drugs which has not succeeded by any measure."

Another major player in Prison, Inc., is the private incarceration industry. What are the prospects for transitioning to a post–Drug War economy with the cooperation of the executives in this expanding sector? Not great, if history is any judge. The big

TOO HIGH TO FAIL

problem is a revolving door between the industry and government. One recent conflict-of-interest example is the "revolving so fast she must be dizzy" Stacia Hylton. She went, in rapid succession, from the Department of Justice, to a $112,000 consulting gig with billion-dollar private prison giant GEO Group, before returning to serve you and me as head of the U.S. Marshals Service. The good folks at that agency, of course, oversee private prisons.

We've already discussed America's dubious honor as the Most Incarcerated Society in History. Most are nonviolent kids who have run afoul of the War on Drugs. We've managed to quadruple the prison population in twenty years, ballooning from the 600,000 dependents on Prison, Inc., we fed and housed in 1991 to the 2.3 million prisoners currently serving time.

So, looking at Ms. Hylton's career trajectory, we can continue to follow the money for insight into why this increase came about. What is not in dispute is that both use and supply of illegal drugs have hardly changed in the same ensuing quarter century. But a couple of million kids now get a full-tuition ride at the University of Hardened Criminality. Some private prison contracts with municipalities even guarantee incarceration rates.

These statistics were already dancing around my head. But it wasn't until attending a preliminary hearing of Cohen's Northstone Two in Sonoma County on May 12, 2011, that I saw them: the people the Drug War most commonly imprisons. On that day, a dozen very frightened-looking young men in navy jumpsuits filled an unused jury box and tried to look tough while awaiting, no doubt, the single public defender who would be on call for all of their hearings. This, of course, is another reason Cohen's employees, Harwood and Tangney, are fortunate to be defended at company expense by Panzer, one of the most prominent cannabis attorneys in the state: they actually met their attorney prior to trial day.

Statistically speaking, of the dozen defendants seated in the courtroom, at least three were there for a nonviolent drug offense. And again, I'm not talking about pharmaceutical sales reps marketing antipsychotic medicine off-label to children. I mean the kind of crime that actually gets prosecuted. This in a state whose prisons are so overcrowded that inmates are winning constitutional violation claims and Supreme Court–ordered plans are under way to release some of the overload. Los Angeles County jails are slated to run out of space by December 2011, according to *The Los Angeles Times*. The proposed solution is simply to let "potentially thousands" of inmates go free.

Most of the navy-suited youngsters I saw in Sonoma didn't look like fellows I'd be scared to pass on the street at night. And that, to me, was scary. But it was nothing compared to the jolt I felt when the large bailiff leaned over my spectator bench and interrupted my reverie at that moment with the gruff demand, "Who are you and who are you with?"

I bolted upright. "Um. Doug [mumble]. Independent journalist . . . in a public courtroom. Um, why?"

"You need to turn off that laptop in here."

"Oh!" I said, immensely relieved not to be joining the kids in jumpsuits over some online petition I once signed against fracking. "Right. Sorry."

"And take that hat off too!" another bailiff screamed from the other side of the courtroom.

If this civics lesson seems like something out of *Night Court*, please know that Cohen and Panzer can confirm every word. More importantly, I briefly caught the eye of one of the kids in the dock, but I couldn't hold it. I didn't know what would be most comforting to him. A helpful shrug? A thumbs-up?

From an economic standpoint, unless you consider America's young men to be a sacrificeable resource for the benefit of GEO Group and the rest of Prison, Inc., these needlessly incarcerated young men represent not just a policy run amok, but an obscenely gaping money pit—a financial shot in the foot to the United States' overall world strength. I mean, as a taxpayer, I'd say, "Keep half the current annual Drug War Budget and use 80 percent of that for real education and treatment."

Just do almost anything else with young men other than turn them into criminals. Let's not devour our own youth. I'd rather train them to make solar panels. Start 'em at seventy-three thousand a year, for all I care. You'll still be saving billions annually compared to current Drug War spending. Effective policy will bring thousands back into the fold as productive citizens. Which most of them probably were prior to arrest.

As for the hardworking detectives in the narcotics divisions of our nation's law enforcement agencies: I assure you you'll still have plenty to do if you just focus on meth manufacturers and wayward pharmaceutical executives. If current trends hold, their actions are still going to be illegal in five years. Johnson and Johnson is the latest drug giant to pay a billion-dollar fine for off-label marketing (for the antipsychotic Risperdal), a fine that amounts to 5.6 percent of the drug's sales, according to *Businessweek*.

The Drug War game is so visible, the incarceration/industrial complex's tactics have been applied for so long, that those who profit from it seem content to live in another galaxy while the rest of the nation wakes up. As the poll numbers supporting cannabis legalization continue to rise, the Drug War motors on as though nothing has changed. Ten years from now it will seem incredible that the Northstone Two were facing criminal charges for delivering cannabis. "The public is way ahead of us on this," is how California Republican state senator Chris Norby puts it.

Even today, if you're a prosecutor who's got to face a Mendocino County or a Sonoma County jury, arresting legitimate providers whose cooperative can afford attorneys quite simply will backfire. The public doesn't want that, and it's only going to help the cause of changing drug policy.

If the momentum of the legalize cannabis movement and economy is a bull, the Drug Warrior legal strategy, as of 2011, is best described as a determined flea on its spine. Or, as Sheriff Tom puts it, "Medical marijuana passed in California in 1996. And some of us law enforcement folks thought, 'My God, the sun still rises. There is still an America. The world didn't end.' For the others of my colleagues who refuse to notice this, perhaps it's time for them to retire. Because it can be legal or it can be illegal. But marijuana isn't going away."

Indeed, when I covered the well-intentioned Operation Full Court Press interagency law enforcement raid in the Mendocino National Forest in July 2011, I got lost finding my media contact, who worked for the state Department of Fish and Game. He had given me a set of GPS coordinates, but I couldn't get phone service. I *did* find and get promptly ordered off my public lands by an armed U.S. Forest Service enforcement fellow in fatigues. Perhaps it was my hemp sun hat. In his eyes I recognized, from documentaries, the look of the career sergeant just trying to do his job (think Vietnam circa 1971) despite what everybody knew about the eventual outcome. Despite the current appropriations. His whole demeanor shouted, "Heard anything about this year's budget negotiations? Because this is my job, until I'm laid off." Punch in, punch out.

And, really, how psyched could this hardworking fellow be, when a week later *The Willits News* reported that none of the "at least twelve foreign nationals" arrested during the operation were still listed on the Immigration and Customs Enforcement website as being in custody. All Quiet on the Northern California Front.

# TWENTY-FIVE

## Lucille Harvest Emergency

This is Nick with the Mendocino County Sheriff's Office again, just reminding all the farmers about erosion control. The rains have started and if any of you have not implemented erosion control techniques yet, it's a good time to start. With the new rains, it is the most ideal time to lay down non-invasive erosion control mix. People have had good luck with clovers, barley, and sweet peas, but make sure whatever species being used is not invasive to the natural plant life. Other useful erosion techniques include laying down waddle rolls and erosion blankets. As always, hope everything is going well, and good luck with the rains. E-mail me back or call me if any questions arise.

—October 4, 2011 e-mail to permitted 9.31 cannabis farmers
from Nick Arendt, assistant to Mendocino County Sheriff's
Department sergeant Randy Johnson

**T**he 2011 cannabis growing season afforded me plenty of opportunity to visualize how it must've been for those first farmers in the Fertile Crescent. Maddening, often, is my guess. Punctuated by periods of formal, medically aided ecstasy.

I envision a lot of midfield fist-shaking at the Creator, followed by profound apology and cloth-rending several evenings later, when everything turned out OK again. Then the dancing began. Particularly after a strong harvest. Food for a year! That was akin to paying off the mortgage today.

As for the dancing: Somewhere there was a statue of the fellow who figured out what happens when you heat cannabis. Perhaps he or she was a time-erased prototype-Buddha. Because I'll wager my journalistic reputation that very few Paleolithic humans objected to what we today sometimes dismiss as "recreational use." That was almost certainly a synonym for "spiritual use." Have you *seen* some of the Anasazi pictographs? Archaeologists call one near my ranch "ceremonial." Above a corn storage bin, it features a man with a giant spiral head raising his arms toward the heavens.

In fact, I sometimes ask myself, "What is it exactly that anti-cannabis folks fear about a plant most cops consider a peacemaker?" What it seems to come down to is this: Cannabis in our bodies encourages the human system's natural non-punch-clock way of thinking about time. A day is just a day, is the realization. Carve it up any way you like.

On the one hand, this might be interpreted as the classic unambitious stoner outlook. Gotta stay focused, busy, and worried in order to succeed. But I think it worth noting that it's also a time view shared by the high achievers of this millennium: the digerati. This is a very cannabis-friendly demographic. It's why Seattle and San Francisco have both in practice legalized cannabis.

Steve Jobs called his psychedelic experimentation "one of the two or three most important things I've done in my life." And he went on to say that Microsoft would have been a more creative company if Bill Gates had just chilled out and medicated in a forest every now and then.

What we're broaching here is the topic of nonabusive cannabis use for healthy people. Health maintenance. *Homeostasis* is the medical term. What is the line? Humans throughout history have similarly asked, "What's just the right amount of celebrating, of encouraging non-punch-clock views of time?" This is why our various cultures have written in between one (Hmong) and 52 (Catholic) festivals during which "recreational use" of various time-alterers is called "religion."

We're talking divinely ordained medicating and dancing, people. Often with goats playing some philosophical role. This is how it's usually been. Even for many of the American Founding Fathers.

Having now lived on both sides of the subsistence lifestyle line as a child of the surburbs who then called rural Alaska home for years, I can say I prefer the less synthetic one. The closer to Paleo-lithic the better. Sure, you give up 3-D theaters and Frappuccinos, but you get to live by the seasons and notice shooting stars. And therein, I believe, dwells mental health. A Zoloft prescription isn't going to do you much good in a lion's den.

For my family and me, at least. Warning: This lifestyle might not be suitable for everybody and nothing contained herein should be considered an endorsement of any demographic choice. Wouldn't want too many folks buying up all the pictograph paint.

Still, no reason the neo-Anasazi home can't employ a solar-powered electric fan. Which I mention because there's nothing like four straight months of triple-digit, epidermis-melting sunlight to make a farmer forget that there's this thing called rain.

The fall rainy season began abruptly on September 29, 2011 in Mendocino County, and didn't stop for nearly two weeks. Then there was a surprising Indian summer lull. What this moisture meant for my family was a collective "Yee Haw!"

For one thing, the massive Pacific frontal masses had a washing-the-air effect. All the dog poop and blackberry residue were gone from my running trail. Bigger picture, as desert-dwellers, my family dances at any precipitation. We don't get many amphibians back home. We were prepared to bid the sun good-bye until New Year's, even though by October 5 I could already feel my vitamin D reserves slipping away into the spongy air. And I suspected (incorrectly) that both the defogger and the four-wheel drive would be employed for the duration of my California research. My kids puddle-splashed on a daily basis. They had the boots for it now.

Mendonesians looked at the slightly too-early coming of the rains very differently. The local view can be summed up in two words: *harvest emergency*. If I had taken that overflight in Sandy's aged Cessna three weeks later than I did, I would've thought I was in a nearly cannabis-free county. In practical terms, what the rains meant is I got a borderline panicky text from Tomas on October 1 reading something like: *"Lucille needs to come down tomorrow. Immed. mold risk from botrytis. Can U make it to Eagle's Nest to research?"*

Also in my in-box were terse, urgent e-mail exchanges between Tomas and scientists at his quality testing company, Halent Labs (he'd cc:d me). The company charged Kama Collective four thousand dollars for their work on the entire 2011 crop, including two site visits from the company headquarters in Davis, five hours away.

| | |
|---|---|
| From: | tomas@kamakush.com |
| Subject: | Re: Great to talk to you Colleen Halent |
| Date: | October 1, 2011 8:01:45 PM |
| To: | c.brand@halent.com |

On Sat, Oct 1, 2011 at 10:08 AM, Tomas Balogh <tomas@kamakush.com> wrote:

Colleen,

Great to talk with you the other day. Sorry for the delay in getting back to you but the early rains have had me in a mild panic. We discovered some botrytis and have had to begin harvesting early.

That said, let's get that call scheduled for early next week (Monday or Tuesday) and get the ball rolling. I'd like to get you guys out here to gather samples of every strain (12 total). Is it a problem if I (start to) harvest (half the crop) this weekend? The diesel strains and GDP won't be ready for a couple more weeks. Should I leave one plant of each strain in the ground so you can take a live sample? . . . Please advise.

Thanks and have a great weekend!

-Tomas

On Oct 1, 2011, at 7:16 PM, Colleen Brand <c.brand@halent.com> wrote:

Hello Tomas,

   I don't know if Nick got thru to you yet but here is his feedback. He suggests you harvest as you said as you're getting more rain early next week. Please feel free to contact him about the mold & any other questions you have. Please cc me so I stay on top of any situations that might come up & I can be sure we get you answers right away.

Thank you,
Colleen

This was weeks before one-step-at-a-time Tomas had been planning for harvest. And the harvest of hundreds of pounds of a perishable crop requires, to put it mildly, preparation. In the only recent conversation we'd had even touching on the topic, Tomas merely asserted that he was dedicated to avoiding the nightmare personnel issues surrounding the trimming of the flowers.

As has been the case with seasonal harvest cultures the world over from time immemorial, Mendocino County's population doubles around mid-September as the troupe of—in this case—professional bud trimmers begins drifting into town.

Cannabis flower maturation is to the seasonal employment picture in Mendocino County what the salmon run is to Alaska's. I started to see the workforce congregating in the park across from the Willits Safeway around September 15. You can't miss them. That thin strip of lawn and picnic tables becomes Shakedown Street each fall, and the Safeway parking lot itself often transforms into quite the party in the midnight hour and beyond. All over the place are supercuddly, pointy-toothed, just-weaned dogs whose puppyhoods are going to outlast the relationships of the human couples that adopted them.

In fact, demographically speaking, it's the same tuition- and adventure-seeking kids who once hopped on an Alaskan fishing boat who now hold day-laborer-style signs on the side of Highway 101 offering bud-trimming services. The savviest ones advertise

"Have Fiskars." This shows that they travel with their own industry-standard garden clippers, known for a "super responsive" spring mechanism that, Tomas told me, "just won't quit— otherwise you'd have tendonitis by the end of the first day." I've seen the clippers taped right to the signs. This is just forty miles north of where I was pulled over on the Gauntlet.

Anyone who's visited a suburban Home Depot early on a work-day will recognize the human clusters in Mendocino County towns in the fall. These are migrant farmworkers, essentially. Only with a higher than usual percentage sporting dreadlocks.

There is thus, in the fall, a lot of what you might call Seeker energy here. Youngsters, as they should, sniffing out their calling. These are most commonly people barely weaned themselves— more youthful even than the young punks savvy enough to get their own twenty-five clones started.

This is a valuable time of life, and one experienced by field researchers from Siddhartha to Darwin. Hit the road, look into what interests you, and see what happens. The whole "set off and seek your fortune" phase. I remember my own first such expedi-tion, to Alaska, in 1998. Granted I was hopping a Subaru to write a screenplay and not hopping a boat to catch king crab, but still, I did wind up unloading a lot of halibut boats.

You step out of your cabin or your tent each morning and you're a day closer to falling in love, figuring out what you want to to do with your life, or developing the algorithm that's one day going to fit into your innovative software design platform.

The only difference from the Last Frontier is that, this being California, union organizers are already on the case. Indeed the United Food and Commercial Workers Local No. 120, represent-ing 1.3 million workers nationwide, had already embraced the can-nabis employees of Oakland's industrialized indoor grow facilities and were in discussions with MendoGrown.

Matt Cohen thought this was a positive development, given that the bud-trimmer pool is not always the most disciplined workforce. As an employer—and farmers are often no better as bosses than they are as real estate traders—you have to separate a lot of wheat from chaff.

On the wheat side, Sharif Moye came as a trimmer a decade earlier and is now Jim Hill's full-time botanist. Cannabis is a growth industry. Show your worth and you've got a career. But work ethic arguments and trimmer expulsions are common. Perhaps more common than smooth harvest seasons.

"Some people just come up here for the scene and because of the abundance of medicine," George Fredericks told me. Some save their money and some smoke it away. The scene overall reminded me what an old Alaskan river guide replied when I asked him if his gig could provide a living. "Depends if you invest in bonds or booze."

One farmer in Canada considered the situation serious enough that he invented an automatic bud-trimming machine called "The Twister." It looks like the kind of contraption Daffy Duck would sell: a giant generator with all kinds of hoses and tubes. The company motto, splayed across its sophisticated home page, is "Because trimming doesn't have to suck."

Humboldt County has a Twister vendor named Joey Burger, who summed up his very successful sales pitch this way: "Yes, it costs fifteen grand, but it won't hit on your girlfriend when you head out on a beer run." Not sure of the union view on the device.

I should disclose that Burger, a lifelong Emerald Triangle resident and son of hippies, quickly added sheepishly, "'Course, I married a woman who'd come here as a trimmer. But it's the only time we growers in the hills get to meet pretty girls."

But the point is cannabis flower manicuring takes a long time and, without Cupid's presence, is often an employer headache.* Tomas seemed to have already learned these lessons when he summed up his hiring plans for trimming season. "Oh, only peo-

---

* Once Cupid does visit, trimming time is often family time. Lotta summer babies in Emerald Triangle culture.

ple I already know will be here after harvest," he said succinctly back in mid-September.

In other words, call in the Kama Karma Volunteer Brigade. Tomas's 2011 growing season was in the home stretch. By way of visualization, here is where I (finally!) get to insert the "cannabis growing is like golf" analogy I've been waiting to get in:

Becoming a professional cannabis farmer, I realized picking figs at the Eagle's Nest one evening, is like getting good at golf, with its three entirely distinct skill sets of driving, short game, and putting. In cannabis, it's cultivation, processing, and delivery.

Bud trimming represents the short game. You're setting up that crop—that you've doted on for hundreds of hours over so many months—for success. What you can do, if you're a farmer, is bring in short-game specialists. Because the golf world is full of great drivers who never win the Masters.

Jack Nicklaus, in his prime, would hardly ever miss an eight-foot putt in front of eight thousand screaming fans and a TV camera poised a few inches over the hole. That's pretty close to the nerves required for harvesting your yearly income and patients' medicine in two weeks with helicopters but hopefully not rain overhead much of the time.

And make no mistake: Though it's far from rocket science and closer to bonsai, trimming is a significant and acquired skill, especially when it comes to speed and efficiency. In fact, some of the best trimmers are also seasonal grape pickers. As Mendocino grape farmer Martha Barra said in an October 19, 2011, *Ukiah Daily Journal* article entitled, "Grape Pickers in Short Supply," "We don't know if it's because of immigration, or we happened to hit the marijuana picking season. It's easier to work sitting on a white bucket and trimming."

You'd think so, wouldn't you? She's right that all you're actually doing is "cleaning up" the plant after it's dried for a week. Your job is to ensure that it has final "bag appeal." That essentially means snipping off surrounding leaves so only the flower remains: the sticky green bud that had my college roommate so conditioned.

From there the buds can be stored in mason jars or vacuum-sealed in bags for up to a year. Some varieties even age well, Tomas said—with "curing" or "finishing" another similarity to vitaculture. But I was to learn that a sitting-down job is not necessarily an "easier" one.

A note on "bag appeal." As a sustainability journalist and organic rancher, I must say that the parts of the plant that must, as of today, be removed prior to "packaging" seemed like a tremendous waste as I witnessed the 2011 harvest. At every farm I thought, "Man, these folks clip off more cannabis than most patients have ever seen." When I mentioned this to botanist Sharif Moye, he took it even further: "It's possible that the natural-leaf-matter-to-flower ratios deliver beneficial cannabinoid balances that we're losing in the trimming."

The more I thought about it, the more the image of makeup and body shaving came to mind. No one can explain why it's thought more attractive in some Western nations for women to shave their legs and apply blue paint to their eyelids, but not too many question it. "Bag appeal" similarly seems to me to be arbitrary. Quite like a crew cut. I have heard it argued that when prices are high, people want to make sure that what's going on the scale packs the maximum punch, and buds have more THC than leaves do.

Still, it strikes me as likely that one day—particularly if cannabis prices drop with legalization, as many predict they will—many people will start asking where the rest of the plant went. Today it goes mainly into the edibles side of the industry—the tinctures and cookies and lozenges. So it's really not wasted.

But as many of the other cannabinoids besides THC are revealing themselves as having manifold medicinal properties, folks are going to start requesting the special ones by name. "Untrimmed" or "natural cut" cannabis might be quite the value-added product for people who today shop at Whole Foods or their local organic food co-op.

In 2011 even the most educated cannabis consumer is probably aware of only two cannabinoids: You basically have cancer-fighting CBD as the Avis to appetite-increasing THC's Hertz. But soon there's going to be Enterprise and Dollar and National on the menu too. Like the old Ragú spaghetti sauce commercial used to assure us: It's in there.

That's also why the pharmaceutical isolating or synthesizing of single components of the cannabis plant doesn't work well. The laboratory mind-set of "find something medical and concentrate it ten thousand times in a pill" is not one that maps well to a plant with which the human species has been coevolving for at least ten millennia. This is not merely the view of your Mendo crunchy herbalist. The widespread patient conclusion is that synthetic Marinol simply is not as effective as smoked cannabis or edible cannabis made from the plant itself.

Trimming, physically, is a deceptively easy process. Preservation of the trichome crystals on the bud is essential. It's a make-or-break process, as the THC resides in those crystals. And patients know it. Trimming is not conducted with the reckless abandon one associates with barefooted mushing of harvested grapes, although you do get the barefooted women involved.

Tomas wasn't about to take trimming, even emergency trimming, lightly. So much can go wrong even *after* a successful cannabis crop harvest, and everyone moves without cease, for fear of seizure, until the massive job is done. It's a tense, fast time.

As Tomas put it in October, "I don't think I'll really sleep well until all this medicine is on the other side of the Gauntlet, stored and starting to reach patients." That meant about a month as a zombie.

While Lucille could arguably be said to be peaking at the beginning of October—or close enough—Tomas had some tough decisions to make about some of the other, less locally hardy strains, like Casey Jones and Bubba Kush. The former was the high-THC, sativa-leaning prima donna of the garden. The wide receiver. At the time of his emergency text message, Tomas said that these strains "could use another week or two." But with frequent glances up at the saturated clouds, the Mendocino farmer motto in October 2011 was clearly "better a little early than never."

Botrytis, also called bud rot, is a fungus that can eat a plant from within overnight. Generally speaking, farmer Gabriel Martin said in a harvest lecture at his Leonard Moore cooperative, "You harvest when the plant looks autumnal." I'd noticed the same thing with the local blackberries.

Moye was a little more scientific. "It's a balance as the plant's chemistry matures to a peak level without overaging on the vine," he told me during a harvest-season visit to Jim Hill's Jurassic garden. "Similar to grapes—when it fruits or flowers, the plant loses its defenses against mold and mildew. I choose to watch very closely. In the end, I think you have to feel it, to know when the time is right to harvest. In the wine world, some farmers use sophisticated instrumentation to harvest at the ideal day or hour, and you might one day see that with cannabis."

What everyone knows, though, is that you only have those few days of peak plant moisture content to get the flowers harvested and ready for trimming. How long to let the flowers cure after trimming is a big topic of discussion. Moye finds this astonishing. "How is it after thousands of years of farming this plant, and thirty years as a local industry, we don't know how best to harvest it yet?"

"Sounds like you favor an end to cannabis prohibition," I observed. "You know, for research purposes. Conventions and networking and whatnot."

Otherwise known as Friday night at the Ukiah Brew Pub. Tomas also said that habitués of cannabis-growing blogs are usually very forthcoming with advice. Not long after I arrived in Mendocino, a time locals now referred to with an eye roll as *last* rainy season, I asked Matt Cohen if one had to be a particularly skilled farmer to grow cannabis. His answer surprised me. "Nah—so much of it is genetics by now," he said. "These are plants that know it and love it here. Anyone can learn the basics and do it."

The bottom line for this industry, then, is that Rock and the other Mendocino County Gregor Mendels are good at what they do. That's what it all comes down to: you want a strain that can hack it if it rains before harvest time. Better yet, you want some strains that will be ready for harvest before even early rains would come. This is why Cohen wanted to see MendoGrown have the same kind of legal territorial origination protections that Champagne and Parmesan do.

As usual, it was the terpenes that hammered home the point. Man! I had thought the world smelled terpeney *before* harvest season. As soon as I arrived at the Eagle's Nest for her harvest on October 2, I saw and smelled once again that Lucille loved the local climate.

I noticed that Tomas had pared her down—the term is *coring*—so that she could concentrate all her energy on final flower production. Still, the finished Lucille looked like a Renaissance nude, with heavy buds—some two-foot-long *churros*, some like gaudy hunks of turquoise on an urban cowboy's ring—visibly pulling her branches downward like urgent cherubs leading the way to the Bright Light. This plant developed so quickly, my photos from each visit looked like they were taken in time lapse.

When Tomas had stepped beside me with what looked like rose-pruning shears, it hit me that Lucille was about to be harvested and turned into medicine. It seemed a little abrupt. I'd known her for six months. There would never be another Lucille.

Well, OK, there would likely be hundreds of thousands of her genetic clones. But she was the only 2011 Cashmere Kush at the Eagle's Nest.

Tomas said, "Thanks, Lucille," and began sectioning her into three-foot branch clusters. In minutes he had her loaded onto a wheelbarrow, with her zip tie on top of the piles of bud-dense limbs. Every flower from every plant on every 9.31 farm gets stored with its uniquely numbered zip tie. Stella was stacking the trimmed buds by strain with color-coded cards affixed to the outside of their plastic bins while they cured in the basement. These turquoise and gray cubes were their home while they awaited the Halent Labs visit, where they would be sealed inside crinkly, silver,

UV-blocking, space-age-material bags. Tomas just didn't have time to collect enough giant glass mason jars.

To determine which plants to harvest first, Tomas said, "I look for a plant that might be giving a sign with a dead leaf or two. I check it out, and if the bud—usually the cola [top flower]—has a spot that looks like a spiderweb or cotton candy, I go into code red. Harvest right away and survey the damage. So far it's been very light. I think we got in gear in time."

Back outside in the drizzly garden, Tomas took one of his final strolls through the aisles of emerald flowering plants. Around me hand-shaped oak leaves twisted slowly to the ground, pausing with each upturn in a decidedly autumnal breeze. Hard to avoid the impression they were waving. It was very quiet.

Tomas told me later that in the garden he was thinking, "I'll have such a better baseline knowledge next season—about which strains like what conditions, especially."

After a while I stopped typing notes and met Tomas at the garden gate. Locking it, he observed, "I feel connected to this garden. It's allowed me to be outdoors all summer. I used to just want to get out of my indoor garden. The quiet's been good for me. I'm gonna miss these girls."

# TWENTY-SIX
## Trimming with Buds

*Concentration is the factor that causes the great discrepancy between men and the results they achieve.*

*—Owen Swett Marden*

I arrived October 8 at an Eagle's Nest farmhouse quite literally filled to the rafters with hanging cannabis branches. I'm talking about from basement to bedrooms. I had to duck under a row of Reggie Noble/Organic Cowboys even to find Tomas and still one more Sonoma childhood friend at the dining room table, wearing surgical gloves and trimming more buds than I ever imagined could be in one place. Their finished bowl—bigger than a spaghetti pot—badly needed to be transferred to the plastic bins waiting for them in the basement. The floor was a fractal-pattern carpet of leaves.

I just couldn't believe how productive these plants were. Lucille's cola bud alone was close to a quarter pound. How much of a horticultural achievement is that? Let's call it a lifetime supply for a monthly migraine medicator, or a semester supply for one floor of your average University of Vermont dorm.

It's. A lot. Of medicine. Best farmers of my generation, Michael Pollan calls cultivators like Tomas.

How about of *any* generation? One doesn't understand the true nature of the market system* until one is exposed to the

---

* Tomas, like Laura Hamburg, Matt Cohen, and Jim Hill, said he will run his Kama Collective in a closed loop. "I think it's a huge leap toward becoming a local nonprofit business to be providing hundred-percent MendoGrown certified, 9.31 medicine to our patients," he told me. "Does that sound like a press release?"

supply-chain side of a product, any product. One doesn't understand it because one doesn't otherwise see the sheer amount of
product involved: how much broccoli, cannabis, or olive oil can
emerge from one efficient farm. All you and I generally see are
bottles of oil on the supermarket shelf. We don't see the mile-long
warehouse halls full of the stuff, the presses, or the olive groves
themselves.

I was seeing the groves themselves. A farmload of cannabis was
hanging at branch junctions on a maze of clothesline so as to lose
80 percent of its moisture content at just the right pace. Too fast
brings harshness when smoked, too slow invites mold. It has to do
with biochemical transformations going on even now in the plant.
I thought of a Colorado farmer who made me gasp when he told
me that oversupply had caused him to compost some of his crop in
2010, but "only a few pounds." For me, prior to 2011, when it came
to cannabis, *only* would never be followed with a few *pounds.* Have
I made the point? I would've thought that a pound was a huge
amount of cannabis.

Except in the Emerald Triangle, on the farm. Here, George
Fredericks told me, "a sample isn't an ounce, it's a pound." I pic-
tured James Bond dropping a gold brick at Goldfinger's feet. This
wasn't a sample I was amid now.

At the moment, I was in one of the county's five thousand
warehouses. Just a temporary one, until harvest madness was finished and Tomas ran the Gauntlet. But it was a warehouse that
would provide 100 percent of the eventual Kama Collective membership's medicine for at least a year. For reasons that should by
now be obvious, Tomas said he was dedicated to migrating Kama
to a fully sustainable menu as quickly as possible. He wanted his
collective's medicine "to be medicinal." Any indoor "bridge" crops
he might need for inventory reasons as the collective got off the
ground would be, he said, temporary.

So why all the tension? Besides the rain, COMMET had just
raided the home of a Redwood Valley farmer and his pregnant wife,
and discovered only twenty plants, well within the local limits.

The plants weren't the problem, one of the raiders said in the local media, but the amount of processed bud—seventy-five pounds. That, they declared, was more than the family's current medical needs.

Tomas had a lot more than that stuffed into the Eagle's Nest at the moment. It was a Panzer's Paradox issue. Even in Mendocino County in 2011, there were competing interpretations of cannabis law. When I asked Sheriff Allman about the processed bud conundrum, he told me it was a real one, but that "some farmers in Laytonville get around it by storing most of their harvest preprocessed." Plant branches, in other words.

All part of the game, as Jim Hill saw it. Feed a few farmers to the COMMET sharks, everyone's happy. Didn't hurt that the busted family had a Latino last name to carry into what would nonetheless be his eventual acquittal or dismissal.

Following five days of round-the-clock branch snipping, wheelbarrowing, drying, and processing, less than 20 percent of the Eagle's Nest garden had been harvested when I arrived midday. "You should check out the basement," Tomas said as soon as I'd busted through the cannabis curtain and into the dining room.

So I crawled back under the Organic Cowboys, gasped a deep whiff of oxygen at the front door, and made my way downstairs. I knew I had arrived because all I could see were Super Silver Haze branches—Tomas's old tuition and migraine strain. Hundreds and hundreds of them and thousands and thousands of drying buds upon them. Their crystals caught the light filtering in from behind me.

And it was only at that moment that I knew I was in the presence of medicine. In fact, as naturally as if I'd been doing it for years, I shared a short prayer with my fellow organisms, expressing hope that they'd reach and help patients. I still kept my voice low enough so as not to get pegged as a plant-talker, but I'd kind of become one.

I was able to do this, I think, not just because my head kept bumping into the branches, depositing leaves at every angle on my head and ears, and leaving me looking very much like a cannabis flower. But also because the ceremony mapped onto something I do every Sabbath in offering thanks for my family's bread and fruit of the vine, while extending the concerned cup of grape juice or slice of local sourdough aloft in gratitude. Why not medicinal herbs?

Clawing my way back upstairs under the living awning, I figured it was time to give those Fiskars a try. I found them soaking in alcohol-filled paper cups all over the jungle of the dining room table, like combs on a barber's shelf. I pulled two latex gloves out of a box and ended the visit with forearms and calves added to the normal list of body parts plastered with fragrant terpenes.

Additionally, note taking from that point on proved even more difficult than usual. Let me assure you that it is not so easy to type in surgeons' gloves, even when you're not living in an ecosystem composed mostly of crystalline glue.

The other trimmers watched in awe as I time and again pulled my gloves out nearly a stretchy foot from my phone screen before the latex disengaged from the cannabinoids with a rattail snap. To avoid this, I started pocketing the gloves when I'd built up enough thoughts to record.

If pressed, there was thus a plausible explanation I could have given to, say, a CHP officer at a traffic stop, as to why I would be driving home across Mendocino County during harvest season with five or six forgotten green-stained latex gloves hanging out of the back pocket of my Carhartts. Luckily I found them myself back at the cabin that evening.

"Bud trimming is all fun and social for about an hour," Tomas had warned me way back in the spring before I had ever even been to a cannabis farm. "Then there are several hundred hours to go. That's when it's work."

Concentration, I found, was the real skill here. The rub. Effective trimming is a matter of focus. I wasn't so much bored as distracted within five minutes. I found I couldn't think and trim at the same time. And talking was out of the question.

I forced myself to really do it for a couple of hours. This involved ignoring direct questions posed to me, like "Another Aperol spritz [shot of Aperol, prosecco, lime, and soda water]?" and "Hey, watch out, man—did you know you're holding that clipper upside down?" (The blades have an arch and thus which side is up matters.)

I've just always had a hard time focusing on tedium. This is usually a blessing: When I'm bored my mind provides the entertainment and I wind up writing books. But it's not the skill set for an ambitious young bud trimmer. This is today's version of starting in the mailroom.

Moving in what seemed to be slow motion compared to my research subjects, I estimated that I added maybe six ounces of Lucille's flowers to the giant pasta bowl in the middle of Tomas's dining room table. I did the math, and if I had been responsible for the Kama Collective's harvest, the processing would have taken four years. I even managed, in my short career, to pinch my right palm in the famous Fiskar springs severely enough to draw blood, which pooled in a widening circle inside my glove. Took a week to heal.

You can tell someone whose body is familiar with trimming the way you can tell if someone's a professional dancer. It's a muscle memory thing. As usual, Stella was the secret weapon. She could trim three entire plants with Mr. Miyagi precision while making a soufflé.

Tomas broke the silence by asking me if I thought he should hire a security guard to patrol the garden until harvest was complete. "An organized team of Rippers could hop the fence and cart a bunch of plants down the hill," he said. "A guard's really not that expensive. I looked into it."

I advised against it. "Brother, you told me you wake up when a deer steps on a pebble."*

---

* A few days later, Stella noticed a strange truck parked at the Eagle's Nest ranch gate. She (of course) got the license plate number. Tomas called 911, rightly considering county law enforcement his ally, and deputies showed up within twenty minutes. By that time, an underground cannabis farmer neighbor

But then I realized what the question implied. When I observed that it really looked like he'd have a significant crop to protect, Tomas, midharvest, finally broke the Ultimate Farmer's Rule and made a prediction. "I think the Collective will get three hundred pounds from the Eagle's Nest farm, at least," he said in the tone flight attendants use when they don't want passengers to hear their jump seat conversations. He allowed a slight smile, then leaned back over his Fiskars. It was as though it was difficult for him to frame the words.

He knew I knew what that meant. It meant, conservatively, a nine-hundred-thousand-dollar nest egg for the Kama enterprise. Once patients had reimbursed for the entire crop. It remained to be seen if any of it would come to Tomas in salary, given the collective's overhead, but it was a darned strong debut season.

Good thing, too, because of late Tomas had been expressing concern about his finances. "Nail-biting" might be a more apt description of his fiscal outlook, particularly when it came to liquidity. I'd be learning more in the ensuing months about what the increasingly likely initial year success meant for the collective's future plans, for its tax documents, and for Tomas's own prospective income.

What he said now was more philosophical. "It's a weird model we're developing here. On the one hand, it's not free market capitalism because patients are involved in the decision making, and we're not-for-profit currently. It's about patients' health. Un . . . what would you call it? Unmitigated profit-making is not the primary concern. Financial health and a fair living? Sure. On the other hand, I'm approaching it as a start-up—working my ass off and not getting

whom Tomas had warned of the invasion via text had fired three "warning blasts" from a shotgun. These terrified Tomas until he was informed of their origin and purpose. But they evidently did the trick. The truck was never seen again, though the deputies said the plate was traced to the East Bay city of San Leandro. Very unlikely a lost driver. "Rippers've worked this neighborhood before," Tomas said. The deputies did not ask Tomas his line of work. Tomas's subsequent concession to harvest season security imperatives: locking his ranch gate and posting a Beware of Dogs sign.

paid. I would love to see the medicine as close as possible to free in a way that's still a workable business model. One day federal health care will cover it. Meanwhile I have no idea if this model will work. I don't even know if most farmers sell their entire harvest."

"You mean, 'get reimbursed by their patient members.'"

"Right. Like at the food co-op. What do you think a fair salary would be for farming and managing this collective?"

"I once stopped donating to a hunger organization in Africa because the CEO in D.C. was taking home two hundred fifty large," I said.

"So, what, a hundred? In a good year where all the medicine is used?"

I told him that was slightly less than what other farmers had shown me on their federal tax forms. I told him that sounded quite fair.

The highest-salaried cannabis farmer I met was Jim Hill, who raked in a combined $128,000 as an executive team with his wife, for supplying and managing a farm and two growing collectives, providing 5,050 members, many elderly, with medicine. That's about what the head of Doctors Without Borders USA makes. Gail McGovern, President/CEO of the American Red Cross, took home a $1,032,022 package in 2011, and United Way CEO Brian Gallagher earns $1,037,140. Oh, and the CEO of those for-profit health care specialists GlaxoSmithKline, Andrew Witty, deposited $10.6 million in 2011.

So, are there Ganjapreneurs in the 9.31 Program? Yes. Sinsemillionaires? Not many, yet. Not among the rank-and-file farmer, anyway. A crop might be worth three quarters of a million dollars or more, but there's a lot of overhead. As with every gold rush (and this is the region's third, in just the past century and a half), it's the behind-the-scenes suppliers and financiers, on Wall Street and in retail, who are making the real money. It was dry goods providers of flour sacks in 1849, today it's the grow shops and compost peddlers. In between, various rushes spawned Levi Strauss and sent Sears, Roebuck public.

At the same time that Mendocino County supported twenty-two grow shops, farmer George Fredericks was facing foreclosure and needed a strong harvest to avoid it. His ducks, as yet, weren't laying golden eggs. Still he happily paid his $8,500 in 9.31 fees and inspection costs. "This is the way it should be," George told me. "I hope it works and other parts of the country use the model. Be prepared for paperwork, though."

At the Eagle's Nest trimming table, it was one of those big picture days, where we had time to imagine the Pax Cannabis. A few minutes after the financial conversation, I watched Tomas toss a bare, trimmed stalk the size of a skinny snowman—pure cellulose—into the compost bin next to the trimming table. "That's America's energy future you're throwing away," I told him. I'd been reading about producing alcohol from biomass to provide petroleum-free fuel. "Think MendoGrown will sponsor a county-wide fermentation facility someday?"

Tomas thought about it for a moment, while trimming more buds than I would in a month. "Maybe once the cost of the flowers comes down."

Moving away from industry prognostication, I noticed the table developing a trimmer-only sense of humor. The Fiskar-clutchers were laughing at things, hours into a session, that were immensely funny to those in the trenches, but not necessarily to anyone else on the planet.

For instance, we briefly did a blind scent test of five strains—with the nasal palate cleansed by a whiff of coffee grounds between samples. Tomas had been talking the vintner's talk about "pine-infused" Sour Diesels this and "fruitier" sativas that. Several of us wanted to see if, when it came down to it, he could really tell the difference between strains. He got three of five right. Stella got two. I got one.

"You're, ah, snipping that bud in half," Stella had to remind me soon after my turn.

I examined the result of my incompetence. This made me feel

like Jack Kerouac on his first, humiliating day of rural living with his migrant farmer girlfriend and her son in *On the Road*:

> I knew nothing about picking cotton. I spent too much time disengaging the white ball from its crackly bed; the others did it in one flick. Moreover my fingertips began to bleed; I needed gloves, or more experience. . . . My back began to ache. But it was beautiful kneeling and hiding in that earth: if I felt like resting I did, with my face on the pillow of brown moist earth. Birds sang an accompaniment. I thought I had found my life's work. Johnny and Terry came waving at me across the field in hot lullal noon and pitched in with me. Be damned if little Johnny wasn't faster than I was!— and of course Terry was twice as fast. They worked ahead of me and left me piles of clean cotton to add to my bag—Terry workmanlike piles, Johnny little childly piles. I stuck them in with sorrow.

I was saved from further embarrassment when the technicians for Halent showed up. I watched them stick samples of Lucille's flowers into various sealed envelopes for cannabinoid potency and purity testing, while Tomas filled out the form headed "Cashmere Kush."

And the clouds leaked on. Tomas was almost on the putting green, if he could nip this botrytis in the bud. There would be no rain delays.

# TWENTY-SEVEN

## The Stigma Front: Should Storefront Cannabis Dispensaries Be Relegated to Red Light Districts?

What I would take away from it is maybe there should just be a little bit less fear about having dispensaries. Hopefully, this injects a little bit of science into the discussion.

—Mireille Jacobson, health economist and lead researcher for a
2011 RAND Corportation study (later retracted, following law
enforcement complaints) that found a 59 percent increase in
crime within three-tenths of a mile of a closed cannabis dispensary
compared to an open one, quoted in a September 21, 2011,
*Los Angeles Times* article headlined, "RAND Study Finds *Less*
Crime Near Pot Dispensaries"

While Tomas was stuggling to get the Kama crop in out of the rain, I was learning about another business in the cannabis sector: the storefront dispensary. In typical Mendo fashion, local dispensary managers were not prone to hiding in the warehouse and quickie mart side of town. They're activists, like the rest of the players in local cannabis culture.

They have to be. It is a public, and thus a currently risky, sector of the industry. First off, it's important to mention that any dispensary operator, if he or she chooses to be legal in the state of California, must also be a patient with a physician's referral for cannabis. This is a policy that grower George Fredericks calls "like requiring a headache to sell aspirin." Dang states rights, it's different in every cannabis program: In New Mexico, for example, state-sanctioned cultivators don't have to be patients. In Michigan, you can grow cannabis in your garden or obtain it from a caregiver, but you can't obtain it at a dispensary.

So the California cannabis patient/dispensary manager sits at a workplace, the address advertised in the local news weekly. Because of the federal risk alone, you can see why he might want to keep a low profile.

But like nearly all of Mendocino County's storefront managers, Gabriel Martin didn't hide. Instead he preferred to, in his words, "wear it." That is, the "a known, local, high-quality cannabis source is a positive thing for our community" robe. This was a philosophical stance anchored in Martin's mantra, "I'm offended that anyone would try to force me, a small farmer, into a red light district."

The reason Martin felt the need to operate this way is because 185 California municipalities had banned dispensaries by 2011, according to the Associated Press. Providers in New Jersey are having a difficult time finding a town that will let them operate. "Minds needs to change," Martin said. In other words, thousands of Americans still associate cannabis with crime.

Martin thus focused his activism in what you might call the realm of cannabis zoning. He in 2011 set up his top-shelf and Cannabis Cup–winning Leonard Moore Cooperative smack dab in upscale, coastal, and almost painfully rustic Mendocino Village, where everything seems to be made of driftwood and spires. This is a town that is home to a yarn store *and* a bead store. An entire shelf in the "Harvest Market" is devoted to brie, some of it local. Of more concern to a ganjapreneur, local zoning officials generally give a knee-jerk response to a petition for so much as an unconventional downtown doorknob: "Not in our town."

Martin thus was wrestling intentionally with big issues like Cultural Zeitgeist. In fact, Martin's establishment sat directly across the street from the tourist-friendly Mendocino Chocolate Company. The half-dozen times I parked on the block, the Leonard Moore Cooperative was generally far quieter and less busy than the chocolate shop—except during the hoppin' herbal and neurochemical seminars. Not to give Congress any ideas for new Schedule I controlled substances. I wouldn't want to have to get a doctor's note for my absolutely medicinal daily cocoa fix.

All of this existed under a wonderfully relaxed Mendocino Village vibe. I always feel like I'm moving in slow motion here. Residents know they are living the good life. The hamlet is a universe away from the meth-troubled former logging town of Fort Bragg, nine miles up the coast along Highway 1.

Martin's answer to the predictable "who will think of the children?" pushback that started popping up at county zoning discussions about his choice of location was "You must be talking about the pharmacy up the street with the dangerous drugs. What we provide is an ancient blessing of an effective herbal medicine. To help people."

And as for his cooperative being an attractive nuisance, Martin said, "We believe sunlight erases that mode. Shine a light for children and teens to see what cannabis is. That's what prevents abuse. We have a kid area in the collective. Bring your whole family."

The 2011 California legislature did not agree. In August, it passed a bill, which Governor Brown declined to sign, that would have restricted dispensaries and cannabis collectives from setting up shop "within a 600-foot radius of a school" or residential area.

But cities and counties can, arguably, ban dispensaries flat out.* In 2011, Mendocino County was in the process of establishing a 9.32 ordinance governing medical cannabis providers in the county. Thus municipalities, too, and not just district attorneys, can try to forge a wet county/dry county model akin to Utah's liquor laws, according to the *East Bay Express* newspaper.

And yet, in Mendocino Village, after what he described as "a flurry" of concerned calls from constituents when the Leonard Moore Cooperative opened its doors, the county supervisor for the district, Dan Hamburg, said he hasn't had a single complaint

---

* A 2011 state appellate decision in a Long Beach case known as the Pack ruling brings into question whether municipalities can regulate a federally illegal industry at all. But that decision, like so much in cannabis law today, is still being wrestled over, now by the California Supreme Court.

about the cooperative. Which is housed, by the way, in an impeccably restored downtown Victorian.

Martin intended to fit in. "We're not a sin industry—why should we be regulated like one?" he asked me rhetorically. "Cannabis is a medicine, not a sin."

And thus, make no mistake, Martin's front line advocacy helps cultivators like Tomas Balogh and Matt Cohen on the crucial propaganda front. Simply by fitting in. By not grabbing headlines.

In fact I've noticed that Cannabis dispensaries in California tend to reflect their community mind-set, architecture, and even fashion. Jim Hill's Wilbur OC storefront in Southern California, for example, had the kind of security camera coverage you'd expect for a warehouse scene out of *Beverly Hills Cop*. Nor do you find the tattoos and dreadlocks there that one might more commonly see in, say, a Bay Area facility. As Wilbur OC's manager Craig Raimondi put it, flipping his tie between his fingers, "The Che Guevara T-shirts are discouraged here in Orange County. That's one way we keep it to real patients. When we get a membership inquiry I can tell right away if it's genuine or someone trying to supply the black market."

Martin's Leonard Moore Cooperative, named for a late local artist who had to go to the black market for his AIDS-related pain medicine, cultivated a far more urbane feel. He out-Mendocinoed his village of Mendocino neighbors with ubiquitous displays of fresh-cut flowers, hardwood flooring, and original art inside the cooperative's homey storefront.

In 2011, Martin was explicity and daily engaged in smacking down the notion that there is something, anything, a cannabis provider or patient should be embarrassed about, let alone should be zoned to the wrong side of the tracks about. The Leonard Moore Cooperative's common area, in other words, was the bubble within the bubble within the bubble within the bubble. Any more progressive and it would be clothing optional.

And it was in that common area, at one of Martin's comprehensive how-to lectures—this one on harvesting and curing cannabis,

I believe (Martin missed his calling as a high school science teacher)—that I met that most demographically surprising Mendo grower, sixty-five-year-old Buffy Madison. I mean, I was already getting familiar with the concept of the granny patient. But the granny *farmer*?

I don't know how well I disguised my "but you're not a kid!" surprise that day, but we've stayed in touch. During our first conversation, I found it interesting that Buffy's lessons about the benefits of cannabis came by way of her daughter.

In fact, one of the reasons she was now so willing to conduct her essentially life-or-death experiment in herbal healing (in addition to the insurance realities earlier mentioned), is that "one day when she was in high school I confronted [my daughter] Lucy because her grades had suddenly improved—by a lot. I wanted to know why that was. You know, to keep it going. She told me, 'I'm smoking pot, Mom.' I was stunned, of course. Ya know, fearful like we're trained to be. And then I saw the reality: The meds she took for ADD were no help at all. Ritalin and the rest of that junk. I'd been a nurse since the sixties, so I knew what I was seeing: I was seeing effective self-medication. So now, ten or twelve years later, my doctor is proposing an anti-inflammatory cannabis regimen, and I'm open to it."

Such is life north of the cannabis Mason-Dixon Line. It's a fertile cannabis business and patient climate as much as it is an agricultural climate. And because minds are so open in Mendo, the more extreme voices of the cannabis world are particularly vocal here.

For instance, now that his kids were grown and the collectives he created and managed paid his legal fees, Jim Hill had become even more of a thorn in the side of, well, pretty much everyone, instituting lawsuits like the one against the Orange County city of Laguna Hills based on a writ of mandate. This challenged municipal officials there to, in his words, "either find that we're not a legitimate entity or obey Prop. 215 by treating us like any other business." The city did not reply by the court-mandated date to close Wilbur OC down.

He'd also sued, this time unsuccessfully, to overturn Ordinance 9.31, since he was of the school that believes "the people of California voted in 1996 that patients should be able to get medicine, and it is not up to the state or municipalities or a policeman at a traffic stop to decide how much is enough medicine."

For the more centrist, pro-9.31 Matt Cohen, a man who was still making his way in the world and not yet in his day-trader phase, his conflict-based activist days were behind him when we met—the Northstone Two case notwithstanding. Though he benefited from the battles Gabriel Martin is fighting on the stigma front, Cohen himself lived by a "stigma? What stigma?" code. He operated with the casual certainty of the true believer in any creed.

He felt that he had the law on his side, for one thing—Sergeant Randy attended his October 2011 birthday party—and he knew that he had his conscience on his side. Plus he had venture capitalists falling all over themselves to get a piece of his action, and two Mendocino County Sheriff's deputies, in part still employed because of his own industry, dropped by to "make sure everything's all right" when he had a security system malfunction. Twice.

Now, it seemed, all he needed to do was improve the rainy-season parking situation at his farm and cooperative's headquarters. The venture capitalists' Bimmers were likely to provide even less torque than my Ford truck.

# TWENTY-EIGHT
## Bubble Breach

In a wide-ranging interview, he could not say that his approach
had made Mexico safer. "What I can say is Mexico will be safer,"
he said, "and to have not acted, it would have deteriorated much
more."

> —Mexican president Felipe Calderón, discussing his nation's front
> of the Drug War on October 14, 2011, quoted in *The New York
> Times*. According to the article, that conflict has claimed forty
> thousand lives since 2005, while garnering $1.4 billion in U.S. aid.

It was a great mistake to put routine drug offenses into the federal courts.

> —U.S. Supreme Court Justice Antonin Scalia, October 5, 2011

We ask that these laws be changed. It is time for a different,
more effective approach. That's why we endorse Initiative 502,
which would decriminalize marijuana in our state and make a
long-overdue change for the better in public policy.

> —Katrina Pflaumer, former U.S. attorney for the Western District
> of Washington, Robert Alsdorf, retired state Superior Court
> judge, and Anne Levinson, former Municipal Court judge and
> former deputy mayor of Seattle, endorsing cannabis legalization
> in Washington, in *The Seattle Times*, November 11, 2011

In October, right at harvest time, cannabis activists in California
got a kick in the body part Sheriff Tom doesn't get off of when
encountering mere pounds of cannabis. Specifically, federal prosecutors, including Melinda Haag of California's Northern District,
started sending threatening letters to both cannabis providers themselves and to landlords of collectives' storefront dispensaries. The
letters ordered the closing of dispensaries within forty-five days.

Then, all four California U.S. attorneys held a press conference

October 7, claiming that medical cannabis had been "hijacked by profiteers" and they'd "yet to find a single instance in which a marijuana store was able to prove that it was a not-for-profit organization." Similar menacing and blatantly mendacious gestures were being made in Oregon and Montana. 2011 saw federal raids in seven states that allow medical cannabis.

Coming from a federal prosecutor, I found the second track (that people profit from cannabis farming), to be a tellingly losing argument. It admitted intent matters, and ignored that federal law says, "No cannabis at all—it's more dangerous than meth." Plus, Colorado was operating a state-managed for-profit cannabis industry that had as yet drawn minimal federal attention. When seeming to recognize that the average thinking person might spot such holes in a new phrasing of the basic premise of the forty-year-project, the desperate Drug Warrior will often revert to the "who will think of the children?" screed. Thus U.S. Attorney Haag at the big October 7 press conference:

"The value of their inventory presents a danger that the stores will become a magnet for crime, which jeopardizes the safety of nearby children."

Welcome to the argument that, to endure, we must demand the RAND Corporation retract a study concluding otherwise. And the RAND study isn't the only one to draw such a conclusion. In Colorado Springs, I spoke with a dispensary manager who lives next door to his place of work specifically to ensure that any crime (there has been none) would be reported immediately. The dispensary is 435 feet from an elementary school. Like tens of thousands of liquor stores are nationwide.

Looking for sound reason in the enforcement of federal drug law is often a time-waster. But some decision, almost definitely in Washington, D.C., had been made. There was no turning back, at least for a news cycle.

The October 2011 timeline entry for a future history book titled *Final Days of the U.S. Drug War* will now read, "Facing record-high oppositon to the war, the Justice Department begins multiagency attack in California, Oregon, elsewhere." Given that the initial press conference announcing the offensive came on the same day that—indeed sharing the same front page on which—the *L.A. Times* announced, "U.S. jobless rate stuck at 9.1% for 3rd straight month," it's not hard to imagine that, ten years from now, citizens will read those words and wonder, "Why did this happen? How could they not see that they'd already lost a war that shouldn't have been fought anyway? Why was our government actively costing American jobs?"

The first assault in the October offensive had already been unleashed in the barrage of threatening "go away or go to prison" notes sent to dispensaries and—even more constitutionally scary— to landlords who had nothing to do with cannabis. Is the landlord of a Manhattan office building threatened if a banker commits insider trading from his leased space? Is the operator of a convention center threatened if a vendor at a traveling gun show sells a Glock to a felon?

One recipient of a nasty-gram was Lynnette Shaw, operator of California's longest-active dispensary, the Marin Alliance. She "has been paying state and federal taxes for fourteen years, and they have cashed all the checks," her attorney, Greg Anton, told the Associated Press on October 6. "All I hear from Obama is whining about his budget, but he has money to do this which will actually reduce revenues."

"It was very ominous," Shaw told Bloomberg October 7. "It informed [our landlord] there was medical marijuana dispensing on his site, and that he had forty-five days to evict us, or possibly face forty years in jail, forfeiture of the property, and any money we had given him."

Another dispensary operator whose landlord received a threat, wheelchair-using Charlie Pappas of Divinity Tree in San Francisco, said in *The Bay Citizen* on November 7 that although his establishment is 594 feet from a park, the U.S. attorney's office issued no letter to the strip club, multiple liquor stores, and massage parlors that are even closer.

"We've never had any complaints," Pappas told the paper.

While the bloggers melted their DSL lines debating the meaning and impact of the unfolding "crackdown," I oberved a great big yawn in Mendocino County. People noticed it, sent e-mails, even talked of organizing a rally in Sacramento to protest the federal posturing. But no one I spoke to in the 9.31 Program, or outside of it, for that matter, addressed changing any actions or policies. It was harvest season, man.

To get into Tomas or Buffy or Sharif's head in early October, call to mind your busiest day recently. The one where you were asleep before your head finally, in the wee hours, hit the pillow. Then imagine living it every day for a solid month and a half. With helicopters overhead. "It becomes like that movie *Groundhog Day*," one farmer told me. "You wake up and realize, ugh, more trimming."

The Halent technicians didn't even bring up the feds when they visited the Eagle's Nest. I remember a moment of silence for Steve Jobs and at one point Tomas swapping some theories on native soil microbiology with Colleen and Craig from the testing company. Other than that it was all about the day's business of packaging flower samples for testing, including Lucille's.

For one thing, everyone associated with the cannabis industry had seen this all before. Ho-hum, another swing of the Drug War pendulum. "We won the Drug War because we wanted it more," the seventy-something cannabis farmer Sarah told me while we were on line for the kale salad during those halcyon August days of the Gaia Festival.

Sarah'd been farming in the county since 1979. She'd seen the start of seizure law and all the cycles since. She even survived Nancy Reagan appearing in the schoolyard to tell Arnold to Just Say No on that very special *Diff'rent Strokes*.

"We're already showing how you can live openly when it's officially over," Sarah said, not with a flower actually in her hair, but with a brooch in the shape of a lupine blossom. "There will soon be federal legalization and regulation."

As Oakland-based cannabis attorney Robert Raich put it in the San Francisco neighborhood newspaper *Mission Local* in early October, "the U.S. attorney will try to make an example of a few in an attempt to create fear, but the genie is already out of the bottle. It's an efficient way to make people scared."

Tomas and I took our Cannabis Tourism overflight as planned on October 7, with pilot Sandy announcing herself over the radio to the unmanned tower at the county airport at Ukiah. Cost us three hundred dollars for ninety minutes, and Sandy said her Pacific Air Taxi gets calls for such amateur cannabis-spotting flights "all the time." It was exactly as I remember glacial flightseeing in Alaska: a nice cottage industry supporting a bunch of local jobs.

The scope of the industry should serve as a wake-up call to politicians on how cannabis prohibition affects votes. Again, it's the Green Economy, stupid. Ignore it and your fate is the same as that of any politician who for a second forgets that any election hinges on the candidate's perceived personal impact on individual voters. When it comes to President Obama's stance, many cannabis activists get it: You know you've won California, so why appear soft on "drugs" in an election year?

But the activists I spoke with consider that sentiment to reflect overconfidence and to run counter to nationwide polling. OK, they acknowledge of the incumbent they want to like, you're running for president of Ohio and Michigan and Florida. But Ohio and Florida, like everywhere else on Earth, is plenty enough procannabis. And Michigan is already a medical cannabis state. "Mr. President," the Drug Doves argue, "cannabis is a safe issue. It's a strong issue. It's the country's favorite herb. Capitalize and trademark that, like you did *Organic* if you like. Be 'The Country's Favorite Herb' candidate."

They have a point. Guess which seven states at least floated medicinal cannabis legislation or proposed initiatives in 2011? Ready? Florida, Kansas, Arkansas, Oklahoma, Indiana, Ohio and, wait for it, Courtenay Cohen's Alabama. Montanans also will be voting on a sort of reform/reaffirmation initiative of their

Republican-disrupted program in 2012. At least half a dozen other states are debating the issue, too, with Arkansas and North Dakota on the Marijuana Policy Project's list for medical approval in 2012.

It's not like this demographic is hiding. The multiple online Town Hall embarrassments were just the beginning for the poor Obama administration. Even more recently, when the White House posted a petition contest of sorts on its home page in September 2011, promising a formal response to any question receiving five thousand signatures, cannabis brought in the first qualifying question, with seventy-four thousand signatures. It read:

> We petition the Obama Administration to: Legalize and Regulate Marijuana in a Manner Similar to Alcohol.
>
> We the people want to know when we can have our "perfectly legitimate" discussion on marijuana legalization. Marijuana prohibition has resulted in the arrest of over 20 million Americans since 1965, countless lives ruined, and hundreds of billions of tax dollars squandered and yet this policy has still failed to achieve its stated goals of lowering use rates, limiting the drug's access, and creating safer communities.
>
> Isn't it time to legalize and regulate marijuana in a manner similar to alcohol? If not, please explain why you feel that the continued criminalization of cannabis will achieve the results in the future that it has never achieved in the past?

The response came October 29, from Drug Czar Gil Kerlikowske, who is prohibited by a 1998 law from advocating the legalization of a Schedule I controlled substance. It read, in part:

> As a former police chief, I recognize we are not going to arrest our way out of the problem. We also recognize that legalizing marijuana would not provide the answer to any of the health, social, youth education, criminal justice,

and community quality of life challenges associated with drug use.

What a strange nation we are when it comes to leadership. We guide the world's attention to the tablet device, but can't agree on a solar- and wind-powered energy future. I guess with three hundred million people it's amazing we act on anything. The result, though, is that on some issues we lead, on some we drag.

In 2012, the cannabis plant's long-recognized analgesic properties are hardly questioned outside of the United States (even if the laws vary per country). The Israeli position, for example, summed up in the *Haaretz* newspaper in 2011, is typical of Western democracies: "Of approximately 6,000 Israelis currently being treated with medical cannabis, most suffer from chronic pain and terminal illnesses. The therapeutic potential of cannabis has been known for many years and is recognized by the Health Ministry."

The White House online petition and the earlier Town Hall questions are the ones coming from the people, not from talking points at the news conference. Cannabis wins every time the agenda is unscripted, no doubt with digerati hackers helping in some robo-voting way.

The sense of alienation felt by traditional friends of the president is captured in this letter from attorney Anton, posted all over the cannabis blogosphere on October 14, 2011:

> An Open Letter to President Obama:
>
> This is not a challenge or a threat, only a sad personal statement.
>
> I am an attorney, my wife is a doctor, we have five adult children. Support for the Democratic Party in our family goes as far back as 1972, when my father was a campaign manager for George McGovern.
>
> We, as a family, did everything in our power, financially and spiritually, networking with people around the country, to help get you elected president.

We feel this recent assault by the Federal Government on medical marijuana patients is;

1)  An abhorrent waste of our precious law enforcement resources;
2)  An unwarranted intrusion into State's rights to regulate medicine;
3)  Perpetuates criminal activity;
4)  Results in making marijuana more available to children.

For the first time in over forty years, we as a family withdraw our support for the Democratic Party.

Greg Anton
Santa Rosa, CA

If it was noticing at all, I imagine the Obama reelection brain-trust was at this point thinking, "But, you know, that's only seven votes in a pretty blue state." Or at most, "If only another poll would come out to show Americans' views on cannabis heading into this election season!"

Back at the Eagle's Nest, by contrast, the discussion topics during trimming were terpene-related, not DEA-related. Cannabinoid balance. Patient strain preferences. Cannabis bouquet tests.

As much as anything, the shrugging of the trimmers had pretty much convinced me that no matter what the legal status of cannabis, it will always remain a valuable medicine to vast numbers of people. As it has been for getting on ten thousand years. The truth is the truth, I thought as October changed my footgear back to rubber boots: It's over.

Then I got the message that some in power do not as yet agree. In fact, one fairly immediate problem arose with the "ah, they'll only make a few examples" assertion: One of the first "examples" in October was perhaps America's number one poster child for legal, taxpaying, patient-providing cannabis farming. And I knew him well.

At six A.M. on October 13, 2011, six DEA agents and two local law enforcement officers raided Matt Cohen's house and the Northstone farm, "machine guns blazing," Cohen said. He and Courtenay were asleep.

"Matt woke up when he heard the vehicles," Courtenay told me the next day by phone. "He bounded downstairs to meet them, pulling on his boxers, and I dashed off a text to (Northstone employee) Lauren that said, 'Raid. Don't come in.' Then I heard Matt shouting, 'You don't have to bash the door—I'll open it'. So I ran downstairs, yelling, 'Please don't shoot the dogs! Please don't shoot the dogs!' 'Cuz our dogs were of course going pretty crazy. I was scared. They had machine guns. All in all [slight giggle], not the way you want to wake up on a Thursday."

Turned out that text message was hugely important, because Courtenay and Matt spent the next eight hours separated, in handcuffs, deflecting questions from a DEA team leader intent on making them out as a for-profit business. Or as Matt Cohen put it via cell phone, "Then they found out I've hardly even collected a salary yet."

"But wait," I thought. "At the press conference they said they were going after the profiteers who hijacked medical cannabis. They promised! Maybe they got the wrong address."

"Some of them trashed our house and even scraped out the chimney while the others went outside and chainsawed the garden down, zip ties and all," Courtenay said. "Then they calmed down and got more civil as the day went on. But they also kept getting more and more frustrated that there were no illicit drugs, no weapons, no money. They dissed the [9.31] program as a sham, and said that [the recent California] *Pack* [case] made local ordinances illegal. They tried to get me to admit that not all our crop goes to patients. But I kept telling them, 'Um, it's really true. We provide medicine to sick people.'"

In custody, Courtenay said, she mostly just meditated. "I sat there listening to the chainsaws and I thought, 'There's a reason this is happening. It'll just make us fight harder.'"

I found out about the raid an hour after it started—and seven hours before Matt and Courtenay Cohen were allowed to call their attorney Panzer. That I and the rest of the world heard about an unfolding DEA raid so quickly from the mailing list of the Drug Policy Forum of California (DPFCA) is, for me, one of the major journalistic lessons of this book.

The moment the October raids started across the American West, list moderator Dale Gieringer (who has an engineering Ph.D. from Stanford and is also California director of NORML) was on top of every news report and planned response. Calls for unity in the sometimes fractured cannabis activist world were mostly heeded.

Two weeks later, President Obama faced a coordinated protest from cannabis activists when he visited San Francisco for a fundraiser—it was covered by the Associated Press, alongside other protests against the proposed Keystone XL pipeline. That e-mail list is the reason hundreds of cannabis supporters gathered to insist that their vote wasn't a certainty.

I was at a prior commitment in Connecticut that day—one of fourteen states to have decriminalized all uses of cannabis, by the way—so I wasn't at that protest (there would be others), but Tomas texted me a video. Looked, you know, like a San Francisco protest rally.

My New England hotel gave me a *USA Today* that morning. The cover story was about prescription "pill mills"—doctors setting up in strip malls around the nation while pharmaceutical lobbyists fight tracking software that would prevent multistate operators. Matt Cohen, incidentally, is a vocal supporter of cannabis DNA testing, to ensure "every ounce" gets to appropriate patients. And Aaron Bluse of the Altitude Organics dispensary in Colorado voluntarily uses such tracking software, called Biotrak THC.

That same newspaper's business section that day ran a graphic that charted "hospital revenue growth" over twenty years. Wait. For-profit hospitals and pharmaceutical firms can reap immense windfalls, but cannabis farmers must be nonprofits? The explicit duplicity of this dichotomy reminded me of something Cohen had posted on the MendocinoCountry.com website back in 2009 when 9.31 was in the formative stage, public input was being taken, and he was trying to rally farmers around the idea of legitimacy. The title of his contribution was "A Greener Future for Mendocino County":

> Bringing medical marijuana out of the shadows would create jobs, raise much needed funds in our county, bring hard-working citizens into the lawful taxpaying world with worker rights [and] workman's comp. benefits, and finally shed new light on the county's largest grossing crop.

That crop contributed the aforementioned hundred million dollars in sales tax to California's general fund in 2006. A spokesman for the Obama reelection campaign took but didn't return my call asking if the president was aware of the October 25 rally outside his seven-thousand-dollars-a-plate fundraiser.

Which is all very fine and grassroots, so to speak. The point is that the cannabis world's central information repository was in place before its constituency knew there'd have to be a rally. The cannabis activists are nimble. Thus some people believe the clerks win wars.

But the glaring, unmissable lesson of October 2011 was that it was premature to call this particular war over. Believe it or not, the raids weren't the only problem facing the cannabis industry as the 2011 harvest got nervously under way. On October 3, the IRS issued a ruling against the eighty-three-thousand-member Oakland dispensary Harborside Health Center, saying that, as drug traffickers, the facility's operators were not entitled to take payroll and other standard deductions when they paid their taxes.

We'll *take* your taxes, was the message. But you can't operate with the same tax model as every other taxpaying business. Says it right there in section 280e. Seriously, that's the section, basically the same kind of thing the feds used to get Al Capone. Only, I know Harborside's pigtailed founder, Steve DeAngelo. He's been an activist since I was nine years old, even peddling navy surplus hemp in the 1980s. "I couldn't keep it in stock, it sold so fast," he told me when we spoke at length in his Harborside office back in March. He's not a gangster. And he wants to pay taxes.

Though being appealed, of course, the ruling translated into a suffocating $2.5 million tax bill for DeAngelo's dream operation. When I heard that one, I thought, "Maybe now the truism will be 'The accountants win wars.'" The IRS stance was also affecting smaller collective and dispensary managers with whom I spoke. One referred me to his accountant the way an executive would once have brought a chief strategist into the conversation.

And, giving the eerie sense that there was something coordinated going on in some subbasement on the Beltway, the U.S. Bureau of Alcohol, Tobacco and Firearms (ATF), in a move I can say as a gun owner was met with hypocritical NRA silence, declared a new policy in September: ATF officials sent a letter to gun sellers saying cannabis patients no longer have Second Amendment rights. That's right: In the United States of America today, it is illegal for playing-by-the-rules, state-registered medical cannabis patients nationwide to bear arms. Whacked on OxyContin? Shoot away.

My friend Carl Reid, the New Mexico 'Nam veteran, cannabis patient, and concealed handgun permit holder, was apoplectic: "I have a houseful of guns," he told me by phone a few weeks after the ATF action. "Probably eight or nine. I can't wait for someone to take this to court. I can't believe I lose my Second Amendment rights because I'm receiving treatment. I defended this country's freedoms."

That same month, not incidentally—and assuming a similar violence rate as the previous year—more than a thousand people were killed in drug cartel violence in Mexico, and the head of the same ATF, Kenneth Melson, was about to be "reassigned" over a gun scandal involving supplying arms to those very cartels. In one grisly incident in September, the *Guardian* reported that masked gunmen "have blocked traffic on a busy avenue in [Veracruz] and dumped the bodies of thirty-five murder victims in front of motorists."

Closer to home, on October 22, it was reported in *The Willits News* that the summer's massive, multiagency, weeks-long Operation Full Court Press had resulted in one cannabis conviction.

But, you know, other than losing their constitutional rights and tax parity, how was October going for members of the American would-be legal cannabis industry? For most, nothing was as stunning as the Northstone raid. In going after Matt Cohen, the federal prosecutors chose to take out the peacemaker. The man dedicated not just to creating a workable model for a safe cannabis industry but equally dedicated to rooting out the punks and organized criminals who won't come on board. This is why Gieringer's response to the Northstone raids was to call it "a victory for the cartels."

Matt was the fellow whose confident "that's right, I provide an ancient medicine, what do you do?" posture was leading the responsible Green Rush. He was comfortable in his ganjapreneurial skin and had the pro bono legal representation to prove it. This was a fellow who didn't seem to me to be worried. Why should he be? Local law enforcers came to his birthday party. Renegade growers despised him for ruining the tax free-for-all. Let's put it this way: There was no need to wonder what Cohen's mother thought about his work—she was part of the Northstone co-op staff.

If I had any lingering faith, as a journalist, in the ultimate good intentions of the War on Drugs, what I saw when I visited the Northstone farm on October 23 dispelled it. Strolling past the last of Courtenay's tomatoes, which were still on the vine near the goat fence, naturally I started to wonder why such a raid would have been ordered here at this hard-to-find property in a county filled with thousands of cannabis farmers.

Could a decision maker still be serious about this war, and yet clueless enough to go after the most aboveboard operator in the state? A national board member for the NCIA lobby group who had only for the past three months started collecting a four-thousand-dollar monthly salary? That's not going to look good in the newspapers.

It reminded me of when Northstone Two defendant Tim Tangney wandered out of the courtroom wondering if maybe a Sonoma narcotics detective was actually testifying for the defense. Could the Justice Department's CSA enforcement deciders actually be funded by NORML and secretly working to end federal cannabis prohibition? Seemed unlikely, even with Soros on board. Thus the conclusion I came to was that the Northstone DEA raid was either nothing short of malicious or almost unfathomably ignorant. Imagine declaring war not just on your voters but your contributors!

As Matt gave me the grisly tour of Northstone's ninety-nine stumps, I tried to force myself to think of the War on Drugs as just a game, like Matt's fellow federal raidee Jim Hill insisted it is. OK, 99 percent of cannabis reaches markets unhassled. Law enforcement budgets get renewed. Politicians don't look weak on drugs. All constituencies and unions are satisfied. North of the border, at least. The show goes on. Prices go back up and the unsafe, untaxed cannabis market thrives.

Except it's immoral. Public policy should be honest and conducted with the best interest of (duh) the public in mind, not departmental budgets. Furthermore, if you want to keep emotions out of it, it hurts the legitimate American economy by costing jobs and eliminating tax revenue. Dan Harwood, one of the Northstone Two, is now collecting unemployment.

I still, in that sad garden, saw a way for everyone to win. The cannabis game as played for the past forty years just needs a minor rule tweak. Instead of hovering around a 1 percent "success" rate, winning should now entail saving the taxpayers billions, creating massive domestic agriculture, manufacturing, and energy industries, and honoring civil liberties. That's still drug enforcing, albeit reinforcing.

A quick read of the DEA mission statement reveals that the agency is not planning to change its name to the Drug

Reinforcement Administration (DRA) anytime soon. The DEA exists "to enforce the controlled substances laws and regulations of the United States and bring to the criminal and civil justice system of the United States, or any other competent jurisdiction, those organizations and principal members of organizations, involved in the growing, manufacture, or distribution of controlled substances appearing in or destined for illicit traffic in the United States."

Knowing that this was a policy that had somehow been used to cut down Northstone's plants, on a farm I knew to be following state and local law, I took some small consolation during my post-raid visit to the Cohens in the fact that it looked as though Courtenay had told them where to park. Someone had clearly and recently had trouble getting off the property. I recognized the amphibians splashing in the huge tire gashes. Though I must say that it was distressing, as a patriot, to see an American citizen's farm left by the DEA in a trashed condition not all that different from the one in which Tomas's punk Eagle's Nest predecessors had left that landscape.

The chainsawed garden itself didn't leave much for a friendly Mendocino County deputy to check up on. With sharply angled stumps it looked like Isengard under Saruman.

Beyond the stifling of new tax revenue that will benefit everyone, in those stumps I saw my own taxes being wasted. That's a pet peeve of mine. If you ever want to set my blood boiling, show me one of those exposés where contractors get $1,220 for a toilet in the Pentagon or corporate absentee "farmers" are paid $97,000 by you and me not to grow soybeans. This was the same thing. Worse, actually. The War on Drugs, as the Students for Sensible Drug Policy slogan puts it, is a war on us.

In order to keep a wartime economy humming, our nation has taken the unusual step of declaring war on a hundred million of its own citizens. Even Secretary of State Hillary Clinton seemed to unintentionally admit as much when she told a Mexican interviewer in February 2011 that ending the Drug War by legalization in either country wasn't a good idea because "there is just too much money in it." Her other comments seemed to suggest she was referring to cartel profits, but even if so, she missed the point that the existence of the illegal market is explicitly why there's so much money in it for criminals.

In general, I wake each morning a renewed optimist. And though the title of this chapter is not "The Day the Bubble Popped," the scene at the Cohens' goat and cannabis farm was causing this Drug Peace believer to phone in his optimism for a couple of days. The best possible immediate conclusion I could draw about the Northstone raid was that cannabis activists already know that they're on their own—they're forging ahead whether federal policy changes next week or in twenty years. As Vonnegut's holy man Bokonon puts it in *Cat's Cradle:* "Pay no attention to Caesar. Caesar doesn't have the slightest idea what's really going on."

But that's not how Matt Cohen wants to live. He's a proud member of this society. And that was also not an option for Tomas, who found himself midharvest overseeing a cannabis-stuffed house, listening to the Black Keys, and close to freaking out. With Rippers to the left of him and the feds to the right, he took Cohen's punishing hard.

"How am I doing? The freakin' DEA is robbing Matt," he said about two hours into the raid. "I feel personally attacked. He's a fellow MendoGrown board member. My head is spinning. I am so disgusted by the actions of the federal government; that people can go to jail for cultivating a benevolent plant like cannabis. I am just so motivated to change. And also pretty scared that they'll come for me next. [Pause] Damn! This was gonna be my first day off in a month. I have tickets to the Cal-USC game tonight."

"You should still go," I said from my redwood-enshrouded office.

"I am. Already am, actually."

Given that he was en route to the Bay Area, I asked Tomas if he'd called that day's trimmer, Jared, to warn him to take caution.

"Why, do you know something?" Tomas asked me with a forced laugh. Strikes deep, paranoia does.

Tomas was not alone in his reenergized activist mode. Even Courtenay was saying within days that the raid was a blessing in disguise. The silver lining came in the immediate national pushback. For one thing, a PBS crew was in the trashed next room interviewing Matt when she and I spoke. By the morning after the raid, the Northstone matter had reached Washington, and cannabis activist e-mail networks were humming:

> Less than a week after the U.S. attorneys in California announced that they'd waste your taxpayer dollars by raiding and closing state-legal medical marijuana providers, the DEA used paramilitary tactics while raiding the Northstone Organics co-op in Mendocino County. Please e-mail your assemblymember, state senator, Governor Jerry Brown, and Attorney General Kamala Harris, asking that they publicly denounce federal interference with the California medical marijuana program. Once you've sent that e-mail, please call the White House and respectfully ask that they allow states to implement and regulate medical marijuana programs.
>
> The raid on Northstone is especially disturbing because, by all accounts, they went above and beyond to ensure that they complied with state and local laws and regulations. In fact, Mendocino County Sheriff Tom Allman said Northstone "appears to have followed all of the county's regulations, which cost the cooperative about $8,500 a year." . . . Send this alert to your friends and family and (help) end this nonsense.
>
> Sincerely,
> Robert Capecchi, Legislative Analyst
> Marijuana Policy Project
> 236 Massachusetts Ave., NE,
> Suite 400
> Washington, D.C. 20002
> http://www.mpp.org

And the Northstone Facebook page was inundated with support, including this October 17 post from one Dave Shore:

> We at Magic Growing fully support you, and if you come back to grow next season, we will hook you up with an incredible deal on Magic Pots. So sorry you got picked on, please keep us updated with your situation!

Mendocino County supervisor McCowen called Cohen's raid "outrageous . . . Cohen was the first medical marijuana advocate in Mendocino County to call for regulation of the cultivation and dispensing of medical marijuana to prevent black market diversion."

OK, several growers told me, maybe the Northstone harassment will prove a giant leap forward for the movement. But as is the case in every war, it is the civilians who suffer most. In this case, Northstone's seventeen hundred patients.

"We're beside ourselves—it's especially scary to not know if my partner is going to get his [cancer] medicine," Northstone patient Diane Fortier told me. He was the one who missed two days' delivery thanks to the Northstone Two's Sonoma quagmire. And he only got it the third day because Matt made the delivery personally.

On October 13 it looked like there could be a Northstone Three or Four. This about a week, by the way, before Temple University researchers concluded in the journal *Anesthesia and Analgesia* that the cannabinoid cannabidiol (CBD) "completely prevents" the onset of nerve pain associated with chemotherapy treatment.

"Imagine if you went to the pharmacy not knowing if your prescription could be filled," the sixty-one-year-old Fortier told me. "Finally there's a safe source and the government is taking it away? It's causing mayhem in our lives. I would do just about anything to get Northstone back on its feet, because we're vulnerable. Now I have to go to sources I worry about for Bill. Living in pain is not something I'd wish on anyone."

Indeed, Fortier had had reason to think her partner could rely on Northstone-grown medicine. Just five days before the raid, the co-op's thousands-strong mailing list received an e-mail with the subject: "FALL HARVEST COMING!" The note itself promised fifteen strains, some new, including Pineapple Thai and Red Cherry Berry. The Northstone menu also included a link to a Reschedule Cannabis petition.

Instead, by this interference with a law-abiding cannabis farmer trying to deliver the medicine, these law-abiding senior citizens, these health care consumers, could be forced to meet with a criminal. It's either legalize cannabis or keep enriching the cartels. In a formula few could misread, the feds in 2011 were choosing to favor the illegal market. Again. Prices were already heading up as I finished my research in Mendocino County. Though in a troublingly ironic twist, there's since been talk of a steep, if likely temporary, decline in Mendocino County outdoor wholesale prices, since the raids are forcing legitimate growers back underground, flooding the black market.

Seventeen hundred patients are yanked along when Matt Cohen is Punished with the Process. But wait. Did the raid of a 9.31 farm violate the game as played between federal and local law enforcement? Back on the morning of the assault on the Cohens, after hanging up with the jittery Tomas—and Cal lost big that evening, completing a terrible day for him—my next call was to the sheriff's office, perhaps three hours into the raid. Tom called me back within forty-five minutes on his cell phone.

"In the game of life, not every step is a step forward," he told me poetically. Evidently the Mendocino County Sheriff's Office only learned of the raid target at five A.M.—an hour prior—when a deputy liaison accompanied the DEA team to pick up the county dump truck that would haul away Northstone's crop. The deputy called Allman as soon as he realized where they were heading. The sheriff told me he told the deputy (who was not Randy Johnson) to "take good notes."

Sheriff Tom explained the reason for his venture into metaphor: "My sphere of influence is thirty nine hundred square miles. The DEA's is the whole nation. So I have to be very careful what I say. I don't want to say anything that would create a rift between me and the DEA. We have a good working relationship right now, and I wouldn't want to bring any more attention on this county than there already is, if you know what I mean."

I thought I did. To make sure, I asked him how the Northstone raid would affect the 9.31 Program. He said, "I don't have a crystal ball."

I was stunned. Reeling. "They went for the Boy Scout instead of the criminal," Leif told me when we spoke soon after.

"Ask him if he's still in the program" was Jim Hill's suggestion for when I caught up with Matt Cohen. "Remember, that wasn't his medicine they took. It was thousands of patients' medicine. Your government and mine is attacking sick Americans. With guns. And it's the patients' prices that go up."

Mendocino supervisor McCowen likes to point out that everyone in Mendocino County is "in the same boat." Linked by this industry. So it's safe to say everyone was badly rattled this day. I didn't get a return e-mail from Sergeant Randy for a week, and that basically said, "I'm busy for a few weeks working on a new computer system." I took that to mean, "We gotta wait to see how all this plays out."

Around lunchtime on the day of the Northstone Raid I needed a break. My Sweetheart found me outside in lotus position in a redwood circle and asked why I had pulled down our last tomato plant. "Best to avoid miscommunication in case anyone gets an address wrong," I said. A distant helicopter was doing its ululating yodel. "One farmer I just spoke with told me he's chopping down his whole crop today. He's wondering if he, or maybe everyone in the program, is next."

"Wow," I thought while my Sweetheart went inside to make me some tea. "Intruders have penetrated the Bubble within the Bubble within the Bubble."

# TWENTY-NINE
## The Thirteen-Billion-Dollar Economic Hit

Medical marijuana dispensaries are helping our economy, creating jobs, and most importantly, providing a necessary service for suffering patients. There are real issues and real problems that the U.S. Attorney's Office should be focused on rather than using their limited resources to prosecute legitimate businesses. . . . Our law enforcement agencies—both state and local—should not assist in this unnecessary action. Shutting down state-authorized dispensaries will cost California billions of dollars and unfairly harm thousands of lives.

—California state senator Leland Yee, October 13, 2011

**B**y midafternoon on the day of the Northstone raid, not even their attorney Panzer knew anything about the Cohens' fate. The couple was being held incommunicado. There was nothing for me to do but be a journalist: keep following the money.

That was easy. There were four groups of people this law enforcement offensive benefited. They were a) the black market growers of whom the Camo Cowboys croon—along with their cousins, the fly-by-night strip mall dispensaries in the Stocktons and Burbanks of the world, b) Mexican cartels, c) pharmaceutical interests opposed to cheaper, better competition from an ancient plant, and d) prosecutors who perceive Agressive Drug Warrior to be a résumé item.

Putting aside patients for a moment, among those directly and immediately harmed by the federal action late in 2011 were the state's already suffering municipalities. As Sacramento's Fox40 quoted Ron Mullins, manager of a local collective called J Street Wellness, on October 14, "We paid forty grand . . . in license fees, plus a four percent tax." These fees, incidentally, were not being returned to cannabis collectives and cooperatives whose managers chose to stay in the program while Sacramento froze its permitting process in light of the 2011 turmoil. The city's financial managers' explanation for hoarding the cash was essentially "We're not canceling. Just freezing."

That was real money that had been coming in to bare municipal coffers from one dispensary in one city. Sacramento's Economic Development Department employees agreed that the local revenues were two million dollars for the previous year. Most statewide figures call California's cannabis industry a thirteen-billion-dollar one. Annually. And remember, NBC Los Angeles estimates that there are currently one million Californian medical cannabis patients, paying that hundred million dollars in sales tax.

And yet in the broader county, Sacramento officialdom didn't seem to mind, bragging to its own e-SacCountyInfo mailing lists in October that "63 [of] 99 dispensaries have closed" in Sacramento County. This reflects that, California being California, municipal reaction to the federal offensive ranged from jubilant to horrified.

It should be noted that this lost two million dollars for Sacramento doesn't even count payroll taxes, property taxes, and income taxes. The two collectives Jim Hill managed paid seventy thousand dollars in payroll tax, one hundred thousand in sales tax, and forty thousand in property tax in 2010.

"Never had a single issue with law enforcement," he told me. "No bars on our windows." I should add to that statement, though, that Hill's automated eight-foot-high farm gate, a monument to prohibition, was located in one of Mendo's cell phone black holes, and when I'd arrive to do research, I routinely had to blow some of my kids' soap bubbles over the top to get at least the dogs' attention.

But the point is the October federal posture was shutting down taxpaying American business. And not-for-profit ones, too, in California, claims by the U.S. Attorney's Office notwithstanding. It's a tactic that seems to be saying, "We'd rather be a bankrupt nation than legalize drugs." But what cannabis activists insist is that, if the public could see the minutes of policy meetings at federal agencies (and know the players), the tactic is actually saying, "We'd rather be a bankrupt nation than allow cannabis to compete with pharmaceuticals and close prisons."

Given that the stated Justice Department raison d'être for the offensive was "profiteer hijacking" of the medical cannabis industry, while on the ground the DEA had instead raided a man who personally made less than fifty thousand dollars from it in three years, I wanted to know how Northstone could possibly be characterized in court as for-profit? Even the star prosecution witness in the state Northstone Two trial had called the cooperative's prices below retail.

So I called to ask U.S. Attorney Haag with what I thought was a simple question: "Why has Northstone been targeted?" Though I couldn't get an answer from her spokesperson, Jack Gillund, his no-comment was revealing. "I'm not going to discuss an ongoing investigation," he told me after asking me to spell the name of the cooperative. "And we don't discuss policy. If we did that, people would know how we did stuff and why we did stuff. So we have to draw a line there. But if you have any other questions, I'd be happy to bring them to the U.S. attorney."

"Hmm," I thought. "You're right. We the people *would* like to know how you do stuff and why you do stuff."

I told Mr. Gillund I'd try to think of drug policy questions that didn't deal with policy and follow up by e-mail. The only one that came to mind was "Was Ms. Haag aware that a member of local law enforcement had recently testified under oath in a state trial that the Northstone Cooperative was a paragon among lawful medicinal cannabis providers?" But, dang, that concerned an ongoing investigation. So no luck there. She'd probably have gotten all technical about federal law trumping state law anyway.

When I asked DEA spokesperson Payne why Northstone was raided he said, "Never heard of them, but they were raided because they broke the law. If you want specifics you should probably talk to the U.S. attorney."

I hung up the phone hoping that deep down, federal prosecutors feel that as Americans, we're all ultimately on the same side: the side of a strong, safe, prosperous, and free America. I know this sounds like basic "what we all believe" stuff, not necessary to bring up. But I think it is important to remember that the Drug War's U.S. front is a civil war. Whatever your view of cannabis, Americans are the casualties. That's not good. Plus, most cannabis defendants aren't breaking any other laws; they're law abiding except for a plant. Yet homes are seized. Kids taken. Businesses bankrupted. That makes the issue deadly serious.*

Before I had left the Cohens' farm following my postraid recon, I stood in the spot near the goat corral where, seven months earlier, Matt had told me that his farm's alarm system was intended for Rippers. Hope it came with a money-back guarantee. Because those ninety-nine Northstone plants, days from harvest, were gone now. Ripped or seized, the difference was academic for Northstone Organics. Same chainsaws. I asked the DEA's Payne where the medicine was, and he said the dangerous controlled substance was as a practice warehoused as evidence and would later be burned.

When I first spoke to him on his new cell phone four days after the raid, Cohen was not only still a believer in 9.31 permitting, he told me that the program, if anything, needs to strengthen its guidelines. I should say, though, that when I initially asked him if his crystal ball showed a future for 9.31, Cohen paused so long I thought a wiretap was interfering with the call.

Then he said, in a measured, shaken-but-not-broken voice that

---

* Michael Pollan famously parried early Obama administration overtures to run the Department of Agriculture. To avoid that tragedy in the Drug Peace efforts, I would humbly like to offer my services to President Obama or his successor as drug czar, but only if the position is renamed drug shaman and, additionally, only if the president's Office of National Drug Control Policy is redubbed the Cannabis Economic Development Office and Center for Addiction Recovery and Retraining (CEDO-CARR). Or better yet, since we are talking about a plant, let's fold the ONDCP into the USDA and either I or, if he's now willing, Mr. Pollan, can run the show until we get frustrated and resign two years in.

TOO HIGH TO FAIL

actually frightened me a bit because I'd never heard him lack certainty about anything cannabis-related before, "I do think there's a future for permitting. With conditions. I think there needs to be even more oversight and compliance. Because I suspect they could probably have found medical providers who diverted to the black market. There needs to be more organized response from our community, demanding that everyone grow responsibly. We have real providers next to total thugs. We need to weed those people out.

"As for 9.31," he continued, "maybe we'll look back in five years and say, 'The first few years were a bit bumpy, a raid a year or so, but then it took off.' Or maybe we'll find that confidence is shaken and farmers aren't joining in as large numbers as they did this year."

Ryan Landers agrees with Cohen about bad apples spoiling the basket. An AIDS patient who worked on Proposition 215 in 1996, he told the *Sacramento News and Review* on October 20, "People blew it out of control. Now, did [the feds] have to come in so heavy-handed, and threaten patients and jobs? It's things like that that creates more harm for patients."

But Jim Hill does not agree with blaming cultivators. I called him so early during the Northstone raid because I knew he was someone who understood what the Cohens were at that moment going through—and he in fact predicted exactly how many hours they'd be held before the DEA made tracks and left.

He told me of Matt Cohen's predicament, "See what happens when you sign up and let the government tell you how much medicine patients need? In Mendocino County this year, you had a higher chance of getting raided by the feds if you were a 9.31 grower than if you weren't. You think they won't come asking for 9.31 farmers' records?"

Cohen's comeback to that view, at least when we first spoke after the raid, was that if 9.31 endures, it can return even better suited to support an emergent cannabis industry. This is an example of the forty-year "if it doesn't kill me it'll make me stronger" approach to fighting the Drug War. I remembered Cohen's earlier, casual take on his Northstone Two's troubles: "cost of doing business." I asked him if his recent federal visit was likewise just a part of the cost of doing business.

"Well, federal business is different than state business," he said with a laugh. "Right now, anyway. But forward progress is inevitable."

But by the time I visited his farm to survey the damage on October 23, Cohen had fairly radically changed his tune (aka spent a lot of time talking to his lawyer).

"I'm not a cannabis farmer right now," he told me on the same spot where Tomas had given me the "we'll do it or die trying" pep talk back in the spring. "I'm a lobbyist. They can charge me at any time. So I can't cultivate or market or distribute or any of it. Financially, the raid basically bankrupted the co-op the same way as a robbery would have. I sunk all my savings into it. If we reopened now, I'd have to accept other farmers' medicine on consignment. That asks a lot of other growers and I couldn't guarantee quality. I don't want shitty Yelp reviews. I only want to do it in a closed loop—farm to patient."

Here Cohen sighed deeply and reached out to pet one of his dogs. Then he shook his head. "We finally cracked the code of how to make this sustainable cannabis model work and then we got raided. Even to replant, we'd need angel investors. And I can't be around the farm until the federal cloud goes away. I just don't know if or when I'll be planting cannabis again. So I think I'm going to spend a year working to fix the laws on the state and federal level. Billions are at stake for the economy, and patients need their medicine."

One word came to mind when I heard Cohen's position: understandable. Ten years in a cage just doesn't sound like that good a time. The cages close when federal law changes. A federal prosecutor's job is to prosecute. A DEA team leader's job is to raid. Douglas Adams calls this the "shouting and killing trade," and it's part of society. They'll evidently continue to raid easy cannabis targets until the Controlled Substances Act tells them that the target is no longer domestic cannabis cultivators who are following state law. Meanwhile, there went another chunk of the hundred million in cannabis sales-tax dollars.

In addition to doing practical harm to the citizens his administration is supposed to be governing, by mid-October, pushback against the federal offensive was mushrooming beyond the cannabis industry network and into a publicly discussed bad election move for President Obama in California, Oregon, and elsewhere. Drug Policy Alliance (DPA) executive director Ethan Nadelmann said in the October 13 *San Francisco Chronicle* that he could not understand why the Obama Justice Department is willing to alienate real estate agents, property owners, gun owners, and the Democratic base.

"Typically, as an advocate," he said, "your best opportunities emerge when the other side overreaches." Indeed even the conservative-leaning *Orange County Register* blasted the federal raids in an October 22 editorial:

> We continue to believe that Prop. 215 was good medicine, and that medical marijuana should remain a state matter. . . . The Obama administration should return to its original stance of noninterference in state medical marijuana policies. It should concentrate on the deficit, debt, high unemployment, and the numerous ongoing wars, leaving other matters to the states. We'd also like to hear what the Republican presidential candidates would do on this issue. As to [a proposed 2012 legalization ballot] initiative, we'll check it out should it advance to a ballot.

Nadelmann, who has been fighting to end the Drug War for twenty-five years, also told Reuters, "Instead of encouraging state and local authorities to regulate medical marijuana distribution in the interests of public safety and health, [the Obama] administration seems determined to recriminalize as much as possible. It all adds up to bad policy, bad politics, and bad faith."

That's exactly why I wanted so badly to figure out how high up the food chain this October offensive went. Who was responsible for a cannabis policy that was being widely considered worse than Bush's? The worst in history, many in the blogosphere were concluding. I put out invitations for off-the-record discussions with Justice Department operatives* but couldn't get a definitive answer to my question about where the buck stopped.

I did get two conflicting clues. The first came from a source that, based on other comments I'd read of his over the past year, seemed to be an unofficial Office of National Drug Control Policy mouthpiece. Kevin Sabet, a former advisor to Drug Czar Gil Kerlikowske, currently describing himself as a "consultant to drug prevention and policy organizations," told ABC News on October 26, "All actions have to be approved by Attorney General Holder."

But then Lucia Graves floated this in the *Huffington Post* the same day, quoting California-based U.S. attorney spokeswoman Lauren Horwood: "The only D.C.-based official with whom California U.S. attorneys coordinated was Deputy Attorney General James Cole." Maybe someone in reelection headquarters in Chicago realized before that bleak month of October was out that more than seven votes were at stake.

For his part, Cohen said he believes his raid is connected to the Sonoma DA's office frustration with the Northstone Two case, and indeed Panzer said in the October 30 *Sacramento Bee*, "The very day that [Sergeant Johnson and Supervisor McCowen] testified was the day that the DEA did a flyover of Mr. Cohen's property."

Cohen's take to me was "You get the U.S. attorneys declaring open season, and the DEA probably has some discretion to go

---

* I extended some of those feelers via a well-connected attorney, who told me, "I know many of the rising stars at Justice understand the issues because I was passing joints to them in law school."

after someone they just don't like. I was on *Frontline*. I'm in the media all the time. The 9.31 program is embarrassing to the DEA, and [Sonoma assistant DA] Jamar has nothing on our delivery guys. It's totally about dogma. Personal beliefs of bureaucrats on an issue that Obama doesn't want to use political capital on. It's not about what's right." In *The Sacramento Bee*, Jamar denied siccing the feds on Cohen, calling it "merely speculation."

When the dust settled, the Northstone raid proved to be, like tens of thousands before it over the past forty years, just another of what cannabis cultivators call a "smash and grab" of ninety-nine plants and some computers. No one was arrested. No charges have been filed. Just a little more Punishing with the Process. I guess you and I own the crop now. Don't know where the computers are.

It was a simple governmental theft of cooperatively owned medical property. And thus now, two months later, it sure sounds like, yes, a game to me. An old one. One side wins a round or two, and then the other counterpunches. "Not every step is a step forward," as the prophetic Sheriff Tom put it. He's seen dozens of these skirmishes. Almost no one remembers 2002's raids or 1999's cannabis activist court victories. That's just not how the Californian memory works.

An example of a then-resonant moment on the Drug War timeline: the day in 2001 when the Supreme Court unanimously ruled that federal government could in fact force the closure of an Oakland cannabis dispensary. Big news at the time. Another one that got people excited was the 2010 settlement whereby the federal government agreed to stop raiding a Santa Cruz cooperative if its lawyers would stop suing it.

The lesson to me is that the politics of the moment are almost irrelevant. The cannabis market stays right where it is: America's biggest agricultural commodity. Yell and scream all you want. This plant is not a pendulum. It's a pillar.

This is why cannabis activists believe they've already won the war. They'll never give up, and eventually they'll outlast their opponents. It'd be like the actual World Series not mattering in baseball. If the trophy went, permanently, to the team that kept showing up without fail every year. One year the other team is going to stop showing up. "Could be twenty years of this, though," NORML's Gieringer told me.

When Cohen next got his chance at bat, the day after the raid, he got off a professional note to the Northstone mailing list saying that the closure would last for seven days. This was a vital piece of information: Patients needed to know if and when they'd be getting their medicine. But the update that went out on October 22 read:

> **Northstone Organics operations are suspended indefinitely due to a DEA raid on our farm. We are so sorry that the Federal government feels it is necessary to spend our hard earned tax dollars on disrupting safe access to medical cannabis patients.**
>
> **Monday, October 24th, two of our drivers will be back in Santa Rosa (not related to the recent raid) court for the continuance of their preliminary hearing. Yet another saga unjustly executed by Sonoma County law enforcement and DA. We feel the recent raid on our farm is possibly tied to this ongoing case in Sonoma. Please show your support.**
>
> **600 Administration Drive, Santa Rosa CA 95403**
> **Room 5 @ 9:00am**
> **Monday Oct 24th**
> **As always, Northstone Organics thanks you for your membership and support, and we continually strive to find better ways to serve you!**

So I suppose that I should have known that Cohen would be speaking in the past tense a lot when we toured the farm on the twenty-third. Though it was a past tense peppered with hopeful future tense. It was only the present, Cohen's grammar suggested, that sucked.

As Homer reminds us, in any war, no one can know what will

happen after the first volleys are fired. The clear message from the tumultuous October for cannabis was "Fasten your seat belt, this war is about to take off." Buffy Madison seemed to have a cogent take when she told me, "In the Civil Rights movement, the segregation side stepped it up at the very end. Right before they gave up."

This was also the sentiment of Northstone Facebook page poster Carol Borden on October 14:

> Thank you for standing up in the face of fear. They can't win, ultimately, but they can sure destroy a lot of lives in the meantime.

If 9.31 represents the cannabis Declaration of Independence, October 2011 began the period when the British won nearly every battle and lost both the strategic advantage and most hearts and minds. If those 2011 raids don't prove to be the final flourish, then they definitely caused renewed defiance in the face of bombs bursting in air. "It's coming to a head" is how Jim Hill put it.

Hill doesn't envision being a federal outlaw for long: "You've got to work to change a law that's wrong. And at the same time you've got to live as though it's already changed. Then when society catches up, suddenly you're just a citizen again and no one can remember the crazy law that would let hospice patients die without access to medicine that would ease their pain and allow them to say good-bye to their families. To me, telling the truth about the inhumanity of federal cannabis law is just being rational. You can call it activism if you want."

Hold on tight. Both sides are laying it on the line, like the fourteenth round in an Ali-Frazier fight. The official federal policy, if there was a coherent one in late 2011, was "We're not going to even give you a chance to do it right." Beyond that, "We're going to spend millions of taxpayer dollars fighting changes to the Controlled Substances Act." The cannabis industry's response, not counting the fly-by-nighters who run whenever the heat gets turned up a notch, was "(Sigh) Will you stop already? We already won."

Whether or not you believe the RAND study on crime or the health studies on cannabis, it's hard to imagine that the Drug Peace Era could be worse for America, Mexico, and in fact the whole world than these forty years of war have been.

Meanwhile, while Matt Cohen considered how long to extend his hiatus, the "nonsense" Robert Capecchi referred to in his Marijuana Policy Project appeal continued. Here's the Santa Rosa *Press Democrat*'s "Road Warrior" Column of October 7, 2011:

## Mailbag: Drug crackdown on Hwy. 101
by Road.Warrior

We've received a few e-mails lately from readers asking why they're seeing Santa Rosa, Rohnert Park, and Petaluma police stopping motorists along Highway 101 from Windsor north of Cloverdale. For example, JD wrote in:

"I am a courier for a pharmacy and have seen Santa Rosa police squad cars pulling vehicles over the past few weeks on 101 well north of Santa Rosa. Would you have any insight as to why they are that far away from Santa Rosa? Are they perhaps part of a training situation? Just very odd seeing them that far from their territory. I have always seen sheriff vehicles enforcing the rules of the road, but rarely have I seen city vehicles on state highways especially away from the city they represent."

Asked about the traffic stops, a Santa Rosa police official paused for a bit before saying, "I can't talk about it."

Well, then, who's in charge of the operation?

"I can't tell you, and they're not going to talk to you about it."

Another Santa Rosa police official also declined to discuss the operation, saying it was "sensitive."

**TOO HIGH TO FAIL**

But another law enforcement source said several Sonoma County agencies are participating in an antidrug task force. Sheriff's deputies for years on north 101 have been stopping vehicles that they suspect are being used to transport marijuana. Those stops often are successful. Now it appears other agencies are joining in.

So the Gauntlet was proving dangerous as usual just weeks before Tomas had to run it. Although Andy Cash might no longer be casting the net. Here's Sonoma County's *Windsor Times* from two days prior to the Road Warrior column:

### Officer Andrew "Andy" Cash is Windsor's New School resource officer.

Windsor students may think twice about misbehaving at school this year after the Windsor Unified School District welcomed a new Student Resource Officer to campus.

Officer Andrew "Andy" Cash joined the Windsor force this year after 16 years in law enforcement, starting as a police cadet, working as a deputy then joining the Sonoma County Sheriff's Department in patrol before most recently working in Narcotics.

Hmm. Was that shadow I was seeing on the horizon in fact the pendulum already on its way back? Less than a week after the Northstone raid, a new Gallup poll reported that for the first time American support for full (not just "medical") cannabis legalization had reached 50 percent. Three days earlier, on October 14, the trustees of California's largest medical doctors' group, the California Medical Association, representing thirty-five thousand physicians, voted unanimously to endorse legalizing cannabis.

The drafter of the policy, Dr. Donald Lyman, told the *Los Angeles Times* on October 16 that drug law to date has "proven to be a failed public health policy."

There, in one long weekend, were your poll numbers and your medical evidence for ending the Drug War.

And yet the game for some reason continues, a little closer to legalization with every pendular cycle, even if each swing hurts at least as many legitimate operators and patients as it does criminal operations. If enough signatures are gathered, California voters might have their choice of multiple full cannabis legalization initiatives in 2012 (though 2014 looks more likely), and one (or more) is on the 2012 ballot in both Colorado and Washington.

In November of 2011, the medical cannabis advocacy group Americans for Safe Access began circulating a draft cannabis bill for the 2012 California legislative cycle, which among other provisions would codify the legality of (duh) collective members paying for cannabis with money. On October 27, 2011, the same group filed suit in federal court, arguing that the month's raids constituted a tenth amendment violation of state's rights. One of the plaintiffs is a Northstone Organics cancer patient named Mark Perillo Sr.

The premise of the suit is that the Justice Department is not affording California cannabis farmers and patients equal protection under the law. Hard to argue with that. There is no question federal enforcement is ultimately selective.

The message in the lawsuit is clear. Real Americans are sick of hiding from their own federal government, and even angrier that the aggression appears to be coming from the presidential administration for whom they campaigned so hard. In other words, no, those aren't Civil War revisionists, antitax crusaders, or the NRA making the state sovereignty argument. They're California cannabis farmers and patients.

And in Mendocino County, they're as law-abiding as grape farmers. Here's proof. Late on October 26, Tomas heard another pair of Rippers, this time closer to the house. Just outside the orchard. On this occasion the Ripper team had been inadvertently tipped off about the bounty by Tomas's landlord's Realtor, who had been giving tours while Tomas was trimming. During one Eagle's Nest showing, a young mother had entered from the porch and said, "Yum, does it come with the smell?"

"Terpenes," I explained.

In perhaps the final sign of Tomas's conversion to True Mendonesian, he told me that after he was rousted to the back deck he "saw the guard deer that sleep under the fig trees weren't spooked, so they couldn't have come that far. That meant I had time to call the sheriff."

This, remember, was *after* the Northstone federal raid. When the responding Mendocino deputy, arriving within a half hour, this time asked if Tomas grew cannabis, he said, "Yes. Yes I do. Would you like to see my permit from your department?"

The deputy essentially said, "That won't be necessary, sir," and went on to stop and question the Rippers, one of whom Tomas recognized as having been on a tour of the Eagle's Nest a few days earlier. The duo had been scared off by the now familiar neighbor's shotgun blasts after Tomas had confronted them with shouts.

"I can't remember exactly what I said, but the message was, let the word go forth to the Ripper community," Tomas told me when he recounted the story during the final Halent bag-sealing session on Ocotober 28. "Rural folks notice their surroundings. And in Mendocino, the sheriff will come and apprehend you if you try to rip someone's crop."

He shook his head in wonder at being part of this miracle. "It's a huge change for cannabis in America. The sheriff works for all of the citizens of the county. All of them."

Sergeant Randy monitored Tomas's second trespassing call on his radio. "This," he told Tomas, "is why 9.31 matters, why it's gotta continue: When cannabis farmers can call the police, on any issue—domestic abuse, trespassing—we have a safer community."

The days of Frontier Justice in Mendocino County might finally be numbered. Every politician longs to say he's fighting crime. He throws border patrol agents at a problem by the thousand. Here, in some yellow zip ties, is crime reduction in action. A local solution that's not just inexpensive, it's revenue generating.

By the end of the 2011 season, Tomas was a welcome member of his neighborhood watch, embraced by cannabis and grape farmers, retirees and law enforcement. A local. It's just one county in one state. But it's a working model.

Whatever his own cultivation future, Matt Cohen remained adamant in the weeks following his raid that the poll numbers and the zeitgeist shift they represent hadn't emerged too late for the MendoGrown citizen farmer model. "We'll get there," he said, his posture a little more stooped than I was used to as we toured his cooperative's hacked-down garden. "It'll take a lot of work, especially on the federal level. But we'll get there."

# THIRTY
## Meet the Patients

I will prescribe regimens for the good of my patients according to my ability and my judgment and never do harm to anyone.

—Hippocratic Oath (original)

[The 2011 federal cannabis offensive] is tantamount to a government bailout for criminal gangs and violent drug cartels. . . . For some reason, the federal government wants to force legal medical marijuana patients toward a dangerous criminal market and away from an above-ground industry that pays over $100 million per year in state taxes and provides jobs for thousands of our citizens.

—Retired California Superior Court judge Jim Gray, cosponsor of the 2012 "Regulate Marijuana Like Wine" California ballot initiative, in an October 17, 2011, press release

There's nothing that anyone can do to stop me from providing this medicine to people who need it. Unless they lock me up, chain me down, and put me in a box, I will keep on doing this.

—Steve DeAngelo, founder of Oakland's Harborside Health Center, after receiving a $2.5 million supplemental tax bill, quoted in the *San Francisco Chronicle*, October 7, 2011

On the rest of Mendocino County's, I dunno, let's call it five thousand small farms, harvesters weren't pausing to gauge political winds. They *were* noticing the suddenly and stunningly sunny breezes that followed the premature start to the rainy season. In other words, feds aside, the trimming must go on. Only faster and more tensely even than usual.

And, on many farms, with a palpably renewed sense of mission. I was back at the Eagle's Nest October 18 and October 28 to witness the final Kama Collective harvest push. With ex-military

man Adam back on duty and providing prowling nighttime surveillance, Tomas's "now that I've had a week to calm down" perspective on Cohen's federal raid came from a higher altitude.

He wasn't the paranoid wreck I expected to find madly stuffing
flowers into turkey bags. He sounded, actually, like he was a quar-
terback who'd just got an inspiring pep talk from a legendary coach
while down after three quarters.

"I'm no longer just a medicine grower and deliveryman," he
said, hauling some Grand Daddy Purple stalks from the lower garden, sandals gone and in boots for the duration. "I'm a catalyst for
change. I'm fed up. It's gotta stop."

"So you're lobbying too?"

"*And* providing. For a while there last week, I definitely gave
some thought to whether cultivation was where I could make the
most difference. And I decided it was."

This exchange took place on the fragrant Eagle's Nest porch.
Two just-weaned deer had greeted me when I parked the truck
under long-angled autumnal light. They were now munching on
the pink pulp from fallen figs. Someone—my money's on Stella—
had carved jack-o'-lanterns, which were scattered about. One
appeared to be smoking a cigar.

Inside the cannabis-hanging warehouse, Stella had prepared a
prosciutto-and-fig lunch, with balsamico drizzled on top and fresh
mozzarella slices on the side. It was the "an army marches on its
stomach" philosophy in action, and Tomas knew it. "Happy people
are better trimmers," he said.

In addition to the massive trimming quantity still to be done,
and the eight plants—all late-finishing Casey Jones strains—
waiting to be harvested and carted inside, Tomas, as vice president
to Matt Cohen, now had extra responsibilities at MendoGrown.
So he was on the phone discussing protest marches and drafting
mailing-list calls to action and even discussing Sustainability
Standards Committee work to help keep his mind off the "five or
six" Gauntlet runs he had to make to get the medicine stored in
the Bay Area.

"I'll do one or two," Stella said, knowing she was unlikely to be profiled.

"No, I have to do it," Tomas said.

"I'd take the Audi," I suggested. "Never thought I'd hear those words coming out of my mouth."

"Man, I am not looking forward to that," Tomas confessed, looking around the flower-stuffed room.

"Well, at least Andy Cash appears to be preventing locker vandalism in an upscale high school," I posited.

At that exact moment, there in the Eagle's Nest's bud-filled basement, Ben Harper's "Burn One Down" came on Pandora.

> Before you knock it,
> Try it first,
> You'll see it's a blessing and it's not a curse.
> If you don't like my fire,
> Then don't come around,
> 'Cuz I am gonna burn one down.

"Or three hundred pounds down," I quipped in a Ben Harper falsetto, "the freeway."

Gone would be the Eagle's Nest posse on those nerve-racking October and early November runs. It would be all Tomas then. That is to say, getting Kama's medicine out of Mendocino County was a gut check among gut checks.

When I drove down to accompany Tomas on a November 6 patient delivery, I realized that he must've felt like a wildebeest crossing a crocodile-clogged stream. Safety only in numbers. Two local cop cars—I couldn't see from which town—had someone pulled over near my billboard, which had been changed. Now it hawked alcohol in a different way.

The best plan for the Gauntlet, farmers told me, was to wear a cloak of invisibility. Which is probably why I couldn't help noticing that the Willits car wash was a popular spot throughout harvest season. Tomas power-washed the Audi three times. It looked to me as though his "Cal Alumni" license plate holder had been hand-polished.

Whatever he did, it worked. Turned out it took five staged Gauntlet runs, but the 2011 Eagle's Nest harvest made it safely past Sonoma County. In fact, some of it made it *into* Sonoma County.

"They stop you or they don't," Tomas said of the experience. "It was a little stressful the first few times, then I got used to it. Set cruise control. No phone."

I asked him if crossing into Marin County on each run felt like entering the Promised Land. "Just getting past Windsor did," he said. "Now I can think about getting medicine to patients." I forgot to ask him if he framed the first bud.

Since he didn't plan to have the Kama website launched until January 2012—along with the associated marketing campaign designed to build a patient base—Tomas decided in the interim to donate some of Kama's debut medicine to needy patients. It reminded me of when my fishing buddies and I'd return the first salmon of the season caught in our net to the Alaskan fjords. Make a sharing gesture right out of the gate.

The very first patient delivery, which I accompanied, had an undeniably poetic appeal. Not only was Tomas bringing medicine into Sonoma County itself—the county in which he was raised, the county whose district attorney's office personnel were harassing the Northstone Two, and the county whose Drug Warriors had frightened me—but Lucille's first flowers themselves were going to none other than twice-deprived Northstone patients and AARP members Diane Fortier and Bill Harney.

The fog had been so low and thick on my drive south that by the Mendo-Sonoma border my headlights were having little effect. Accompanied by yet another story on the radio about California budget cutbacks and layoffs, I arrived in Sonoma County doing some math. What would the Drug Peace dividend really be? Harvard's Miron said the tax revenues alone would be $6.2 billion annually and an MIT newspaper editorial calculated a ten-year economic boost of $500 billion.

Tomas and I met at the Flying Goat coffee shop—his, I thought, considerate choice, given how much I missed my Pans and their milk—in the heart of Santa Rosa on the morning of November 6. We had both, amazingly, after a year of exposure to Mendo Time, remembered the previous evening's time change. I wore my cowboy hat, to emphasize "Redneck" over "Hippie." To be in touch with my inner Sonoma County PAL supporter.

We arrived at the Valle Vista Senior Subdivision where the couple lived at eleven A.M. The time was set because Diane and Bill were later that day throwing a party for an eightyish-year-old with dementia named Clay who lives on their block. "He's not really sure how old he is," Diane told me. "Frankly, he's not really positive it's his birthday, but somebody's got to look after him."

We crossed through the small, neatly xeriscaped front yard and into a literate and spiritual household. My eye caught a pre-movie edition of *Cold Mountain* on the shelf and couldn't miss the dresser-top stone Buddha of the early Indian variety—from his thinner and trippier-finger-position era. The living room coffee table was covered with one of those six-foot birthday banners that everyone's supposed to sign.

This was where Tomas and Diane sat down. No sign of Bill yet. Even though Tomas's was a donation of what looked to me to be at least an ounce of Lucille's Cashmere Kush flowers—in a one-quart mason jar—to make it unquestionably legal in the state of California, Diane and Bill became members one and two of Kama Collective (outside of anyone who joined so as to "collectively cultivate" over the summer, per current California law).

Tomas explained the privacy policy, and Diane showed Tomas not just both her own and Bill's doctor referrals, but a detailed and at times graphic medical history for both of them. Then she signed and dated the agreements for herself and Bill, for whom she had power of attorney.

After that, there was the briefest of awkward lulls. I wondered if I was the cause. Needless to say, it was a little uncomfortable for me to pry into a stranger's health care process and ask, "How's this plant working for your debilitating arthritis and your partner's pancreatic-cancer-related appetite problems?"

But Diane was one of those high-energy, "tomorrow could be my last" kind of people who don't like wasting a moment when it could be spent hugging someone. So, after mentioning that she had been feeling it from her neck to her tailbone that morning, she walked me right into the spare bedroom where Bill was in a sick-bed, watching an Elizabeth Taylor film and having a bad day.

"I'm so sorry I can't get up," he said. "It's frustrating." He looked healthy to me—good skin tone, plenty of flesh on his bones, and I told him I wouldn't have guessed he was feeling sick.

"See, that's what cannabis does for me," he said. "A year ago I weighed a hundred and eighteen pounds. Now I'm up to a hundred fifty-five."

Bill still had the port in his body that would likely be used again for chemo treatment. He had yet another doctor's appointment the following week. From the tone he used to recount each treatment horror, I could tell he was well into the cancer drill.

"How did you come to cannabis?" I asked him, not knowing how many questions I'd get in.

"My oncologist here in Santa Rosa told me about it," he said, laughing weakly. "I wasn't eating and he knew that meant I was going to die otherwise. Before that it wasn't really in my life. Very occasionally socially. I'm a polite Catholic at heart. If someone passed me a joint at a party once in a blue moon, I'd take a little puff. Now you can see why it was so difficult to have my delivery disrupted. I haven't eaten much in three or four days."

That was it for Bill's energy that day, and Diane was feeling pain, so she went to the master bedroom, beside a blind, good-vibed dog named Marian. There Diane pinched a scented, thimble-size piece of Lucille's flower between her fingers, and a moment after an expert joint-rolling, the room started to fill with the sweet, dense fragrance of Mendocino County's signature crop.

Lucille, as she transformed into her final gaseous state, carried me back along her journey from Rock's lab to Leif's greenhouse to a bumpy U-Haul ride to the Eagle's Nest Farm to the sheriff's office for zip ties to the trunk of an Audi to, finally, this enchanting herbal smell circling around Diane's close-cropped hair. Ever let your nose and face really absorb the steam from a cup of just-picked mint tea? This was a similar sensation. A police car screamed past outside, pursuing crime. There was none here.

Though she was smoking a joint, Diane told me she was shopping for vaporizers, especially for Bill. She and Tomas had a professional discussion about healthy delivery methods. What I took from it was that vaporizors represent the cutting edge in heated cannabis delivery.

The devices, sometimes sophisticated electronic tabletop units, sometimes handheld and battery-operated, burn the medicine at a temperature high enough to activate the THC and other heat-sensitive cannabinoids, but low enough not to burn the plant matter. Thus it's both a purer delivery method and easier on the throat. Plus, no smoke, though you still get the smell. They're often available at dispensaries, and are easy to find online. The medicinal joint-smoking era, in other words, might be drawing to a close.

Diane went to check on Bill to see if he had the energy to smoke, but returned to say he was asleep. She promised me an update after he medicated. As for herself with Lucille in her body, she said, "She definitely has an impact on the pain. But it's smooth and milder than some of the other indica strains I've used. Gentler. And that could be just what many patients want. I have a friend with glaucoma—a doctor, actually—who talks about how he's looking for qualities like these. I see why it's called Cashmere."

This is yet another granny figure saying to the medical-industrial complex, "You know what? Keep your expensive ineffective regimen. My partner needs his appetite restored." Even Bill's doctor agrees with this course of treatment. Does your congressperson and do your senators? If you call to ask, you might tell them lives are at stake.

When she called the next morning, Diane said that after a first medication, Lucille hadn't yet made Bill want to leap back into the

Pop Tarts, but that he'd keep at it. Two days later she called again and said he was scarfing "ravenously," following a first-ever craving for beef Stroganoff. "It still hasn't really had a munchies effect on me," she reported. "Not that I need it for that. I'm actually kind of grateful."

Mental note for Tomas if consulted by doctors or patients: Cashmere Kush is evidently a mild analgesic, but not a tremendous appetite stimulant for everyone. Possibly indicated for patients who want to be functional on the job while reducing pain from glaucoma or nervous system effects from MS. "No couch-lock," Diane agreed. "But my joint swelling is way down." Just as Rock intended in the barn laboratory.

Back in the senior subdivision, as Tomas pocketed the paper-work and I closed my laptop, Diane broke down. She hugged us good-bye and said to Tomas, "You don't know how kind it is what you're doing." She also said she had lots of senior friends who'd like to sign up to be Kama Collective members. Right in Diane and Bill's alcove, I asked Tomas if he consciously planned for karma payback like that in life. "At a certain point you realize it benefits you to help others when you can," he said.

"This," Tomas continued, settling into the Audi. "Is what it's all about."

He was relieved for about three seconds. Then his mind began racing. Since it was a donation, Diane and Bill had been willing to try this new Cashmere Kush strain. Even for loyal patients in a competitive marketplace, though, he felt he really needed to think about samples. "I'd like people to be able to squeeze and smell and try new strains," he said as we pulled out of Valle Vista. "Since they need to figure out what works for them. Gonna have to get those really small bud-sized mason jars."

In other words, now Tomas had a business to create. "All I want to do is make sure that Kama is around to provide again next season. I just saw that the medicine is fine."

And so, back to the Bay Area to bring in the lawyers and the accountants and the Web designers. It was "be careful what you wish for" time. Starting with a quickly sapped sixty thousand dollars, Tomas and a silent partner who preferred not to be named in this book—though I met him several times, and trust me, he's not part of a cartel—had been leaking capital throughout 2011.

Credit card bills were piling up, and even Tomas's mom wound up chipping in. Leeni is a retired librarian with a fairly thick Finnish accent who now keeps chickens on the suburban plot where Tomas was raised. When I asked her if she supported her son's work, she said, "I do—more than I thought I would. The more I learn, well, I am very angry about this Drug War."

Tomas's finance problem wasn't lack of investor interest. Plenty of his indoor-growing friends wanted to help the Kama cause, but, in Tomas's words, "I don't want people throwing duffel bags of cash at me. I want everyone to know what they're putting in and what they can expect to get back. And I want it to go very smoothly if our books ever get scrutinized." As a result, he told me, "Kama made it to delivery time by a hair."

Hey, I've seen mortgage banks with less realistic business plans. Tomas, in his MO, more than once reminded me of those centenarians who say their secret to longevity is "not letting things get to them." Accordingly, he recognized that it was a good thing that he was worrying about business matters in November. It meant harvest was done. It meant he had reached a stage where he could plan for the future. Every successful entrepreneur eventually comes to this astounding question: What if this crazy dream really comes true?

What Tomas knew for sure was that Kama will be a completely Web-based cannabis delivery service, as well as "a medical resource site for patients with questions about their health care and where cannabis fits into it. Each strain will be accompanied by its full cannabinoid profile. The fact is, most of America's thirty million regular cannabis medicators aren't open about it yet. When they can be, I believe they'll be looking for a high-end, sustainable source like Kama."

I managed not to make a pipe dream pun. Actually, my journalistic analysis of his prospects is cautiously optimistic. Most start-ups in any field fail. Kama has leapt some hurdles but it is just out of the first turn of a long race. The current dispensary die-off in California is only going to benefit those who endure. Enduring with a sustainable marketing plan, it seems to me, will only be a plus.

What mattered to Tomas at the moment, the only thing that mattered on November 6, was that the crop that he had worked on for eight months was reaching patients. When he dropped me off back at the Flying Goat, he said by way of parting, "I think I'll sleep tonight."

"You sank the putt," I agreed.

# THIRTY-ONE

## Pharmakon and the Complex Molecule

Our study did not find increases in adolescent marijuana use related to Rhode Island's 2006 legalization of medical marijuana.

> —Dr. Esther Choo, of Brown University, lead author of a report based on a survey of 32,570 middle school and high school students in Rhode Island and Massachusetts, and released on November 2, 2011

Say no more. I'm going home right now to give my kids some marijuana.

> —Satirical newspaper *The Onion*, October 20, 2011, quoting a "systems analyst" named Emma Barstow in a "Man on the Street" segment about the California Medical Association's call that week for cannabis legalization

Lucille's first cancer patient, Bill Harney, medicates with cannabis every day, and has been doing so for getting on two years. That is, ever since his quest for wellness became his life's priority. Prior to that, as he said, cannabis hadn't been much in his life.

Is that addiction? I think most of us would agree almost certainly not. Particularly compared to the current alternatives, of which pretty much all are much more addictive and possess more and more serious side effects than cannabis. I won't repeat a popular mass media error by miscategorizing today's pop-a-pharmaceutical medical regimen as the "traditional" option. As Carl Reid puts it, "There is no dependency like prescription painkiller dependency."

So what do we do about the one in five Americans who, *USA Today* reported in 2005, suffer from chronic pain? More than five million of them use prescription painkillers, according to the

National Institute on Drug Abuse, or more than 2 percent of the population.

Carl, Navy SEAL Mike Knox, and tens of thousands of ill or injured veterans like them, for instance, had been hooked on prescription painkillers like Vicodin for decades, all with disastrous health consequences. Painkiller dependence is even more pervasive for veterans of recent wars. Pain prescription numbers are up 438 percent for service members since 2001, according to the Department of Defense.

Each of the veterans I spoke with is contributing more to society, in taxes and energy, since substituting cannabis into his medical regimen. Rather than addicting him, Iraq vet Jamie Brown told me, "I actually don't really feel like I'm treating for PTSD anymore: I think the cannabis helped me get past it. Not that I love loud noises, but I haven't hit the deck in several years."

Still, despite the plant's safety and broad medical effectiveness, this book wouldn't feel complete without my attempting to draw at least a rough picture of responsible relationships with cannabis versus addiction. Whatever adjective you choose to categorize your cannabis intake, be it medicinal, spiritual, health maintenance, or social, as with alcohol, there is a line for every person between healthy and unhealthy use. Medicine and poison.

I was sure in the right place to do a field study this past year. By which I could accurately mean Planet Earth. But I'm referring to Mendocino County's openness about the plant. I saw no shortage of indisputably top echelon, ambitious, highly educated folks' undisguised relationship with the plant all over the American West, in fact—and a present but much lower level of what I would consider irresponsible use.

The most common view I heard in Mendo was that when it comes to areas like job stature and parenting, whether your preferred varietal is Riesling or Super Silver Haze should make no difference—if your relationship with the fruit or herb in question is healthy and responsible.

Of course, excessive use is an issue, as are the social and crime realities surrounding an expensive illegal crop. But once the ONDCP and the U.S. Congress land on Earth and the Controlled Substances Act reflects something close to reality, most people I met in Northern California believe that we will see it all comes down to personal and parental responsibility if one wants to keep on the healthy side of the *pharmakon* equation.

Our society can only hold together if we have some basic faith in the choices of ordinary people, the argument goes. Human beings have, the research seems to be showing, evolved to make use of this plant, after all. As Abigail Tucker noted in an August, 2011 *Smithsonian* article, "The ancients were liable to spike their drinks with all sorts of unpredictable stuff—olive oil, bog myrtle, cheese, meadowsweet, mugwort, carrot, not to mention hallucinogens like hemp and poppy." They were also liable to have built their yurt from the cannabis stalk, and eaten the seeds.

Now, for those ill-equipped to act responsibly, our society must contribute health care. Education and treatment. Duh. European and Canadian readers of this paragraph are scratching their heads and thinking, "Does he seriously have to explain that?" My response to that is "Hey, 1980 Ice Hockey, you pinkos. Only wimpy societies care for their weakest, poorest, and sickest. Cool societies give that money in tax breaks to hedge fund managers."

Kidding aside, most cannabis farmers desperately seeking legitimacy would gladly contribute yet another tax toward treatment for what they consider the very small percentage of people who will abuse the herb. Because the ones I interviewed don't equate use with abuse.

If a daily glass of wine at middle school is considered medicinal in Marseille, I would often hear in Mendocino County garden chats, an argument can be made that the mother who shares a weekly 4:20 cannabis ceremony with her nineteen-year-old daughter at the Willits Farmers' Market is engaging in a similar healthy ritual. Journalistically speaking, I'd need much more information about the specific situation in which the family lives in order to make such a determination.

Tomas told me, "Addiction doctors hate the healthy-glass-of-wine comparison, because it implies any ritualized use of cannabis can be healthy."

I spoke to a lot of people all over Mendocino County about cannabis in their lives, from the pregnant woman whose use is limited to making her own muscle salve for application during prenatal massages, to a prominant general herbalist who, asked at a seminar about children's use of cannabis, said simply, "Sick kids have cannabinoid receptors too." She's an herbalist for whom cannabis is just another plant on the shelf. Kind of like Dr. Mom in Laos.

In other words, if you ask some folks in Mendocino County, "Should regulated cannabis use be limited to adults over age twenty-one?" the answer is a tough one and not unanimous. When all currently conventional options were exhausted, a Ukiah oncologist in 2008 advised a county couple to give edible raw cannabis a shot at reducing the brain tumors in what he considered their four-year-old's terminal cancer. The parents complied. The doctor gave the girl six months. She's still with us today.

At the same time, Mendocino County, like (fill in your own county's name) does have a problem with adolescent substance abuse of all kinds. Particularly among at-risk kids—like my magenta-haired goth neighbors—who lack adequate parental communication lines. The Leonard Moore Cooperative's Gabriel Martin, as we've seen, believes decriminalization will actually reduce that problem vis-à-vis cannabis, by eliminating its forbidden-fruit allure.

Another Mendocino cannabis collective operator, Sherry Glasser-Love, goes even further: She takes community parenting into her own hands, out of necessity. Responding to a school administrator at a zoning meeting who objected to downtown cannabis collective storefronts in the county, Glasser-Love stepped to the speaker's podium and said, "Anybody who wants to help a kid in this county would do well to spend time with one. That's what I try to do. If their parents aren't doing the job, that's the problem. That's why they're running wild and disrupting our communities. Cannabis and cannabis collectives are not the problem."

And what Glasser-Love describes is an increasingly serious problem across North America. *Parent*, too often, isn't treated as the verb it should be. A kid can get information from home about any aspect of life, or he can get it in the schoolyard.

Now, rereading these last few pages, I realize that it takes some adjustment for me as a new parent to even contemplate a time when smoked cannabis might be in my children's lives. Yet there has been long debate and much study about whether, for instance, the French relationship with wine leads to ultimately healthier attitudes about alcohol (i.e., less long-term alcoholism) than the typical American high school binge-drinking introduction. There've even been indications in recent research that cannabinoid treatments can be effective in combating alcoholism, including reducing withdrawal. Navy SEAL Mike Knox credits the plant for getting him off methadone.

What I can say for sure is that I wouldn't want my kids, at any age, to have *any* medicine in their lives on a daily or weekly basis— other than perhaps vitamins as part of a health maintenance regimen. But cannabis clearly hasn't hurt half the population of America. Regulation of cannabis for adult use at twenty-one seems high, because 70 percent of college students try it now. I'd rather see that group presented with a responsible, legal model, perhaps starting at nineteen. I'm of the "if you can fight for your country and elect your congressperson, you can have a beer" school.

Somewhat confirming this view for me were the five sign-waving members of the group Students for Sensible Drug Policy's University of Rhode Island chapter whom I met at a Stop the Drug War rally in L.A. in the fall of 2011. They had paid half their way to attend the associated policy conference. The school's club budget paid the other half. All of them were undergraduates. "Any candidates out there looking for an issue to mobilize the youth vote?" one of them asked me.

One of their signs concerned recent approval ratings. It read, "Cannabis: 50%. Obama: 40%. What are you, jealous?" I asked the history major carrying the sign why he cared so much about green, leafy vegetable matter. "I've been lied to about this plant," he said. "I've been told it's bad but I learned on my own that it's good." The speaker they were cheering on with their signs at the moment was with a group called Moms United to End the War on Drugs.

That reminded me that a computer engineer friend of mine in San Jose named Mick, when his nineteen-year-old son expressed interest in cannabis, took him to a nearby dispensary and they joined together (not sure for what maladies). The point is communication, Mick told me. "I believe he'll wind up using it more responsibly and ultimately using it less than if he had to hide it. And he knows I'll always give him a ride. We've actually spoken a lot about all aspects of it. Moderation. Sobriety. Peer pressure."

Since I've been looking at the supply side of cannabis from an economic perspective while holding the quaint belief that any businessperson has a moral obligation to only peddle widgets that are safe, my conclusion after a year of study is this: Unless you are prepared to state that alcohol, tobacco, nicotine, and most prescription depression and pain medicine should be aggressively and immediately prohibited in our society, you have no case arguing that cannabis does. It is safer and provides more benefits than any of these. Dr. Larry Bedard, who is past president of the American College of Emergency Medicine, told the *San Jose Mercury News* that there are seventy thousand hospitalizations in California related to alcohol use every year, but fewer than two hundred related to marijuana. A study published in the January 2012 *Journal of the American Medical Association* even concluded long-term cannabis smoke does not have a detrimental effect on lungs.

Abuse is no joke—everyone knows an alcoholic or has dated the offspring of one; it's one of the terrible things that can happen to a person or a family. But to write a cannabis book about only that would be like writing a history of Champagne and only

covering AA recovery meetings. Any increase in cannabis use following legalization—if there is any increase—can be mitigated a
thousand times over when today's obscene enforcement budgets—
nine billion dollars for intra-U.S. enforcement in 2011—are transferred to education and treatment.

Now, most of us believe that a majority of cannabis fans enjoy
the plant socially, spiritually, or for health maintenance, rather
than as explicit medicine for an illness. Since that, currently, is
illegal in most places in the United States outside the Bubble[3]
(though not in Mexico, which recently decriminalized possession
of the plant), there's a great cloud obscuring our understanding of
these uses, a cloud it will soon be valuable to legitimate businesses
to dispel.

So, to save the inevitable corporate focus groups some time, I
thought I'd ask, "How do real people, other than those like Carl
Reid and Bill Harney who are medicating to treat acute maladies,
actually manifest their relationship with the cannabis plant in
their lives?" By this point, it won't surprise the reader to learn that
I discovered the reasons for and frequency of cannabis enjoyment
in Mendocino County are as varied as the Redneck Hippie (read:
delightfully oddball) place itself.

There were archetypes, though: My first Mendocino County
landlord's relationship with the plant was a common one among
farmers, especially older ones. As soon as he heard what my book
was about, Greg told me in his sort of halting "I've lived in the
hills for two decades and don't talk out loud much" way, "Cannabis
opened the door that allowed me to discover myself, in what I
think of as a very positive way. It was part of my education, really.
It allowed me to figure out what was real in my upbringing and
schooling, and what I needed to study myself. It helped me learn *to*
always keep studying the world. But I don't use it anymore. Haven't
in about eight years."

Then there was the fifty-something farmer, father, and daily
medicator, with what he described as a happy, busy work and family life, who told me the plant was part of a ritualistic start to the

day akin to coffee for him. Paired with it, in fact. This fellow "stopped smoking cannabis consciously to find a partner, only to discover my soul mate was looking for a friend of the plant." He described abruptly stopping his use for those six months after twenty-two years: "It made me grumpy for two days, but I think that's because I gave up coffee at the same time as part of a yoga retreat. Then I didn't think about it."

Many people I met in California in 2011 medicate for the opposite of a coffee effect. A common view expressed to me by a Northern California teacher was "I like to enjoy an indica in the evening, to transition into the relaxing part of my day before bed." She's seeking couch-lock, in other words, but not only that. She went on to describe her cannabis experience as an intentional journey. "I believe that we can create new neural pathways even as adults. Cannabis helps us, me at least, to stay open to charting new territory. To break out of molds. To always evolve."

Sounds like Sheriff Allman's law enforcement career. Not sure if "neural pathway pioneering" is something for which you can today ask for a doctor's cannabis recommendation in California.

Several people spoke of "learning" how to best implement the plant into their lives and/or their health care over time. "When you first come to today's high quality cannabis," a fellow told me in Zaza's Bakery, "it can be intense. So you moderate your use, not just the amount you smoke at one time but the frequency, and you listen to yourself. It might be once a year, once a week, or almost never."

But by my estimate the most common reason for interacting with cannabinoids, if you add up every human who ever has interacted with them since that forgotten first campfire, is best described as sacramental use. Part of the person's journey toward God. That doesn't make the production and distribution of the plant less of a massive business. It just means that with legalization, you might see a lot of openly religious folks at the dispensary. The wise marketer won't ignore the spiritual niche.

And on the other side of the fence was Dot, who was sort of the matriarch of the Willits Food Bank staff. She told me, "I hate drugs. Drugs killed my husband and my son's still fightin' it, wherever he is." I asked her, "Which drugs did it?" and she said, "All of 'em. Cocaine. Booze. Pot."

Less drastically, there was the single mom with a history of mental illness who told me she takes an afternoon puff of cannabis "so I don't have to take Prozac." When I asked if the endgame was to take nothing at all, at least daily, she said, "Sure. It's like any prescription: You don't want to be on it forever."

The fact is, as we've discussed, THC, CBD, and the rest of the cannabinoids are incredibly complex molecules that work on human biochemistry differently from many, even most, other medicines. They affect everyone distinctly, and some not at all. It's why herbalism in general is so hard for mainstream Western medicine to get behind. Mainstream Asian medicine, with its focus on energy flow, is a lot more open to it, which probably explains the relative dearth of cannabis stigma in Asia. Sure, China and Malaysia currently have Draconian drug laws, but the Japanese emperor wears hemp robes at his coronation as a Shinto symbol of purity and godliness.

I can see, though, why Mark Kline, my Mendocino County psychiatrist contact, was reluctant to recommend it, beyond his concern about addiction and social effects: Who you are and when and why you use a particular medicine might affect its potency or even its efficacy? Yeesh. Run *that* one by your malpractice attorney.

And when we speak of any kind of potential for cannabis dependence, of course, we're talking about the psychoactive side of the plant. No one—except possibly a judge seeing how many plants it requires*—would call Buffy Madison's daily raw shake medication excessive use. And the edible raw cannabis shake, mark my

---

* During his Punishing with the Process, Sharif Moye's judge ruled that his case should be tried because the forty (disputed) pounds seized "clearly" represented more than the amount necessary for personal medical use. To which Sharif, sitting in the courtroom, told me he thought to himself, "Huh, that's funny. Judges are M.D.s now?"

words, is destined to be the next California-derived health craze. Invest now.

Accordingly, common sense dictates that there should be no limits at all on the cultivation of and commerce in industrial and nutritional cannabis. Although for horticultural reasons, the medicinal/psychoactive and industrial crops need to be geographically separate: The pollen of the workhorse industrial cannabis (hemp) can dilute the thoroughbred medicinal varieties.

This is why the California legislature in 2011 sent Governor Brown a bill, SB 676, which would have legalized the industrial crop in several counties far away from the Emerald Triangle. Brown hid behind federal law—though he called the law absurd—and vetoed the bill.

Several other state legislatures are now debating industrial cannabis legislation. As I'd lobbied Tomas when I saw his stalks composted, what I'd love to see is a county construct its own fermentation facility to render its entire population energy self-sufficient via cannabis fiber. It can be the regional power plant and the biofuel fill-up station.

It's already happening in Europe with other crops: The entire German farming town of Feldheim today runs on fuel from its biomass facility, according to a 2011 Associated Press article. By producing energy locally, Feldheim has 0 percent unemployment, since a nice percentage of the town works at the biomass facility.

Stateside, I don't care if it's a government or a private operation that takes the lead. If organizations like MendoGrown are able to organize cannabis growers in a region, centralized facilities that produce energy from waste stalks should be no more difficult to establish than bud-trimming facilities.

But that's just silly patriotic me. I'm a fan of sustainable post-petroleum models designed to keep America running strongly into the future. I simply can't wait to pull up to a gas station and say, "Fill 'er up with cannabis, please." Or better yet, to have the pump and the processing facility at my own home.

By the time the 2011 cannabis harvest was flowing to patients and filling California's state coffers as it has since 1996, I could draw a clear conclusion about the healthiest course for America and cannabis: a hundred million Americans, including the past three presidents, have used the plant. They obviously shouldn't be considered drug criminals. Yes, we need to reduce addiction overall in our society, but from what I've seen this past year, responsible adult citizens should be permitted to enjoy cannabis healthfully just like wine, and our laws should reflect this.

Even after full legalization on the federal level, Tomas Balogh said he doesn't see "dropping" the medical identification with the plant. "Let's say we agree it's health maintenance for what we call 'healthy' people," he told me on the Eagle's Nest deck in October 2011, including the finger quotes. "Health maintenance is always cited as the best way to keep health care costs down, isn't it? Preventive medicine? What is the glass of red wine enjoyed by the fellow on his deck after a hard day of investment banking? I think that's documented to be health maintenance. A long-term cost saver. An evening cannabis pipe or cracker is the same thing for some people."

Millions, actually. To the extent that it has upsides and downsides like anything from aspirin to bicycles, cannabis offers significantly more good than it does harm, both socially and economically. In his 2011 *Forbes* piece, Progressive Insurance's Lewis calls out those who hide the cannabis in their life, saying, "One way to win this battle is for people to just be honest. If everyone who used marijuana stood up and said, 'I use this; it's pretty good,' the argument would be over."

Few worries there in Mendocino County, whose culture pretty much continuously shows that cannabis can be a part of an American society that plots an optimistic course for the future.

And when the War on Cannabis ends, the whole continent will be safer. As the author of the Mexican cartel book *El Narco*, Ioan Grillo, said on NPR's *Fresh Air* on October 26, 2011, legalization would take away "hundreds of billions of dollars . . . from organizations that are carrying out terror, hurting families, and destroying communities" in Mexico. Legalizing cannabis, he said, "certainly will affect the cartels. The billions of dollars they make every year [from American cannabis consumers] . . . go to Mexico and end up paying assassins and . . . corrupting politicians."

Oh, and then there's the fact that after hostilities have dragged on for ten times longer than America's involvement in World War Two, the War on Drugs hasn't worked. In accordance with Jim Hill's view of the game, a middle-class American citizen who follows the headlines might even be willing to sponsor law enforcement welfare, the way he or she generally doesn't make a stink about some of the quirks in, say, soybean subsidies, if—and this is an important if—the policy had any basis in rationality. If its continual reauthorizers could make, over four decades and after spending a trillion dollars, any kind of plausible claim of effectiveness.

# THIRTY-TWO
## Visions of the Coming Drug Peace:
## The Tipping Point for Cannabis Reclassification
## and Regulation

> Fifty percent of Americans support legalizing marijuana. Not even one percent of Congress does. Can you think of any other issue with that level of disconnect? . . . Legalize marijuana and arguably 75 percent of the border violence goes away.
>
> —Former New Mexico governor and 2012 Libertarian presidential candidate Gary Johnson, November 3, 2011

Based on the debut Kama harvest, Tomas Balogh's collective looked to pay about thirty thousand dollars in sales tax in 2012. He personally contributed a conservative nine thousand dollars to local business in Mendocino County in 2011, largely in sushi bills and by shopping at Ukiah's Friedman's Home Improvement.

Lucille alone, originating as she did from that four-inch green cutting, will provide patients with more than two pounds of medicine. The final Halent weigh-in at the Eagle's Nest is where I learned there are 453.6 grams in a pound. Her flowers weighed just under 1,000 grams.

This was one plant of eighty-seven in the Kama garden. Some of the 2011 Casey Jones strains—which tested high in CBD—gave four pounds. And Tomas is but one of tens of thousands of small American farmers in California asking for legitimacy; for permission to help the economy and the planet while putting the hit on the cartels and American street violence.

What the revenue-generating power of the Mendocino County ganjapreneurs showed me is that cannabis might not be *the* solution.

But it can and should be part of the solution. Get cannabis seeds into recovering Rwandan soil as quickly as possible: It will improve yields and diets. Get cannabis medicine into mainstream cancer prevention and treatment: It will save lives. Get industrial and nutritive cannabis seeds into the heartland: It will create jobs. Get cannabis biomass into cars, building materials, and energy production: It will help save the planet. Get regulated cannabis into the economy: Crime in cities will decrease. And all the while the multibillion-dollar economy will develop and mature into industrial and medical areas we can't imagine today. It's a valuable plant, is what I'm trying to say.

In fact, the cannabis plant, along with sustainable technologies like solar energy, can power yet another American economic resurgence. We get one of these miracles every three decades lately—the last was in Silicon Valley beginning in the late 1970s. The new Green Revolution has come just in time. In addition to its immediate bottom-line payoff, it can help wean our nation from coal and petroleum energy dependence even as it returns small farmers to a healing agricultural landscape.

Since its harvest doesn't yet get the official crop report that even pork bellies enjoy, I can't quote hard stats on the 2011 Northern California outdoor cannabis season. But the word from the field was that it was the best-quality harvest in several years—a fine, sun-grown vintage. That's the new hip marketing term for the broader outdoor cannabis brand as we go to press: sun-grown.

It remained uncertain whether Tomas would collect a salary for his semiunderground work in 2011. Still, he told me on November 6, 2011, "If there's a [9.31] Program in Mendocino County, and Kama is still in business, and we've distributed enough of its 2011 medicine, I'll be farming here."

"That doesn't sound like an unequivocal confirmation," I said. "Am I going to touch base with you in May and find out you're in law school?"

For a moment he appeared to be considering whether that was preferable to jail but then said, "No, dude. This is what I'm here to do. If I'm successful and patients have received all the medicine,

I'm in 9.31. And we're increasing MendoGrown's outreach this winter: Success is getting aboveground farmer numbers up."

That's because more taxpaying small businesses pave the way for job creation in Tomas's new farming home. We're talking about thousands of jobs and millions of dollars for the local economy if 9.31 returns in 2012 and continues to grow. My estimate from a year of watching the Mendocino County economy is that each cannabis farm creates or supports at least seven local jobs spread across the economic spectrum.

The success and growth of the Zip-Tie Program would slash the unemployment rate, while improving schools, libraries, and roads. It already does do that, only off the books. It would also contribute millions directly into public safety coffers via zip-tie fees.

As one grower from Hopland told me at a 9.31 meeting, "The way to get less than ninety-five percent of cops to oppose this program is to become too valuable to the community's public economy. Pay their salary, essentially. That's how we get treated like any other chamber [of commerce] business."

Continued cannabis legitimacy will also have some less-discussed residual results. One of the most significant is that it will allow named cannabis collectives to sponsor local charities. I guarantee Matt Cohen would love to underwrite the Northstone Wellness Wing at the Ukiah hospital, or that Tomas Balogh would kick in for a Laytonville multisport facility called Kama Park.

This is not just speculation. On my farewell visit to the Willits Food Bank, I told everyone there what this book was about. After the usual "Oh, you should talk to my brother" suggestions were out of the way, one worker said, "You know what the zip ties do? They allow farmers to come down from the hills and donate to us. When we were really short last year, a grower heard about it on the radio and came in with eighteen hundred dollars. Helped a lot." Great story, but it made me feel a little bit stingy for the thirty-dollar holiday fund drive check I was at the moment filling out.

Legitimacy thus matters for more than just the important fact that an American cannabis farmer can for the first time since 1937 pick up the phone and call the cops. Though let's not gloss over how important that is: Imagine if you couldn't do that in an emergency like a robbery.

OK, so will the 9.31 Program grow, in light of a wild 2011 season that saw legal cannabis's best and worst moments? It's entirely possible that fear or threats will kill it and its putative imitators. But the black market is paying attention to the Zip-Tie Program. The Northstone raid certainly didn't help the "declare your crop publicly" effort, but the farmers I spoke to by November tended to see it as a viable model, especially following federal legalization.

My first landlord, Greg, summed up the crossroads when in one conversation, almost in one breath, he mocked the program's bust record and then asked me if Northstone needed any more farmers. I'm not going to cast stones about such ambivalence after what I learned about how our federal Controlled Substances Act enforcement really manifested on the ground in 2011. On the other hand, California recently had a Republican governor who said, upon decriminalizing cannabis, "No one cares if you smoke a joint."*

Under the best of circumstances, it's not likely going to be easy for the MendoGrown board members to politely say to their black market colleagues, "If you'd please stop whining, get a business license, and install an ADA-compliant bathroom in your bud-trimming barn, we can get an industry going here. This is twenty-first-century California. It's a regulated place." That is simply not an intuitive argument to make to someone who has never paid taxes, and is trained since birth to react to the presence of law enforcement like an Arizona GOP legislator reacts to an immigrant: with a combination of fear and revulsion. It's going to take some time to sink in.

For cat as well as for mouse. One well-known Emerald Triangle farmer told me that in a crowded café in 2011, she invited a

---

* The problem with such a policy (as stated by the Governator) is that if you merely shrug at cannabis use, but don't legitimize the producers of the plant, you're really saying, "Unless you grow it yourself, you have to deal with a criminal." There's another term for such a policy: subsidization of cartels.

deputy to sit at her table. "He looked back at the door like I must be talking to someone else. Then his whole face relaxed when he seemed to realize, 'This war is over.'"

Will a second-generation renegade botanist like Rock ever come on board with the Zip-Tie Program? He said possibly, not so much depending on federal law, but rather "if the rules aren't over-burdening and restrictive of my work."

Some cannabis cultivators will probably never come above-ground. If you're in the country illegally, for instance, you can't sign up for zip ties. And the Emerald Triangle culture that created the Redneck Hippie, like the Hazzard County bootlegging culture that spawned NASCAR, is a proud one.

I met a dreadlocked second-generation Humboldt County grower who was still suffering PTSD from raids under the same sheriff that now wants to regulate him. He was sickened by the idea of doing business with specific cops he knows to be bad people. What I heard someone say to him was "It's an Ecclesiastes thing. In any war, someone has to make the decision to end it. You have to forgive and move on to the next phase. You're not going to live in a world without cops."

Or without venture capital. Was the money still on cannabis, even after October's stunning events and big headlines? Could, for instance, Matt Cohen find an angel investor before spring 2012 even if he wanted to? To answer that, I called up MendoGrown's attorney Smiley. And what I heard initially didn't bode well for cannabis activists.

One of the first things he said, in this our third conversation, was "Can you please change my name in your book? And keep my firm's name out of it. I don't want to lose my job."

"Did you think you'd be asking me that in August when we first spoke?"

"No," he said. "I did not."

What really surprised me was the cause for his caution. He said it had nothing to do with a sense that society wasn't ready for legal cannabis. Rather it was his firm's out-of-state, pharmaceutical-company-representing partners who objected when he proposed pro bono work for MendoGrown. There were internal turf concerns.

"The market is ready," he told me. "I'm advising one company that designs cannabis dispensary software and they're moving right ahead," Smiley told me. "Short term, some fly-by-nighter investors might be scared into hesitation after a few raids like this, but the mature venture-capital money is patient and looking at the long view, which is still that prohibition is nearly done."

Is it, though? I mentioned earlier that to ask a bureaucrat to implement a policy that would cut his budget was to live in the Land of Chocolate. Thus Congress has to do it. And that is going to take a lot of citizen noise. Even if, say, a drug czar or FDA commissioner was politically suicidal enough to want to make such a decision in light of, say, Colorado and Washington voters' fully legalizing cannabis in 2012, "there's only so much even a second-term Obama can do if the Republicans still control Congress," the DPA's Nadelmann told me on November 3, 2011.

In other words, most industry watchers in late 2011 believed it's probably up to the voters in individual states for a while longer. Vote in enough state decriminalization initiatives and Congress will have to act, goes the argument. "That's how alcohol prohibition ended," Matt Cohen likes to say. "Twenty-three states independently regulated alcohol." The Marijuana Policy Project's strategy is "Twenty-seven medical marijuana states by 2014." They're actively trying to create that tipping point.

But will even full decriminalization in a majority of states wake up Congress and the White House? It's a little hard to envision either of the 2012 presidential contenders saying, "The people have spoken. Call it off. Bring in the vaporizor for the signing ceremony." (Don't laugh: *Newsweek* intimated that Alaska legislators enjoyed a 4:20 ceremony in the statehouse on the day its members passed cannabis legalization legislation in 1975.)

Tomas, who was wearing an "Obama 2012" T-shirt while reasserting his officially Undecided status during the final Halent packaging visit to the Eagle's Nest in 2011, believes that the incumbent is probably the only choice on this issue, despite everything. Despite the fact that at that moment, the incumbent's U.S. attorney appointee would like to throw him, Tomas, in a cage for what he considers a moral line of work.

"You know, lame duck, second term, speaking fees to come," Tomas mumbled in an intentionally unconvincing tone. "It could be different. Maybe he'll at least reclassify it for easier research."

But there is essentially zero support in the current U.S. Senate for rescheduling or decriminalizing cannabis. In the House of Representatives, Barney Frank and Ron Paul's Ending Federal Prohibition Act of 2011 bill is predictably stalled as of November 2011. And both sponsors are leaving Congress.

One roadblock is that there's a funded school of punditry arguing, "Aw, heck, let's just give it another forty years." I know this because I'm on mailing lists where I receive the rhetoric not just of cannabis activists, but of those dedicated to continuing the War on Drugs. Oh, they speak of "shifting emphasis" from enforcement to treatment and education.

But what kind of education? I know, for instance, that the ONDCP, the executive branch office that controls U.S. drug policy (proposed 2012 budget: $26.2 billion, up 1.2 percent, over the 2010 budget, according to the American Civil Liberties Union of Washington State), is currently teaming up with the leaders of Mothers Against Drunk Driving to start a Drugged Driving campaign.

While I applaud this effort when it comes to the truly astonishing rate of prescription drug abuse in our nation, I have the icky feeling that the commercials are going to feature joint-smoking kids.

By now, everyone's probably heard the basic anticannabis talking points: Isn't a "medicinal" designation a sham for many cannabis aficionados? Shouldn't dispensaries be far from schools? Wouldn't most economic benefits of ending the Drug War be offset by increases in societal health care costs?

These queries seem distinct, but all are really expressing fear. That's what's behind, in former New Mexico governor Gary Johnson's words, this "biggest disconnect ever" between elected and electorate. Fear that a cannabis-friendly mind-set is going to mean a different America than one that obediently buys its Pharma pills. And that such an America will frequent new businesses and require new leaders. Looked at from a business angle, the zeitgeist battle over cannabis is, like the battle within Smiley's law firm, at its core a question of turf protection.

So if you hear a negative societal or health claim about the effects of cannabis, particularly one that also argues for the continuation of the forty-year-old Drug War's failed tactics, the first question always to ask is "Who paid for the study?" Remember, Exxon and BP had no problem finding scientists to muddle the truth by declaring, for a fee, that black is white. That otters cause oil spills, or whatever.

While the pundits slog it out in the media, Congress has to be awakened. That's legislative. In the executive branch, another agency whose deciders have to change their tune, in addition to the DEA, the ONDCP, and the White House–funded National Marijuana Initiative, is the Department of Health and Human Services (HHS), which oversees the National Institute on Drug Abuse (NIDA) and the Food and Drug Administration (FDA). The changing and complex interplay between these agencies surrounding cannabis research approval over the past four decades is a book in itself. A summary: It's way too hard to get approval. It should be much easier, immediately. Especially considering the Big Pharma junk that *is* routinely approved for human study.

Honchos at several of the above agencies, over the past five years, have rejected one effort to reclassify cannabis under the Controlled Substances Act (after sitting on it for nine years) and one prominent effort to gain cannabis research approval. The latter was a proposed medical cannabis research farm at the University of Massachusetts Amherst.

The DEA administrator, Michele M. Leonhart, is a Bush holdover. Which doesn't mean she is evil or bad at her job. It just means that the tens of thousands of people who voted for Obama with cannabis reform as their number one issue found out that they'd actually voted for a Bush third term.

As we head into 2012, in fact, there is explicitly no difference between Republicans and Democrats on the Drug War on the federal level. Ms. Leonhart, a career DEA special agent, was reappointed by President Obama.

Additionally, federal domestic Drug War tactics might be getting even scarier. Andrew Becker and Michael Montgomery at California Watch reported on November 7, 2011, that our nation's intelligence agencies might soon be enlisted to join the cannabis eradication battle on public lands. Yikes! Drones over Mendo?

I've been on the front lines of the Drug War for the past year. I've seen busts of totally upright citizens and cleanups of illicit cannabis messes, and I've spoken to hundreds of largely well-meaning people on all sides of the cannabis issue. My next door neighbor in New Mexico got raided. A nearby U.S. mayor is allegedly a member of a cartel. A U.S. sheriff calls cannabis "much safer than alcohol" if legalized. This is a plant that can bring benefit and—in an illegal economy and absent good parenting—harm.

But wipe away every group's personal rhetoric and you arrive back at one of the more solid truths I've come across over twenty years' reporting on five continents in uncertain times: The Drug War is, along with alcohol prohibition, one of America's worst wastes of resources. It is one of our nation's most awful policies, lumped in with dark episodes of our history like Jim Crow. It is one big constitutional violation, and it isn't necessary. It needlessly and with hardly any real effect—other than causing the Founding Fathers to roll over in their graves—misspends billions that could be otherwise much better directed. Ending the War on Drugs— or at least fundamentally changing it and removing cannabis from the equation—should be a national imperative.

On the medical side, cannabis should be immediately federally reclassified to allow wide study and use, hopefully quickly enough to benefit sick friends of mine. And not in a sneaky, half-assed way that allows some pharmaceutical company to monopolize a concentration of one or two chemicals in the plant. Americans must have broad, diverse access to the whole plant. Schedule III or even V under the CSA seems to make sense when discussing medical use.

Industrial versions of the plant should be grown as a major agricultural crop without restriction, and voters in individual states should be allowed to decide whether varieties intended for human intake should be regulated for responsible adult use like wine.

It's working in Mendocino County. If similar models emerge nationwide with federal decriminalization, it is my journalistic opinion that we will be a more prosperous and a safer America. Probably a more creative one, too, which factors into the Digital Age Superpower formula. This is the Idea Era.

When I covered a computer security conference for National Public Radio in 2005, I learned that in order to lure our nation's best hacking minds, federal recruiters offer exemption from drug testing, in favor of a sort of don't ask, don't tell on cannabis use. That's how important these folks are to the national security apparatus in the age of cyber war.

In other words, the taxpayer-funded bankrupting of someone like Matt Cohen, over sworn testimony of local law enforcement and elected officials, sends one message: Federal cannabis law must change. Everything else is song and dance.

There are tricky policy issues to work out when you get into, say, the work of teachers and pilots. Some states already have motor vehicle rules about percentages of THC in blood. They aren't scientific: Cannabis doesn't affect people uniformly.* These issues can be worked out: When alcohol prohibition ended, the

---

* A current talking point for anticannabis mouthpieces tries to promote the idea that cannabis-related driving incidents are up as well, but not only do some studies actually indicate the cannabis can increase driving proficiency, even the studies claiming otherwise generally indicate that cannabis was in a driver's blood. Which means only that he or she had used the fat-soluble plant within the previous month.

government set policy for the strength of beer, for example. As for cannabis sales, Hoover Fellow Thomas Gale Moore, a former Reagan advisor, suggests (in the June 22, 2011 *Palo Alto Weekly*), "marijuana dispensaries could be permitted in already existing liquor stores, which require a license and where regulations already control sales to minors."

The near future could be very bright or very bleak for the cannabis plant in the United States of America. As with any new idea or species, the prospect of Americans outside of California and Colorado "Grabbing Some Buds" before the baseball game will either prove resilient and spread from the Mendos of the nation or else it'll find other ecosystems less hospitable. At least Tomas Balogh says he's having a good time as a farmer while he witnesses the long, slow transition to Middle America's cannabis acceptance. He believes that Mendocino County's Drug Peace mirrors a positive phase in his own life.

"I learned a lot about trust and community this season," he told me at a raid protest in front of the Robert T. Matsui* Federal Building in Sacramento on November 9, 2011. "When I made decisions based on my better nature—like not bringing a gun on the property—it turned out to be the best for the collective. One day, hopefully one day soon, it's just going to be over. The idea of punishing a farmer, or someone who enjoys a responsible level of cannabis in his life, for any reason, will seem absurd."

There are signs that society is getting there. That normalcy is waltzing in. When Tomas and I met at the Flying Goat before he delivered Lucille's flowers to Kama patients Diane and Bill, we were discussing the lack of support from the U.S. Congress for ending the cannabis war, especially in the Senate.

Tomas asked, with what I thought was an uncharacteristically

---

* Matsui was a groundbreaking progressive civil libertarian, incidentally. He was imbued with the democratic spirit and an unwavering belief in America's progress even though—or because—he grew up as an American citizen in an internment camp.

disheartened tone, "Do you think my lifestyle will ever be mainstream in the U.S.?"

I looked around. "We *have* just been discussing a pending cannabis delivery openly in a small American coffee shop," I pointed out, gesturing to and nearly smacking into the well-dressed middle-aged man sipping an *Americano* at the tiny table next to me.

The man smiled and, eyes closed, gave one of those long, sagacious chin-moving-upward reverse nods. Almost a deep inhale. He'd clearly heard every word. Then he went back to his newspaper.

That, in a gesture, sums up Mendocino County Sheriff Tom Allman's prayer for America's reaction to cannabis. When it is, he told me, he can get back to work on public safety.

# EPILOGUE 2011

Recruit your fire department. Recruit all the people they can't paint as a criminal.

—Dan Rush, political director for the United Food and Commercial Workers Union Local No. 120, speaking at a protest against the 2011 federal cannabis offensive in front of the federal building in Sacramento, California, on November 9, 2011. The union represents two thousand cannabis workers in California and Colorado.

[There] has been somewhat of a de facto decriminalization of drugs—in other words, they're not being prosecuted. And it does not appear that violent crime in San Francisco has risen, so it may say something about the necessity for the war on drugs.

—San Francisco sheriff Michael Hennessey, in the October 30, 2011, *San Francisco Examiner*, commenting on a recent "huge drop" in violent crime in the city

Relatively few adverse clinical effects from the chronic use of marijuana have been documented in humans. However, the criminalization of marijuana use may itself be a health hazard, since it may expose the users to violence and criminal activity.

—Study by the medical insurance giant Kaiser Permanente in the April 1997 *American Journal of Public Health*

A few weeks before my deadline for this book, I went to see if the 2011 harvest of those giant Scarecrow-strain trees was already on Jim Hill's Wilbur OC online menu. There I found that the collective had closed. Guess whose landlord got an eviction nasty-gram from the feds?

Hill told me on November 10, 2011, "Our landlord has been super great and we didn't want to cause friction for him. Plus we think this will be temporary, until saner minds prevail. We're still paying rent. Our patient records are still there. [OC Wilbur manager] Craig is helping and advising patients in the interim." A month later, the San Diego collective closed too.

Welcome to the cannabis industry in the late days of prohibition. Its changes are rapid enough to evoke one of those mind-teasing illustrations that resolve from random dots to Abraham Lincoln's face and back, depending on how you look at it.

Hill, meanwhile, is a volunteer collecting signatures for two of the 2012 California cannabis legalization ballot initiatives, the Repeal Cannabis Prohibition Act of 2012 and the Regulate Marijuana Like Wine Act of 2012. Both are increasingly looking like longshots, and some activists are already regrouping for 2014.

Those interested in whether their local picture is in "random dot" or "Abraham Lincoln's face" phase at the moment can visit the websites of any of the national organizations: NORML, Drug Policy Alliance, Marijuana Policy Project, Americans for Safe Access, Students for Sensible Drug Policy, and the rest of them. Most have regional offices as well. Twelve hundred local NAACP chapters are also now "working to end the Drug War," according to NORML, after the group's national board voted in 2011 to call for the war's end.

On the ground, as I prepared to head home to my New Mexico ranch, folks in Mendocino County seemed to be relaxing a notch after one of the most politically horrendous Octobers in recent memory. Although in the California courts, the recent *Pack* case mentioned in these pages (officially, a state Second Appellate Court decision in *Ryan Pack v. City of Long Beach*), in conjunction with the federal offensive, was causing fearful municipal leaders across California to force the closure of tax-providing dispensaries like OC Wilbur. Every week in October and November saw more forced shutdowns in California. Chico, Albany, Eureka, the list kept growing.

In other municipalities, such as Bakersfield and San Jose, voters were successfully using California's local petition drive system to overturn pending dispensary bans.

Even in the Bubble[3], the *Pack* case was reverberating. Meaning it looked like it might throw a wrench in the 9.31 Zip-Tie Program, the county's unmitigated public safety success.

"My office is still analyzing the effect [of the *Pack* ruling], and we're waiting to see . . . if [the ruling] is appealed," Mendocino County counsel Jeanine Nadel told the *Ukiah Daily Journal* on November 5, 2011. A month later, it was appealed and its ruling that cannabis permitting can't happen because it violates federal law was at least temporaily "depublished." But if it's upheld by the Supreme Court in 2012 or 2013, it's conceivable that past 9.31 permitting fees might have to be returned. 2011 revenue from the program had by the day of Nadel's assessment reached $602,450, according to county administrative services manager Norman Thurston, quoted in the same article. Thanks a lot for threatening this revenue stream, Uncle Sam! You've really struck a blow against those cartels this year.

Then, in January 2012, it got even worse: U.S. Attorney Haag's office directly threatened the Mendocino County government with lawsuits and individual officials with racketeering charges if local legislators didn't kill the Zip-Tie Program immediately. On January 24, the County Board of Supervisors voted four to one to eliminate the permitting part of the program. Plant limits in the county are reduced to twenty-five, zip ties are "recommended and voluntary," and (on the bright side) conditions that formerly applied only to 9.31 permit holders, including the prohibition on illegal water diversion, now apply to all marijuana cultivation in Mendocino County.

"I am way too knowledgeable about the budgetary situation of our county to think we can carry a lawsuit against the federal government," Supervisor Hamburg told the *Willits News* after the vote.

And so the pendulum swings away, ignoring, as always, reality on the ground. No matter the legal milieu of the moment, in Mendocino County, California, the farmers farm. As long as it's illegal and expensive, the Rippers rip. Americans enjoy the cannabis one way or another. That's really the key thing to remember: Demand doesn't change (unless you count the increase when industrial cannabis returns to American farms). The source for cannabis can either be taxed citizen farmers or violent criminals who, it's safe to say, are not researching organic-style standards.*

How you spin that reality depends on your timeline. Longer-term Drug War observers tend to assess the situation this way: An appellate case here or an unfortunate raid there will one day be seen as barely more than speedbumps on the freeway to cannabis legalization.

I can see the wisdom in that unhurried mind-set. Just as the ancient Greeks featured in the War Department's "Hemp for Victory" film provide an enduring democratic model even though the individual philosophers and politicians are gone, the initial 9.31 Zip-Tie Program appears to have been squelched for a little while. But the lucrative, sustainable, patients-first model that the Great Mendocino County Cannabis Peace Experiment provides remains intact. The model stands ready to reemerge not just in Northern California, but nationwide, the moment the exorbitant travesty of cannabis prohibition ends.

At five P.M. on November 15, 2011, just before I sent my manuscript to my editor, DrugSense's Drug War Clock read $35,695,718,424 spent for the year (state and federal). That's a number that could balance a few budgets.

---

* I mention sustainability because Matt Cohen, Tomas Balogh, and the rest of the MendoGrown braintrust explicitly recognize that the locavore farmer-owned business model they're putting forth is not cannabis specific. It can be used as an empowerment model for small farmers and local communities worldwide, no matter what crop the Earth is putting forth.

# AFTERWORD

## One Year Later: The Drug War's Berlin Wall Fell Even Sooner Than I Expected

> It's clear that this thing that has happened [social cannabis legalization in two U.S. states] could bring us to rethinking the [Drug War] strategy.
>
> —Mexican president Enrique Peña Nieto, November 27, 2012

Having a day job that required observing the War on Drugs from the front lines for a ten-month cannabis growing season, I considered myself to be on the optimistic side of the pundit-sphere when it came to predicting how soon and completely hostilities will end. I thought my dovishness was justified: I'd witnessed the Drug Peace era working in action. It raised revenue, created jobs, and lowered crime. But one well-known drug policy observer, who'd been watching the situation since 1972, tempered me by telling me that inevitable though the victory might be, I *had* been reporting from a region that even locals call a Bubble. "It could take twenty years before we see full cannabis legalization," he said.

Or, ya know, one. Three months and four days after the publication of *Too High to Fail*, while the Emerald Triangle's above-ground cannabis farmers—those attempted taxpayers—were just peeking out from their hiding spots after the federal assault recounted herein, America "surprised" the White House by leap-frogging federal law and reversing eighty years of drug policy in one day.

On November 6, 2012, Colorado and Washington voters ended the Drug War. That is to say, voters in both states over-whelmingly legalized adult social use of cannabis (Colorado's new law, vitally, also allows industrial cannabis cultivation). It is no stretch to say that the Berlin Wall of the Drug War fell.

One week later, the departing president of Mexico, Felipe Calderón, said that the U.S. federal government no longer possesses the "moral authority" to fight an international drug war. Two days after that, legislators in four more U.S. states (Massachusetts, Rhode Island, Maine, and Vermont), announced in a coordinated message that they will float full cannabis legalization bills in 2013. Iowa legislators followed suit, an Alabama legislative committee took up a medical cannabis bill, and before November's vote was two weeks old Indiana's state police superintendent Paul Whitesell told state regulators, "[Cannabis] is here, it's going to stay, there's an awful lot of victimization that goes with it. If it were up to me, I do believe I would legalize it and tax it."

Worldwide, drug policy change is now unfolding so rapidly that as I file this afterword in mid-November 2012, I'm certain it will be out-of-date by the time these words are published. In a good way. I already know three Colorado farmers who will be planting industrial cannabis in the spring of 2013, for instance, and I'll be there for fifth-generation rancher Michael Bowman's sowing on the Eastern plains of the Rocky Mountain State. After all, it's a historic moment for America: Thirty percent of us were farmers the last time a legal hemp seed was planted in the United States. Today, 1 percent of us are. I, according to my tax returns, am one of them.* Gotta support the team. By which I mean America, including her economy, public health, and energy needs.

I'm pretty sure the White House thinks of itself as part of that team; that its boss and staff want the best for the country in all of these areas. Yet, shaking off the sand in which its head had been buried for the past decade, prevailing executive branch reaction to the Drug Peace election of 2012 was described in one news report as "completely taken aback." Let's for a moment put aside the question of whether a president who can tell you five factors that led to the 1962 Burmese student uprising could possibly be *that* ignorant

---

* Though not a cannabis farmer, not until I like the way the Controlled Substances Act reads.

about his own nation's forty-years-long civil war. The fact remains that state by state, voters are ensuring that America's worst policy since segregation, her longest war, is finally wrapping up.

The general news pundits waking to the story (after getting past the munchies jokes) are discussing what amounts to peace negotiations: Will the feds raid? Will they sue? Did they get the message?

It doesn't really matter. The American people won. We're done with 2.3 million Americans in prison; 60,000 Mexicans dead; and losing out on a $40-billion-a-year agricultural tax base, not to mention a finally viable source of biofuel. With the wall down, jubilant cannabis investors, social consumers, patients, and fuel researchers are streaming through. The stock of a cannabis peripherals company called Medbox rose from $4 to $20 in the week after the election. They make cannabis dispensing machines.

There's a growing popular awareness in the already bullish financial world that the nation's number one crop is about to become the nation's number one taxed crop. Uh-oh. Time to answer all those recently hypothetical questions. Like "What are we going to do with the Drug Peace dividend?" and "What are the potential downsides to avoid, let's say on the environmental and public health sides?"

I'm not too worried about that last one. I've read a lot of studies over the two years that I've been a full-time sustainable cannabis journalist. If we're sensible enough to really shift to an education- and treatment-based drug policy to address abuse, I think in twenty years we'll see lower across-the-board adult addiction rates and youth drug and alcohol use rates than the historic high numbers we're living with during the failed "war on the user, especially the poor user" model of today. That is, if policy makers allow the real epidemic (prescription pill abuse, and pharmaceutical industry complicity in same, including resisting policies that would cut down on multistate pill mills) to be addressed.

Given that America's cannabis-friendly demographic is about to seize the nation's regulatory reins in a generational shift as philosophically abrupt as any in history (from "What's good for

General Motors is good for America" to "Don't be evil"), an honest drug policy is indeed likely to become a mainstream, cross-party public objective.*

The zeitgeist shift might already have happened: Americans, across the political spectrum and not just venture capitalists and educated digerati, are fired up about a peace dividend. Want proof? Cannabis got more votes than President Obama in Colorado in 2012. Forty percent of Colorado Republicans voted to legalize the plant. Furthermore, Jon Walker of JustSayNow.com crunched some numbers and found youth turnout in 2012 was up 12 percent and 6 percent in Washington and Colorado compared to 2008, versus 1 percent nationally. I think of that as the "duh" statistic.

Even in my remote New Mexico valley (to which I've returned), where the average octogenarian I wait in line alongside at the post office is wearing a cowboy hat and believes Barack Obama was born in Libya because Rush told her so, ending the Drug War is a no-brainer. One such lady, Meg, spied me the other day as the writer whose ridiculously oversize American truck looks right but smells suspiciously liberal (the exhaust is in fact kung pao chicken grease). She asked me what my new book is about, and I breathed deeply and replied, "It's an economic argument for ending the failed War on Drugs by removing cannabis from the Controlled Substances Act entirely and letting states regulate it like alcohol." Without pause Meg came back with, "'Bout time. Pills're the problem. Ask my cousin, Ben. It'll hurt the dang cartels too."

This lady missed Woodstock, people. And I have to say it's a relief to have folks like her and Pat Robertson aboard the peace train. I want as much company as possible on this one. Empowers me to speak the truth in mixed company.

It's hardly ever mixed anymore though. Nationally, a solid (and increasing) majority of Americans, 80 percent of us (imagine 80

---

* I'm more concerned about the sustainability discussion within the infant cannabis industry, especially with Colorado's initial institutionalization of energy demanding indoor cultivation. And of course postprohibition outdoor practices must be sustainable as well.

percent of Americans agreeing on *anything*) support medical cannabis and 56 percent are for full cannabis legalization. And those numbers are climbing every time a new poll comes out, particularly among women. Left wing, right wing, old, young, heartland, city: America knows. Not counting various war frenzies, I've not witnessed anything like this kind of cross-platform agreement in my twenty years of journalism. We're increasingly united on this one. In fact, from what I'm seeing from touring from Missouri to Arizona and on both coasts, 56 percent Drug Peace support sounds about 20 percent too low. I mean, you know you're winning when the *Houston Chronicle* runs, as it did on November 9, 2012, an editorial that reads in part: *"Our country has waged a War on Drugs for forty years, and the only winners seem to be cartel lords and private prisons. Two states have come up with a new plan. Let's see if it works."*

Internationally, it's the same. A Portuguese magazine writer who called me from Lisbon the other day to see if I was aware that the international Drug War was over due to "America's leadership role" in the November 6, 2012, election. The world, in other words, is aware that the social re-legalization of cannabis was a watershed event and represents a sea change in the course of the now forty-one-years-long conflict (seventy-five actually, in the case of cannabis).

Documented believer that I am in the significant economic and social value of the peace dividend, I could be heard startling the coyotes in my riverbed (the same riverbed in which armed authorities bivouacked when my closest neighbor was raided four years earlier) with loud, echoing renditions of "God Bless America" on November 7. "So this is what voting *for* something feels like," I thought. We were all Coloradans that day. *Ich bin ein* Washingtonian.

I thought immediately of the activist-since-the-1970s who'd told me that the war might lurch on for another two decades. His point was that the losers of wars, especially if better funded, don't usually surrender anymore. They "phase out." But not in this case. The peace vote won pretty much everywhere cannabis was on the ballot in 2012, from Grand Rapids, Michigan (decriminalization of social possession), to the entire state of Massachusetts (medical).

Among the few "losses" was in Arkansas, the first Southern state in which voters put medical cannabis on the ballot (despite almost no money for the campaign and massive efforts to throw up legal obstacles to the will of the people): that one lost only 52–48 percent. Just wait until next time, Ozarks—you showed America that the heartland is ready to end this useless war, that the Drug Peace movement is not a coastal or a liberal one. It is a patriotic one. In fact, watch for Missouri, Ohio, California, Oregon, Alaska, Rhode Island, Illinois, and a half dozen other states to declare peace by 2016. The drug warriors don't know where to regroup. They're losing everywhere.

This, as the ganjapreneur Matt Cohen we've met in these pages will never let me or anyone else forget, is how federal alcohol prohibition ended as well: Too many states to ignore spoke the truth. It disappeared nearly overnight, and much sooner than most experts predicted. Bootleggers lost their market, as Mexican cartels soon will. Yes, yes, naysayers, I know the cartels have diversified. Is that any reason not to cut off up to 70 percent of their narco profits while putting American small farmers back to work?

As a parent, what I learned incontrovertibly from studying this war is that the single policy move that will most increase public safety around my ranch is legalizing cannabis and thus ending border drug violence. Make no mistake: Ending federal cannabis prohibition ends the Drug War.

So important, so game-changing and irreversible are these recent poll victories that some of us still-lucky-to-live-in-a-democracy Americans find ourselves almost unable to grasp what a giant leap closer we are to hostilities ending (and on pretty much our best-case terms). You know how people initially react to grief with denial? Sometimes they react the same way to unimagined success. One colleague called me from Colorado a week after the election to say, "It just hasn't sunk in yet. Did we really just win the freakin' war?"

I considered that an understandable reaction. Just that morning, the checkout woman at my local food co-op had asked me if I thought the Mayan calendar odometer rollover would usher in some massive societal zeitgeist shift, and I had joked, "Nothing radical like two states ending the Drug War." When enough of your allies (especially those who depend on cannabis for cancer medicine, or those actually in the industry, both groups even more connected to the recent victories than someone like me, who merely writes about the issue) are resigned to be criminals forever for insane and harmful reasons; when you hear "it'll never happen" enough times, well, you'll understand why I saved this one in a file labeled "Happiest News Story I've Seen In Years" (from *The Daily Chronic*, on November 10, 2012):

> *King County, Washington, prosecutor Dan Satterberg is treating the state's I-502 (ballot initiative) as if it is already law, dismissing 175 marijuana misdemeanor possession cases on Friday.*
>
> *Satterberg said his office is dropping the cases involving people twenty-one and older and possession of one ounce or less. Although the law doesn't take effect until December 6, his office has decided to apply I-502 retroactively, saying it is the right thing to do in light of Tuesday's vote.*
>
> *"Although the effective date of I-502 is not until December 6, there is no point in continuing to seek criminal penalties for conduct that will be legal next month," Satterberg said.*

And thus do our overcrowded prisons begin to empty. Even with the Berlin Wall down, though, it is still a bit—only a bit—premature to call the federal Drug War a paper tiger. I'll leave that for the third, no doubt hemp, edition of this book that I keep lobbying my publisher to consider. All might be getting quieter and quieter on the Western Front—the Obama Justice Department (wisely) stayed mum in advance of Colorado and Washington's legalization votes—but in order for the peace side to declare total victory, cannabis must be entirely removed from the Controlled Substances Act, to allow states to regulate the plant as they wish.

Why? Well, more than 850,000 people were arrested for cannabis in the United States in 2011. The vast majority were otherwise law-abiding citizens. That's one life ruined every nineteen seconds until federal law changes. I met one at a *Too High to Fail* live event: Twenty-two-year-old Chris Diaz had just served nine months in Texas (including 111 days in solitary confinement) for bringing a half ounce of his asthma medicine into the Lone Star State while visiting relatives. A meek kid profoundly shaken by prison, he told me that during his parole in Texas, he was forced to return to the expensive and ineffective pharmaceutical remedies that had driven his doctor to recommend medical cannabis in the first place.

Will the war end during Obama's second term? Let us hope. Better, let us call our representatives, with great dispatch and passion. They're suddenly listening. Activists say they're getting calls from congresspeople since the election, claiming total reversal of drug policy stance and asking for campaign contributions. A few bills mandating that federal authorities leave Colorado and Washington alone are already getting serious committee chatter.

That's the policy-side update. On the ground, during the recent West Coast tour leg in support of *Too High to Fail*, I reconnected with many of the farmers in the book. Which means I got the scuttlebutt on the Mendocino County and overall Emerald Triangle cannabis economy this year. The good news for Californians is that it's been a great season horticulturally, the best crop in a decade and a half, say the farmers. None of the early rains that soaked the pages of *Too High to Fail*.

Yet, lest anyone question whether federal meddling in current state cannabis programs does anything but help criminals, just listen to what one muddy farmer, a permitted Chamber of Commerce member (that is to say, a fully locally legal cultivator in the landmark Drug Peace program we've just explored), told me as she watered her crop amid the redwoods. She said that, buried under a mortgage and other family expenses, she's actually "a little grateful that the feds just jacked up prices [to black-market levels] again. Gives me a couple years' income cushion before the end of prohibition."

Yikes! Remember this any time you hear one of the few remaining drug warrior pundits float one more scary-sounding study about childrens' IQs on pot as an excuse for keeping this war going through another trillion tax dollars: On the ground, in the real economy, *prohibition doesn't work*. Not a new realization, of course, merely an accurate one.

If you carry only one fact with you into your cooler chat about drug policy, I'd love it to be this one, and I am not just culling data here—I witnessed it on the farms: *Not one less seed was planted in Mendocino County in 2012 than in 2011*. The difference is that now the aboveground local economy doesn't benefit. Instead of collecting taxes from America's number one crop, we pay taxes to lose a war against cartels while boosting the latter's bottom line.

Cannabis is to American agriculture today what Silicon Valley was to American industry in the 1970s. It's about to emerge, dominate, and change the culture. When prohibition ends, the realities and responsibilities of taxable profitability will appear before the most skilled Emerald Triangle small farmers. In the end, this is why the U.S. Justice Department's 2011 actions in California should be simultaneously remembered as 1) among the most outrageously counterproductive law enforcement operations in our nation's previous quarter century, and 2) a vital aid in bringing about the Drug Peace victory even more quickly. As NORML's Ellen Komp points out, the more American voters hear that California's northern district U.S. attorney's office is ignoring pleas from Oakland city officials for federal assistance with gun violence and instead going after peaceful Mendocino farmers, the more outraged they are. That's five more percentage points for legalization in Missouri right there.

I was very pleased to report to the farmers on the front lines of the war's final battles that the home front has their backs. Despite their recent legal roller coaster ride, I'd describe Emerald Triangle cannabis cultivators as generally supportive of the message in *Too*

*High to Fail.* Still, every Mendocino County reporter and audience member at my book-tour events had one question that must be answered. It went something like this: "Given that the Zip-Tie Program participant numbers represented a drop in the bucket compared to the total number of farmers in the county (in other words, most of us here at your slide show today), how many farmers do you think would have participated in the program for the 2012 season if the feds didn't in effect work for the cartels?"

I could've taken a page from the sage Sheriff Tom we've met in these pages and said, "I don't have a crystal ball," but that's not a usable quote for an optimist like me. "At least five thousand in Mendo, Lake, and Humboldt counties," I proclaimed over and over on farm tours, at events, in sushi restaurants. "Generating $21 million in fees for local economies."

Three months later, I now think that estimate might be conservative. The Mendocino 9.31 Program model holds immense value, and I now confidently look for it to reemerge nationwide as a key part of the multibillion-dollar postwar economy. Plus, as a sustainability journalist, I'm thrilled at the prospect of a cultivation model for the nation's number one crop that makes sense at once for the local farmer, the larger tax base, and the earth.

However, this is all still theoretical in America's cannabis fields. Mendocino County locals can still smell the exhaust from the feds' helicopters. The Emerald Triangle redneck hippie, emblem of that long-persecuted American subculture, now finds herself facing an almost Tolkienian "darkest before the dawn" narrative. But one-time eager Obama canvasser Tomas Balogh, the farmer whose medicinal flowers we followed from farm to patient in this book, is not burying his head in the interim. Rather, the opposite.

Although he's operating his own collective by word of mouth until it's a wiser time to do an official Web launch, Balogh and Humboldt County activist Kristin Nevedal (along with Cohen and others) have laid the groundwork for the evolution of the locavore MendoGrown trade group you've read about in these pages. The organization has merged with the Humboldt Growers

Association to form the Emerald Growers Association, or EGA (EmeraldGrowers.org). I did a benefit live event for them during the hardcover *Too High to Fail* Pax Cannabis Tour. Why? I believe they represent the future of American agriculture and worldwide fair trade capitalism.

The plan, explicitly anticipating the demise of the federal Drug War, is this: 1) rigorously brand the region as the world's best, local, sustainably grown, farmer-owned top-shelf cannabis; 2) be ready when the aboveground economy allows the cannabis industry to rev its marketing engines; and 3) make sure the discerning cannabis consumer looks for some sort of "Emerald Certified" seal.

"So how's that going?" I asked Balogh just after the election.

"We haven't really got enough farmer buy-in yet," he said, laughing. "I mean, understandably. The feds just shut things down last season. Now we're just trying to keep the organization's head above water with fundraisers. But we're ready to weather a waiting period. We're in it to win it."

There have been some successes: Nevedal has been lobbying at the state level to make sure any cannabis legislation has outdoor farm-friendly provisions and the EGA endorsed a compromise position that was passed in Sacramento surrounding cultivation in city limits.

In Mendo, it's the tail end of bud-trimming season again. Little changes locally no matter what goes on outside the Bubble[3]. If I've learned one thing from the pleasant experience of covering the dawn of the Drug Peace era, it's that farmers farm. That's what they do. Word of the Colorado and Washington votes, locals told me, earned a brief fist bump, and then it was back to work.

Trimming is the most tense time of year and will remain so until the EGA and groups like it nationwide start centralizing payroll, quality testing, and warehousing, and the end of federal prohibition decimates the Ripper (cannabis farm burglar) population. When will that be? It's looking like sooner than my most optimistic projections. Only four months ago, just prior to this book's official release, I think I somewhat startled Conan O'Brien's studio audience midsegment by nervously looking up at the ceiling and blurting out, "I can't believe we've gotten this far and the studio hasn't exploded."

That was late July. Now it's mid-November, and I've been schooled by American public opinion. Instead of recent "do you really think pot'll ever be legalized?" questions from interviewers, now I'm getting calls from business writers and venture capitalists wanting to know "whether cannabinoids like CBD can be synthesized in nonpsychoactive form."

This morning, as I prepare to breed my goats before a brief Thanksgiving break (well, not breed personally unless absolutely necessary—I just serenade the young couple with poorly executed Coltrane riffs on my saxophone for the eighteen biologically necessary seconds), I read that Pitkin County, Colorado, sheriff Joe DiSalvo has told the *Aspen Times* when asked if people will now visit Colorado just for cannabis tourism, "It's going to be live and let live. If . . . that's the sole reason—it's up to them. I am not the lifestyle police."

Wow. Now that the hearts and minds even of law enforcement officials seem to be won, it's down to details. The international treaties that will have to change with the end of the American front of the Drug War, for example, should be relatively easy to negotiate. Here's what Luis Videgaray, head of incoming Mexican president Enrique Peña Nieto's transition team, told the Associated Press on November 8 was the result of cannabis legalization in two U.S. states two days earlier: "I think that we have to carry out a review of our joint policies in regards to drug trafficking and security in general."

Mexico, with ninety-five cosponsors, has also called a UN General Assembly special session on drugs in 2016. I wouldn't be surprised if the result is the adoption of the cannabis legalization suggestions of the Global Commission on Drug Policy, quoted in these pages.

On the other side of the NAFTA trifecta, Kristen Gwynne of *Alternet* reports that Canada is also looking to the United States for guidance, quoting David Valentin, spokesperson for the Young

Liberals: "[The 2012 U.S. election] is an important first step and inspiration to [Canadians] who want to see Canada embrace a smart drug policy."

We are leading the world again. God bless America. I don't mind that the people are dragging their government along toward peace. This issue has reinvigorated me as a patriot. It might even get us off petroleum.

Doug Fine
Funky Butte Ranch
November 22, 2012

# FINAL REPORT
# FROM THE FRONT

> Forty years have gone by, and the entire war is . . . a total absolute failure. . . . [The] U.S. government is way behind its public opinion. . . . It's clear that marijuana harm is much less than cigarettes' harm.
>
> —Former Mexican president Vicente Fox, in *The 420 Times*,
> November 27, 2012

**J**ust when I was ready to celebrate the Drug War's end, new hostilities have broken out. I suppose, having seen up close how this war is conducted, I shouldn't be surprised. But I am.

Readers of *Too High to Fail* will know that probably the number one concern of potential Zip-Tie Program farmers was the question of whether Mendocino County officials would or would not simply hand over local cannabis cultivator records to the feds if asked at a sheriffs' convention cocktail party, let alone if subpoenaed. Guess what? It just happened.

On November 24, 2012, county sheriff Tom Allman confirmed that a federal grand jury was demanding those program financial records from his department—actually, four connected subpoenas were issued a month earlier. A year after being shut down following federal threats to local elected officials, the landmark 9.31 ordinance was under attack again. Exhuming a body is a shady enough enterprise, but, whatever their motivation, federal prosecutors were about to realize that the target of their digging expedition had not expired and, being a successful idea, only benefited from a return to the sunlight.

After three days of intense local huddling and a barrage of

encouraging "no comments" once the subpoena news broke (during which farmer Tomas Balogh's attorney volunteered to defend the county for free if it resisted), Sheriff Tom told *The Ukiah Daily Journal* that while he was puzzled by the subpoenas ("In 2010, I met with U.S. attorney Melinda Haag, and I told her everything about the 9.31 process that I could. . . . She didn't have any kind of concern at the time."), he intended to hand over program documents to county counsel Thomas Parker, since "Every dollar we've taken in has a paper trail."

That decision, though he called it understandable, "ruined my morning," Thomas told me. "Actually, it made me sick to my stomach." But it wasn't the end of the story.

The county board of supervisors, whose members are, after all, the local lawmakers and drafters of ordinance 9.31, called a special closed-door session on December 4. At the public comment period before the board members sequestered themselves, Thomas testified, "Farmers including myself who, in the past, lived in fear of law enforcement are now working with law enforcement in an effort to take back our county from the cartels and illegal growers who were making life miserable for everybody. I reached out to my neighbors for the first time and joined the neighborhood watch, I began to comply with environmental regulations, and I began to pay all of my taxes. . . . I'm asking you to stand up and fight with me."

When they emerged, the board members, still led by the players documented in this book, did just that. They announced in a prepared statement that they had voted to direct Parker to seek outside counsel in order to "take appropriate action" about the subpoenas. A few weeks later, Parker decided that quashing them was the appropriate action. "The scope of the subpoenas is . . . oppressive and constitutes an improper intrusion into the ability of state and local government to administer programs for the health and welfare of their residents," he said in a written statement. There is precedent, in Oregon, for subpoenas of medical cannabis records being quashed in federal court.

In his office at 5:00 the morning after Mendocino County's governing body voted to tell the feds to keep out, Supervisor John McCowen, one of the architects of the 9.31 Permit Program, told me, "It doesn't take a legal genius to see that this is a fishing expedition. I personally believe that the county has an interest in protecting the personal information of everyone who applied for a permit to grow up to ninety-nine plants in full compliance with state and local law. I think it is morally repugnant to brandish subpoenas at people who were trying to protect the community and the environment. In shutting down our program and with these subpoenas, the federal government is on the wrong side of history. They don't seem to be paying very close attention to the recent election results."

I asked Supervisor McCowen—considered, remember, quite the local conservative—if he thought of the board's defiance as a battle in the wider Drug War. "I do think at some point you have to push back," he replied. "If the supervisors take a principled stand on this issue, that's one more incremental step in exposing the failed policy of federal prohibition."

You can imagine some serious political capital was expended when the emotive Mendonesians about whom we've been reading, like McCowen, fellow supervisor Dan Hamburg, and Sheriff Tom, sat down together to come to *that* decision. This was the moment when Mendocino County's political establishment decided how far it was going to push the message of "American cannabis farmers, with complete law enforcement and local government buy-in, have shown that America's number one crop does in the real world become America's number one taxable crop. The Drug Peace works."

Their decision on how far to push that message? All the way. Minutes after the board's vote, I received jubilant texts from Balogh and another of the farmers I followed closely in this book, Matt Cohen. It looks to many in the region like the twenty-first-century vision of the Emerald Growers Association might be coming of age. But Thomas had regained his composure by later that day and told me by phone that "All this means is we get to fight on. This is what we signed up for when we went public. No point in quitting now."

If you hadn't already figured it out from *Too High to Fail*, that attitude is another reason why the ninety-five farmers who came aboveground and gave their names, financial information, and business plans to the county of Mendocino's landmark Drug Peace program should be recognized as economy-stimulating and cartel-battling heroes.

Are they being so honored? Not as yet. The subpoenas came two weeks after the world basically agreed to end the Drug War. Even the Northstone Two, the absurdly charged medical cannabis deliverymen we followed in *Too High to Fail*, have had their charges predictably dismissed. Simply tossed out by the judge before the trial. Someone in the courtroom audience that terrific day texted me a photo of the dejected DA moping his solitary way down the corridor, perhaps on his way home to a federally legal relaxant, like beer or *Breaking Bad*. The Northstone Two themselves, Dan and Tim, slept that night, certain for the first time in more than a year that they wouldn't have to spend ten years in prison for delivering permitted medicine, receipts stapled to bags, to sick Californians.

Of course, a grand jury can ask for whatever it wants. The moral crime that Justice Department personnel are committing is considering bringing a cannabis case against Mendocino farmers at all. Regional media have been speculating that the matter might surround alleged cannabis cultivation on property rented out by relatives of Sergeant (now Captain) Randy Johnson, administrator of the Zip-Tie Program. Man, if you're going to go after relatives of Mendonesians who rent to people who grow cannabis, that'll only end with a ghost county. An independent investigation conducted by an out-of-county team cleared Johnson of any connection to the situation. But since when has innocence deterred the federal Drug War?

I'll of course keep readers apprised of developments in the subpoena battle via my Web site (www.dougfine.com) and social media. My pipe dream is that the president and congress will remove cannabis from the Controlled Substances Act before whatever the U.S. attorney's office in San Francisco has concocted moves forward. I mention this because we're already in pipe dream territory after November 2012.*

At the moment, though, I'm an angry citizen. You don't subpoena people you should be congratulating. These are the very people showing the world how to win the Drug War. They've brought an entire new segment of local residents within the law-abiding fold and created real local jobs.

When I think of the vast swath of North America that's not safe today simply because of the Drug War, my blood runs cold. Especially since it includes my own valley. I'm reminded again of the massive interagency raid of my retired AARP-member next-door neighbor to free a very remote part of borderland New Mexico from something like thirteen cannabis plants that partly stirred me to write *Too High to Fail*. The Drug War and only the Drug War had lured automatic weapons into my riverbed. That is not permissible to this patriot, not for peaceful use of a pretty much harmless plant.

It put my family at risk—and they are on my mind as always this morning, one son in a cape trying to lure the squirrels who live in our woodpile with a carrot, the other giving the cat a piano lesson outside my office. I'm afraid there is no room for helicopters

---

* I don't know that he was listening to me, but in December, President Obama abruptly gave up dodging the issue or trying to giggle it away (two of the classic stages prior to ending big public injustices). In his first big postelection interview, he somberly told Barbara Walters not just that he intended to leave Washington and Colorado alone (leading to the unasked follow-up question, "So if all fifty states were to legalize, the Drug War is over?"), but that he was not "*at this point*" ready to back full federal cannabis legalization.

Those words represent a huge and essentially final victory, but for now they're just hot air. Until federal policy changes—in ink—the reality on the ground will continue to evoke, as I put it in these pages, the final scene in *All Quiet on the Western Front*. Indeed some farmers describe the continual federal assault on their (and their patients') lives in terms of shell shock. We must declare a federal drug peace during this presidential term, for the good of the economy and for the safety of our families.

or men with wires in their ears in this riverbed. It's crowded enough with coyotes.

Wild coyotes or narco coyotes? That's a metaphor for the current cannabis industry crossroads. This plant, or maybe any profitable commodity, can bring out the best or the worst in people and hence their business practices. But the past 10,000 years, starting with the first cannabis roofing stalk that accidentally burned in the campfire and culminating with the stunning U.S. elections this past November 6, show that one way or another we're going to have a special relationship with this plant. My takeaway: From genome and biofuel researchers to solar-powered automatic drip irrigation developers to suburban fledglings who want a reason to return to the land, let's get to work, America.

Meanwhile, the state of Washington's cannabis legalization went into effect today. The Associated Press is reporting that there is "nary a police officer in sight" at the massive smoke-out beside the Space Needle. Peace is so much better than war.

Astoundedly (and thankfully) yours,

Doug Fine
Funky Butte Ranch
December 6, 2012

## ACKNOWLEDGMENTS

I extend sincere thanks to everyone who posts to the blogs and e-mail lists on all sides of the cannabis issue. These heads-ups are so prolific, it's hard to keep up with every trial in Oregon and unfriendly attorney general scheme in Michigan. Along with GoogleNews alerts, these posts were a major asset in the research of this book. Like all online mishmashes, they also provided insight into the Collective Human Mind in general.

Essentially, I'm saying thank you to the Internet and its reach, even though I was working in a redwood grove that allowed marginal speed and access. But I'm also thanking the people passionate enough about the Drug War issue to send their hopes across the ether.

Also valuable for my work was simply seeing what was going on in the rest of the world regarding cannabis—from English hemp concrete senior centers to dispensary lawsuits in Maine to nickel bag arrests for cannabis found in baskets at Nigerian markets. These provided essential grounding and breadth of perspective as I largely tracked one very important microcosm of that world.

The consistently terrific reporting by the staff at the *Ukiah Daily Journal* and *The Willits News*, particularly Linda Williams and Tiffany Revelle, was helpful as I conducted my research. You guys, as you probably know, could be successful anywhere, if you were unwise enough not to live where you do. It says a lot that I have no idea whether you personally share my conclusions about ending the war on cannabis. Your coverage is simply good. Period.

As this book is already dedicated to the people of Mendocino County, I'll risk redundancy by stating the truth that the narrative recounted herein wouldn't have been possible without the generous access to lives that everyone from law enforcement personnel to food bank volunteers shared in that majestic piece of landscape.

I sometimes hear the assertion that what Mendocino County is doing, as a locavore agricultural community, can be done "anywhere." In other words, it's nothing particularly magical that's contained in the Mendo air, soil, mountains, vineyards, dragonflies, ocean views, wild mushrooms, and river currents. If that's an accurate reflection of the planet, we're in better shape as a species than I could have hoped. We're headed in the right direction.

Deep thanks also to my skilled and supportive editor Megan Newman, and agents Markus, Mike, Josh, and Joe. Thanks also to Leigh and Amanda M. for invaluable assistance. And to Rachel Holtzman, for seeing this book's potential early on.

And most of all, I send appreciation to my fifth Beatle, my family: with me every step of the way as usual. I love you and thank you. For the general support as much as for the specific snuggles and crepes.

# INDEX